"*The Heart of Healing* process of healing. Regina wisely explains how a healing process differs from the quick fix of symptom treatment. She describes an ever-evolving path of healing from illness to diagnosis through the bumpy but enlightening road to recovery and growth."

– Aminah Raheem, Ph.D
Founder & Spiritual Director
Soul Lightening® International
Author of *Soul Return* and *Soul Lightening*

"*The Heart of Healing* is a portal inviting all who face life's inevitable healing challenges to join in a guided but personally owned journey toward wholeness. The abundant resources provided will orient even novices to the use of self-renewal practices. Readers are introduced to the wisdom of Regina's favorite teachers, her challenges and hard-won progress, and compassionate observations of travelers on the path toward healing. Come in, explore, partake, and finally come home to yourself, perhaps for the first time!"

– The Reverand Dr. Patricia S. Medley
Pastor, Hope Lutheran Church
Freehold, New Jersey

"The Heart of Healing will provide you with healing strategies culled from extensive experience, traditional wisdom teachings, and personal stories, woven through with an exceptional, loving attitude. Regina takes readers through the process of healing, from the first shock of being hit by a malady to the slow recognition of the patience and courage needed to recover. I highly recommend this book."

– Lydia Salant
M.A., L.AC., Therapist

"A timeless, heart-felt and life impacting book filled with powerful stories and lessons to illuminate a path to healing for every reader. Regina speaks to us from a place of grace, wisdom, and integrity. Her work is the North Star for all of us who wish to heal."

– Lu Pierro
M.Ed, Ed.S, Grassroots Organizer
Worldwide Holistic Day

"As a breast cancer survivor, *The Heart of Healing* offered me priceless Self-care tools and practices that inspired and awakened the healer within me. It led me on a journey that enabled me to understand the connecting link between my mind, body and spirit – my heart – and helped me replace feelings of fear with feelings of peace and hope for my future."

– Deanna Gallo

"This book is invaluable for anyone interested in living consciously from an awakened heart. The tools and reflections in it will help you meet the challenges of being present each moment, and will assist you with making wise, healthy choices. As an acupuncturist with a long-time meditation and journaling practice, *The Heart of Healing* supported the refinement and evolution of my conscious awareness. It provided me with stepping-stones home to my true nature, my authentic Self."

– Betsy Baker
M.Ed., M.,Ac., Licensed Acupuncturist

"Regina's beautiful creation is a gift that will assist you with opening to your unique healing journey. The insightful stories and Self-care practices will deepen your awareness, and help you discover pathways to the wisdom within your heart."

– Kathleen Rose Schival
Licensed Massage Therapist

"Regina Rosenthal has walked through the fire of life and emerged victorious. In *The Heart Of Healing* she eagerly shares how our pains and celebrations expand our hearts' understanding, compassion, and acceptance, and how this leads us to discover our true core of happiness and contentment."

– Peggy Jaegly
www.NurtureForCaregivers.com

The Heart *of* Healing

The Heart *of* Healing

Discovering the Secrets of Self-Care

REGINA ROSENTHAL, PT, MA

The Heart of Healing: Discovering the Secrets of Self-Care
Regina Rosenthal, PT, MA
Copyright © 2013 Regina Rosenthal

Published by: Dimensions of Wellness Press
Holmdel, New Jersey 07733

All rights reserved. No part of this book may be reproduced or utilized in any form or by any means, electronic or mechanical, including photo-copying and recording, without written permission from the publisher.

This book is not intended as a substitute for medical or professional services. If expert assistance and/or counseling is needed, seek out the services of a competent professional.

Every effort has been made to acknowledge and contact copyright holders for permission to reproduce material contained in this book. Copyright holders who have been inadvertently omitted from acknowledgments and credits should contact the publisher; omissions will be rectified in subsequent editions.

The following trademarks, service marks, and certification marks are used by permission of the Feldenkrais Guild® of North America: Feldenkrais®, Feldenkrais Method®, Awareness Through Movement®, ATM℠, FI℠, Functional Integration® and Guild Certified Feldenkrais Practitioner. ℃ᴹ

"Trager," "Mentastics," and Dancing Cloud Logo are registered service marks of Trager International, which licenses their use in the USA to the United States Trager Association.

Quotation by Max Depree: Copyright©1989 by Max Depree. First appeared in LEADERSHIP IS AN ART published by Doubleday. Used with permission of the Sandra Dijkstra Literary Agency and the author.

First Edition, 2013
Book design by Donna Miller and GKS Creative
Cover Design by GKS Creative
Author photograph by Andrea Phox Photography

ISBN-13: 978-0-9885267-0-9
Library of Congress Catalog Number:2012915477

For all courageous souls who seek to
awaken, heal, and remember.

With love and gratitude to Jolie, Mayzie, Noah, and Alec,
children of the Light, who heal through their loving presence.

Table of Contents

Tables

Diagrams

INTRODUCTION
How to Use This Book

If one advances confidently in the direction of his own dreams,
and endeavors to live the life which he has imagined, he will
meet with a success unexpected in common hours.
–Henry David Thoreau

As a child, I often gazed up at the night sky, studded with a vast array of captivating, brilliant stars. I was filled with awe. I felt small amidst the beauty and magic, yet knew on some level that I was also connected with it. I can remember praying at these times, with the innocence of a child, "Please let everyone be healthy and happy." During these moments I became one with the ***Great Mystery**** within the life force that animates the universe, the life force that also animates ***healing***. Though I did not understand the depth and breadth of this until much later, it fascinated me from my earliest days.

---

* Please consult the glossary at the end of this book for definitions of words in bold italics.

1

Spiritual study, *meditation*, *yoga*, and work in the healing arts as a physical therapist deepened my awareness, and I realized that nothing exists in a vacuum. Everything in the universe occurs in relationship within a vast grand design. My personal and professional experiences with healing enhanced my conscious connections within this grand design and revealed:

- We all have an innate ability to respond to healing challenges, an ability that is activated when we connect to the wisdom in our *authentic Self*, heart, and *soul*.

- Healing paths traveled are unique to each individual.

- Healing involves collaborative ventures with ourselves, others, and a power greater than ourselves. This power is described in many ways: G-d, Spirit, Divine presence, universal life force, *Source energy*, and so on. I write G-d in this manner out of respect and reverence for the Divine nature, attributes, and essence of what is nameless, as described in Judaism. I continue this usage throughout the book to remind myself and you, the reader, of the sacredness that surrounds and inhabits each of us.

The Heart of Healing describes the heart-and-soul journey and evolutionary process that occurred as I witnessed and experienced healing. It led me to write this book now, when learning to consciously and actively participate in our healing is so vital. I invite you to join me on a healing journey as you read through these pages, participate in the Self-care practices, and discover what is at the heart of your experiences and healing. Like the constellations above, we are all interconnected and interdependent; we are all conduits of healing for ourselves and one another. Please note that whenever Self is capitalized I refer to your Higher Divine Self, your eternal and unlimited *true nature*, which exists beyond your thoughts and beliefs. I use lowercase *self* to refer to the human self and its associated qualities. This is done merely to help you, the reader, differentiate between the two. Direct, personal experience of the Divine within occurs each time you connect with your authentic Self, heart, and soul. This connection was pivotal to awakenings and healing I have witnessed, and is a core concept within this book.

On your journey you will observe, listen to, and be present with a wondrous source of healing that awaits you within yourself. You will also plug into the limitless source of life and power within the Great Mystery, which interconnects and animates all living things. Healing will challenge you to remember and reestablish your internal and external connections within this grand design. As this life force flows through your whole being, it will endow you with the ability to engage the paradoxes of life and healing – the sorrow and the joy, the efforting and the effortless, the doing and the being. With each reconnection to it, your sense of purpose, aliveness, joy, and inner peace will be renewed and energized.

Why Did I Write *The Heart of Healing*?

The Heart of Healing stems from a desire, a promise, and a prayer.

The desire to participate in healing journeys originated during the earliest years of my life, whenever I stood in wonder amidst the Great Mystery.

The promise emerged during my years as a physical therapist. Clients often urged me to write about our sessions in order to help others. This book is a response to their requests and the promises I made to each of them to bring this forth.

The prayer is for you. *The Heart of Healing* is your story as much as my own. I wrote this for anyone who has been on, or is beginning, a journey of healing. It is not only for those who seek personal healing; it is also for those who seek greater understanding of the healing process as they serve in the healing arts as physicians, surgeons, dentists, psychiatrists, psychologists, social workers, therapists, holistic practitioners, nurses, clergy, friends, or family members.

May your awareness, strength, compassion, insight, and wisdom be enhanced personally and professionally. May your understanding and presence deepen and help establish partnerships in health care with those you serve. We all need continuing education about healing to best support ourselves and one another. This will help us meet life and health challenges with a whole heart, described by cultural anthropologist Angeles Arrien as a four-chambered heart, one that is full, open, clear, and strong.[1]

Begin with me, then, with a desire to heal, a promise to share the journey, and a prayer that your way is illuminated. The journey will be challenging, but remember this: The Latin derivation of *desire* is "from the stars." The world of healing is a vast and often mysterious universe, approached through science yet also needing heart-and-soul presence. Each of us who participates in the process, in any way, are like stars that inhabit the realm, shedding light amidst the darkness, in service to everyone and everything.

What is *The Heart of Healing?*

The Heart of Healing describes the lifelong journey home to our heart and authentic Self that occurs through healing. It reveals how this journey and Self-care practices guide us to empowering discoveries at the heart, or core, of our being. Healing is a continuous *process*, not a single life event, and it is stimulated each time we commit to showing up, being present, and connecting with our heart's pathway. Healing begins with the heart, and all paths lead back to the heart. During my early years as a physical therapist, I came to a realization about healing that has stayed with me to this day – we will experience many healing journeys from the moment we are born. This book is based on a core belief that developed from this awareness – *healing is a lifelong process of growth and development.*

Healing begins with the journey back to our hearts, often initially encountered when we face a health crisis, pain, distress, or **dis-ease** – a lack of ease in our physical, mental, emotional, and/or spiritual being. Too often, our hearts are torn because we have fallen into dualistic thinking and living. Guided by either/or choices, we perceive individuals and situations as good or bad, right or wrong, this way or that way, rather than being open to both options. Returning to our heart transports us to a multidimensional world with beginnings and endings, joy and grief, pain and possibility, love and loss, beauty and the beast.

The healing journey is challenging. During moments of insight, light illuminates the darkness. Comedian Betty Davis stated, "Old age ain't no place for sissies." When I think about the courageous journey that healing is, I am reminded of a client who said, "My tears are like rain . . . they water my soul and enable it to grow." She helped me envision the path that leads to the heart of healing.

The Heart of Healing is written for anyone who finds life turned upside down and difficult in the face of:

- *physical* illness as a result of shock, trauma, dis-ease and/or disability

- *emotional* challenges such as shock, post-traumatic stress disorder (PTSD), depression, or anxiety

- *mental* stress from overload, exhaustion, and **burnout** related to daily living and/or unchallenged attitudes, beliefs, and habits that no longer serve

- *spiritual* dark nights of the soul – an overall sense of emptiness, aloneness, disconnection, loss, and lack of purpose and meaning

The Heart of Healing is written for anyone seeking to learn more about healing, and how to be more active in their healing process. The clients I worked with for more than twenty-five years were empowered through this educational process.

The Heart of Healing is designed to expand awareness about healing as a lifelong journey of Self-discovery and empowerment. Each of us encounters seven universal themes as we explore healing. The return to our heart is at the center of each theme:

♥ Theme One: Healing Involves Showing Up and Being Present

This theme describes how our heart influences showing up and being present during life and healing. As we awaken to our heart, the ongoing heartbeat and pace of our lives and healing shift.

♥ Theme Two: Healing Is a Journey versus a Single Event

This theme describes healing as a process in which life experiences continuously unfold and evolve over time. The heart's pathway is our compass, indicating true north every step of the way. As our heart energy circulates through our body, mind, emotions, and life force, or soul, we will encounter pathways that flow, as well as detours and obstacles.

♥ Theme Three: Healing Involves Self-Healing and Coming Home to Your Heart and Your Authentic Self

This theme describes three aspects of ***Self-healing***: the return journey home to your heart; reconnection with your authentic Self, or true nature; and awakening to your unique heart-and-soul wisdom.

♥ Theme Four: Healing Is a Lifelong Process of Growth and Development

Our hearts reside at the central hearth of our home, our being. This theme describes the continuous process of education healing takes us through, and how heart intelligence illuminates the way. As this intelligence touches and awakens our body, mind, emotions, and soul, the flame that keeps our hearts whole is reignited.

♥ Theme Five: Healing Involves Change and Movement

Our life and whole being changes as we heal. Theme Five relates how healing involves change, movement, endings, beginnings, and many transitions. The journey may necessitate a change of heart and movement along different pathways in our life and relationships. Wise listening, courage, and compassionate presence help integrate heart-and-soul wisdom as we move through change.

♥ Theme Six: Healing Is Stimulated by Life-Affirming Qualities of the Joyful Heart

Creativity, play, laughter, beauty, and **gratitude** are vital to healing. Theme Six illustrates how these life-affirming qualities support easeful, abundant flow of heart energy and provide nourishment for growth, development, wholeness, and healing.

♥ Theme Seven: The Common Denominator in All Healing Is Love

The heart's essence is love. Theme Seven shows how love supports and births us into new dimensions within the Great Mystery, from birth through death on our human journey. Healing involves coming full circle and returning, through love, to our authentic Self, heart, and soul.

Each theme within *The Heart of Healing* will guide you on an individual journey that is about heart and meaning, and a path to your authentic Self. As you learn, grow, and gain insights on this journey, you will find answers to several questions:

- What is healing?

- How does healing impact my whole being?

- Which theme(s) do I encounter during healing challenges?

- How can the themes, expanded awareness, compassion, and *mindfulness* benefit and enhance my healing process?

Your awareness will also deepen as you read, reflect, journal, and consistently participate in Self-care practices at the end of each chapter. These practices will help you discover ways to ground, integrate, and practically apply new insights. Your ability to use internal and external guidance, resources, and support will also be enhanced and will empower you and your healing process.

You will prepare for your journey to the heart of healing in chapters one through three, where you will be introduced to healing stories and three aspects that flow through all seven themes:

- connecting to your authentic Self and others through your whole heart

- self-awareness, seeking answers within, and honoring passages and triumphs on your journeys

- discovering wisdom in ancient practices and traditions, which helps you recover *reverence for life*

In chapters four through seven, you will explore the seven themes through client stories and my personal journey. I have highlighted these narratives throughout the book with headings that signal a call to action relating to each theme, as noted in Table 1. Self-care practices at the end of each chapter will help you apply these actions to your healing journey.

Table 1: Calls to Action & Related Themes

ACTION	THEME
Awakening	♥ One: Healing involves showing up and being present.
Processing	♥ Two: Healing is a journey versus a single event.
Returning	♥ Three: Healing involves Self-healing and coming home to your heart and your authentic Self.
Illuminating	♥ Four: Healing is a lifelong process of growth and development.
Changing	♥ Five: Healing involves change and movement.
Life-affirming	♥ Six: Healing is stimulated by life-affirming qualities of the joyful heart.
Loving	♥ Seven: The common denominator in all healing is love.

At the end of this book you will find further support for your healing journey and Self-care practices. There is a glossary to clarify concepts; glossary words appear in ***bold italics*** when first used. Reference details appear in the endnotes section, followed by a bibliography with additional resources you can consult. Appendix A contains a worksheet for Tool 20 found in the Tools and Reflections section of Chapter Nine. Appendix B contains helpful Internet resources. Appendix C is a questionnaire I used when interviewing individuals in preparation for writing this book. Your responses to this questionnaire may help you begin to map out your journey and guide you to inner wisdom and resources.

Why Does *The Heart of Healing* Work?

The themes, process of Self-inquiry, awareness-tracking tools, and Self-care practices in each chapter are simple, easy to follow, and build upon one another. They can be used independently, in groups, and in self-directed or counseling formats. These supportive and educational strategies expand body-mind awareness and enhance Self-love, confidence, trust, and inner peace. A more purposeful and meaningful life will be manifested as you practically apply and integrate experiences and lessons learned during any healing process.

Practical application and use of Self-care tools will help you remember who you are, why you are here, and what has heart and meaning in your life. My life is renewed each time I use Self-care practices, create time for stillness, and consciously embrace and open to whatever arises within my life and healing process. In these moments, when I reconnect with my heart, soul, and the Great Mystery, I feel nourished and whole. I return to life afterward more centered and grounded. Everyone and everything in my life benefits when I use these practices.

More important than the messages in this book are the powerful questions and answers that will emerge in *your* heart and soul as you read. You will ask yourself:

- How can I remember to listen to my authentic Self during healing challenges?
- How can I integrate and practically apply insights?
- How can I maximize **health** and **well-being** through Self-care?

It is my hope that this book helps to create a bridge for all of us, from where we are now to where we seek to be in our healing process, growth and development, and human evolution. The bridge will be formed from what we discover during archaeological digs and scavenger hunts on our healing journeys, where understanding, answers, and meaning are sought.

As you explore healing, clues will be presented to you through three questions:

- Who am I?
- What do I want and/or need now?
- Where am I going?

These clues are like **Zen** koans, teaching riddles for which no solutions can be attained through logical reasoning and cognition. As with koans, clues temporarily jam cognitive processing to allow deeper awareness to emerge.

As you begin, commit to a clear, compassionate, sturdy, and loving presence with your conscious, aware, wise Self. Know that this presence is supported each time you catch a glimpse of and recollect the Divine presence within you, seen through your heart, soul, authentic Self, and the special, unique gifts you bring into the world. The answers you seek will be found within, as you deepen these connections.

In *As a Man Thinketh*, James Allen states, "A man sooner or later discovers that he is the master gardener of his soul, the director of his life."[2] We are each gardeners in our lives. As we till the soil of our inner being, we reinforce our connection with the natural world and our true nature, our authentic Self. This will help us to harvest and thrive on what nourishes us. Applying the Self-care practices and reflection tools in *The Heart of Healing* will help you tend your life's garden. May you uncover compassionate support and peace within during healing challenges, when chaos and turmoil arise. May your garden be bountiful with life force, your own and that which you discover. May the resources, gifts, and talents you bring forth be blessed, and a blessing for others, during abundant seasons of life and healing. May love touch and heal you as you make and manifest your own healing miracles!

CHAPTER ONE
The Whole Heart

To put the world in order, we must first put the nation in order;
to put the nation in order, we must put the family in order; to
put the family in order, we must cultivate our personal life; and
to cultivate our personal life, we must first set our hearts right.
–Confucius

A Yiddish proverb states, "The heart is the organ which sees better than eyes." After I graduated from physical therapy school, I sent notes to family and friends who supported me, with a quote from Helen Keller: "The best and most beautiful things in the world cannot be seen or even touched. They must be felt with the heart."[1] My heart and mind, working in collaboration, have proved to be a great partnership for life and my personal healing journeys.

Like many of you, I was not always aware of this collaborative process. I needed to recover heart-centered awareness, Self-compassion, and wholeness as part of my healing journey. My return to wholeheartedness involved rediscovering what and who kept my heart open, full, clear, and strong. This became lost to me, as it does to many others who seek healing, when I followed a busy, head-centered lifestyle. As a result, I became disheartened and lost sight of other life options. I closed my heart to survive the chaos, confusion, and uncertainties I faced in daily life. I lost the love of life and sense of play I knew as a child, and participated half-heartedly in my life. I lost connection with my heart and my authentic Self, my true nature, and I doubted my ability to change things. Like many others, I lost touch with what had heart and meaning in my life. I became weak-hearted, and the light from my soul dimmed. Each time I returned home to my heart during rigorous and challenging healing journeys, I realized my heart contained the foundational key from which all healing would begin and evolve.

By the time I completed traditional physical therapy training in my late thirties, a kaleidoscope of life experiences had imprinted on my heart. I had faced challenges such as miscarriages, illness, and the premature deaths of friends and family members. In the years that followed my professional training, my heart was again challenged as I faced two marital separations and trauma after a life-altering automobile accident. Daily stresses accumulated – raising a family, returning to school, and running a private physical therapy practice. My challenge was to learn how to live consciously and joyfully in a complex world. To remain awake, aware, and present, I needed to apply Self-care and healing practices on a consistent basis, while I engaged in "full catastrophe living," as described by mindfulness meditation teacher Jon Kabat-Zinn. I needed to use and embody the heart-centered lessons I was learning, in order to ground my healing process.

In this chapter you will read about the heart's innate wisdom. This wisdom awaits your discovery on your healing journeys and flows through each of the seven themes.

Discovering Our Heart's Wisdom

In today's world we often neglect our heart's wisdom, so vital to life and healing. Unlocking that wisdom and uniting our heart and mind has been at the core of virtually all healing I have witnessed or experienced. In *The Heart's Code*, psychologist Paul Pearsall describes results of experiments that measured electromagnetic fields around the human body. These showed that the heart generates the largest electromagnetic field of any body organ, several thousand times more powerful than that of the brain.[2] Like binary stars, the mind and heart orbit together, the mind around the heart, the heart around the mind. What is most important for healing is understanding how they serve each other in this binary relationship. Our natural inclination is to see the mind and heart as a hierarchy, in which the mind rules the heart or the heart dominates the logical-thinking, rational-acting mind. This is not the map of healing. One does not rule the other. Rather, our hearts and **higher minds** need to be in partnership.

My everyday mind, working mechanically in linear time, has the capacity and intelligence to think and reason. Mind is a dutiful, highly effective source that I can count on to bring plans and goals to fruition in everyday reality. It can also draw me out of focus when my "monkey mind" takes over through attachment to external distractions, emotional upheavals, and/or everyday life and drama. When this occurs, I can use Self-care practices and Self-compassion learned during healing to engage my heart and higher mind, referred to as ***HeartMind*** in Oriental medicine.[3] My challenge has been to ensure that wisdom from my HeartMind informs my everyday mind, versus having everyday mind, conditioning, and defensive ego take charge of and run my life. Heart and mind are both needed, in service to living a full and on-purpose life.

In Oriental medicine, integration of the thinking and feeling self, or *xin*, resides in the heart as HeartMind. It is here that the intelligence and **consciousness** of both the heart and mind are respected and valued. The heart, in Oriental medicine, is considered the emperor or empress of the kingdom, holding the *shen*, or spirit, of the individual. It creates harmony between body, mind, and spirit. When the heart and mind dissociate, and mind becomes head of state, reasoning powers take charge. We disregard feelings and intuitive knowing, see bodily dysfunction and distress as pathology, and treat what arises as the enemy. This split is defined and treated as deficient Heart Spirit in Oriental medicine. In Western medicine, by contrast, the anxiety and depression that results from this are too often treated with drugs that alter physiology and brain chemistry. We seldom recognize the loss of Heart Spirit, and what we don't recognize cannot be addressed.

For a long time, I developed and lived from a conditioned belief that my everyday thinking mind directed my life, with my head versus my heart taking over and running the show. This created a split and dissociation between my body, mind, and heart. The body-mind split did not begin with me, but centuries ago when French philosopher Descartes stated, "I think, therefore I am."[4] In conversation with a Native American chief, Swiss psychologist Carl Jung became aware of the Western world's denial of the heart. The chief demonstrated how his people thought with their hearts versus their heads – the reverse of the norm in Western society. Jung recognized how unconscious he and Westerners had become about the heart-mind split.[5]

I realized this heart-mind split was present one night at work years ago after concluding my final client session for the day. Alone in my office I was dutifully writing up daily patient notes when I suddenly became aware of being amidst a profoundly alive silence. I glanced around the room – bookcases filled with books, walls holding professional certificates, plaques with philosophical sayings, a stack of client charts on my desk. I suddenly and unexpectedly heard an inner voice saying, *None of this will keep you warm at night*. My husband and I were separated at the time, and I had moved out of our home. As I sat in stillness, I became aware of how living from my head, following unconscious habits, and strategizing had disconnected me from my heart. My heart was out in the cold. I became aware that my ego had taken charge while my heart barricaded itself behind physical and emotional armor, in order to survive betrayal (including Self-betrayal) and the loss of a dream. In order to survive, my ego put a lid on unexpressed fear and rage after the breakup of my marriage.

At the time, my ego tenaciously clung to survival behaviors, though in retrospect I see these no longer served. Through therapy and **bodywork,** it became apparent that my mind alone could not handle the stress and overload I experienced. Another language and presence was needed – that of my heart. I had ignored body symptoms such as weight gain and insomnia, pushed through mental exhaustion, ignored feeling depressed, buried rage, and kept busy to avoid any encounter with parts of me that felt overwhelmed or deadened. At the time, I believed life was a huge cosmic joke with no ultimate meaning or purpose. I cast aside my heart, unable to touch upon its painful messages. I was unaware of the wealth of intelligence it also contained, which could serve me.

I closed the door to my heart, which had become inundated with unresolved fear, anger, and grief. It was this rage and grief that would later serve me during therapy and bodywork sessions, and bring me to **edges** where I began to explore and process dark and ominous **shadow** places within. An essential prerequisite, however, involved developing patience and letting go of self-judgment, before HeartMind wisdom could begin to soften and reopen my heart. As I called upon this intelligence during daily living and healing, a more vibrant life force gradually returned.

Today I consider the heart a kaleidoscope that collects, contains, and holographically reveals the many dimensions where change affects our lives. In a purely physical and physiological dimension, the heart is an organ that receives and sends blood to every part of the body. Central to our physical body, the heart pumps blood, oxygen, and life force to every cell, as it guides the flow and integration of this essential energy through our whole being. Our physical hearts are the central, core part of our being, vital for life to continue. When our hearts die, life as we know it ends. By contrast, people may remain alive after being declared brain dead, as their hearts continue to preserve life.

In an emotional dimension, our hearts are the central source of feelings and often nonrational, nonlinear intelligence. This is in contrast to our heads, or minds, being a source of intellect. Emotion, or *e-motion*, can be described as the energy of our hearts in motion. When we engage in something "with all our heart," or when something is "near to our heart," or "touches our heart," we are moved and influenced through this connection with our heart's energy and intelligence.

Psychologists Daniel Goleman and Howard Gardner expanded my awareness of the emotional dimension. They emphasize the need to recognize and include emotional and other intelligences (artistic, musical, emotional, intrapersonal, linguistic, kinesthetic, spatial, and logical) in learning and social interactions. The Institute of HeartMath® has studied links between emotions, heart-brain communication and physiology, and cognitive functioning. Their scientists identified a physiological state that optimizes learning and performance. In this state, emotions are calm and harmony exists between our brain, body, and nervous system. This state facilitates enhanced focus, attention, reasoning, and creativity, which are all vital for learning, achievement, and social interaction. Their work is helping to reduce stress, enhance health and well-being, and strengthen connection with our hearts.[6]

In a mental dimension, what we "take to heart" we consider seriously. Our feeling, sensing, and intuitive natures all bring information to our minds, for our minds to filter and process. This often involves transcending ego mind, which causes us to defend ourselves to avoid pain and suffering. When we are able to use life experiences as vehicles for growth and development, our consciousness expands and embraces HeartMind intelligence.

In a spiritual dimension, we connect with heart intelligence each time we consider what has heart and meaning in our lives. When we bring consciousness to both doing and being aspects of our lives, we are better able to sense when our intentions are clear, when our "heart is in the right place," and when we are in sync with our life path and purpose. One of the longest journeys I have taken in healing has been from my head to my heart. This process involved continuous *lab work* – the practical application and integration of new experiences and insights with current body, mind, heart, and soul wisdom.

Over the past fifteen years, I have been most fortunate to meet and study with cultural anthropologist Angeles Arrien, an award-winning author, educator, and consultant in medical, academic, and corporate settings. Because of the extensive time and respectful relationship we have shared, I refer to Angeles Arrien in this book as Angeles, versus the traditional way of citing sources by last name. Her workshops expanded my awareness relative to my life and heart. Learning to witness and consciously interact with the current state of my life and heart, a process referred to by Angeles as *tracking*, proved invaluable. Tracking helped me develop a more aware, nonjudgemental ego and enhanced connection with my observer, or witness self. Tracking the state of my four-chambered heart helped me realize where I was (or was not) being full-hearted, open-hearted, clear-hearted, and strong-hearted in my life.

You, too, will discover that what you can name and track you can interact with and integrate more consciously into your whole being and life. Tracking is an essential Self-care tool. It develops objectivity, discernment, a sense of safety, and deeper *intimacy* with your authentic Self and your relationships. It brings curiosity versus judgment to what arises and what you focus on, and supports the creation of beneficial change within you and in your life. Using tracking and an Awareness Journal will help you draw wisdom and wholeheartedness from your *wise-hearted spiritual warrior*. This part of you embodies and expresses heart-and-soul wisdom through your visions, commitments, discipline, courage, integrity, and service. It will empower you to become the hero or heroine of your life.

The Awareness Journal, presented as a tool at the end of this chapter, was created by Betsy Baker, acupuncturist and senior instructor of *Process Acupressure*. She developed it to help others explore Self from a place of nonjudgmental, compassionate presence; and to facilitate the healing of pain and suffering that may have occurred from habits, beliefs, and conditioning we accepted as truth. Observing our conditioned minds in the moment, being present, allows us to see what is real. This brings choice to our actions. Betsy's holistic approach to journaling uses all available senses and body-mind signals to deepen awareness. This approach enhances connection with our authentic Self, our heart, and our soul. It helps us become aware of how our thoughts and language often become our biology. The Awareness Journal will empower you to connect with and use your internal GPS in everyday life and on healing journeys. It will also help you set clear *intentions* and *goals*.

In *Molecules of Emotion*, Dr. Candace Pert points out how the body is often treated medically with no regard for the mind or emotions. She notes that psychologists have also treated the mind as separate and disconnected from the body.[7] Through researchers such as Dr. Pert we are reminded of the need to consider healing the body through the mind and the mind through the body. Our heart is always present as the bridge between the two. Healing begins to occur as we come home to our hearts, when we grow from either/or duality thinking (mind *or* heart) into holographic thinking that combines HeartMind intelligence and wisdom. The whole is more powerful than the sum of the parts in this model.

Coming home to your heart and making the trip from everyday mind to your heart is key to enhancing your *response ability*, your ability to respond. Although you may not be able to change what happens to you, you can choose how you react or respond. Response ability is enhanced as you learn and grow through health challenges. This expands your ability to thrive versus merely survive and helps you deeply appreciate moments of renewed meaning and inner peace.

Austro-German poet Rainer Maria Rilke suggests we "be patient toward all that is unresolved in our heart, and try to love the questions themselves."[8] May your heart and mind open to the wisdom within your HeartMind as you read *The Heart of Healing* and experience discoveries in yourself and your life. May this bring renewed Self-love, trust, and compassion to your as yet unanswered questions.

Tools and Reflections

*The road of life twists and turns and no two directions
are ever the same. Yet our lessons come from the
journey, not the destination.
—Don Williams, Jr.
American novelist/poet*

Max De Pree, author of *Leadership Is an Art*, reminds us: "We need to give each other the space to grow, to be ourselves, to exercise our diversity. We need to give each other space so that we may both give and receive such beautiful things as ideas, openness, dignity, joy, healing, and inclusion."[9] May you discover and walk this path through the tools and practices in each chapter that follows.

As you creatively and playfully follow your heart during Self-care practices, you will uncover powerful secrets for health and well-being. These will help you shift perceptions, integrate insights, and bring your inner and outer worlds into harmonious alignment. As you focus on your journey, your heart and soul will reveal guidance and resources during Self-care practices.

Plan for a one-month commitment to using the Awareness Journal that follows. This will stimulate healing and connection with your authentic Self. Devote a minimum of thirty minutes daily to journaling and Self-care practices. Be sure to add a tincture of Self-compassion, love, and joy to bring a lightness of being to your journey. *You* are the gift you have been waiting for.

Tool 1: Awareness Journal*

*When one is a stranger to oneself, then one is
estranged from others.*
–Anne Morrow Lindbergh

Keeping an Awareness Journal will help you slow down, listen to, and compassionately witness yourself and your journey.[10] The process will help you develop a way to plug into your built-in directional system, your GPS. It will enable you to access guidance and wisdom within your authentic Self and will deepen awareness on your Self-healing journey. You will then be able to update your "owner's manual" and wisely bring your unique gifts and talents into the world.

Step 1: For the first two weeks make entries in your Awareness Journal a minimum of four to five days per week. Gently go within as you bring your awareness from outer space to inner space. "Check in" and scan your body, mind, emotions, and soul three times daily: morning before getting out of bed or shortly after you arise, midday, and in the evening before you retire. Use various channels (visual, emotional, auditory, physical sensations, movement, **intuition**) to gather information. Briefly describe what you experience as follows:

- *Scan your body* for sensations and movements. Witness what, where, and how intense these are on a scale from one to ten. Note this in your Awareness Journal.

- *Scan your emotions*. Witness feelings that are present, such as anger, joy, sadness, worry, grief, fear, or guilt. Note these feelings in your Awareness Journal.

- *Scan your mind*. Witness your internal self-talk, chatter, images, or stream of consciousness. Note what you witness in your Awareness Journal.

---

*   Courtesy of Betsy Baker, M.Ed., M.Ac., Licensed Acupuncturist

- *Scan your soul.* Witness any inner knowing or guidance that arises. Note this guidance in your Awareness Journal.

Step 2: For the next two weeks check in daily and scan your body, mind, emotions, and soul. Notice what you witness. Make entries in your Awareness Journal four to five days per week. At the end of each week describe what you are now aware of in your journal. How has this inner guidance affected your daily living and choices?

Step 3: Reflect on your process and discoveries at the end of each day, week, and at the end of two weeks. What perceptions, conclusions, patterns, new awareness, or insights did you uncover? How do these serve your Self-healing process, or not? Notice anything that requires change for your highest healing.

Step 4: Continue this process of developing your witness self by scanning your body, mind, emotions, and soul throughout each day. Make entries in your journal as needed, describing what you witness and want to practically apply and embody. Use your journal to connect with and honor your authentic Self and your heart's wisdom, as revealed through your body, mind, emotions, and soul.

Tool 2: Mindfulness Meditation

Buddhist monk, teacher, and author, Thich Nhat Hanh, describes mindfulness as being in the here and now. The Dalai Lama describes mindfulness as "the practice of bringing our accumulated knowledge, wisdom and insight to bear upon the present moment."[11] According to Rick Hanson, Ph.D., "Mindfulness involves the skillful use of attention to both your inner and outer worlds."[12] Mindfulness is taught at many schools and centers. Appendix B will guide you to resources.

Mindfulness is an essential Self-care practice and a skill. As you develop this skill, your body-mind will become more congruent with your heart, soul, and your authentic Self. Begin with the following mindfulness practice. Take time afterward to reflect on your experience in your Awareness Journal.

Mindfulness Breathing Meditation

Start in a comfortable seated position, where you will be undisturbed for fifteen to twenty minutes. Select a time of day that works best and turn off phones and other distractions. Sit in a chair or on the floor. If you are on the floor, make sure your hips are higher than your knees; use a bench or cushion and cross your legs if comfortable.

Breathe through your nose, and bring your awareness to your breath as it enters and leaves your nostrils. Notice the pace, depth, and temperature of your breath. Sense how your abdomen rises and falls with each breath, and how your breath flows automatically, outside of your direct control. If your mind wanders, or a noise distracts you, refocus on your breath. Let your breath be like a wave that washes in and out over whatever arises. Name and acknowledge any distractions, thoughts, images, and sensations, without reacting or attaching to them. Thich Nhat Hanh suggests we experience the miracle of our aliveness through each breath during mindfulness meditation stating:

Breathing in I know that I am breathing in.
Breathing out I know that I am breathing out.[13]

Slowly and gently bring yourself out of meditation when you are ready. Take a few moments to write about your experience in your Awareness Journal. Allow whatever occurred to be, and notice anything you label "good or bad" or "right or wrong." Be patient with yourself and your process as you cultivate a more conscious presence with your authentic Self, your life, and others, through the Self-care practice of mindfulness.

CHAPTER TWO
The Journey

*The journey of a thousand leagues begins
from beneath your feet.*
–Lao Tzu

T he healing journey manifests in a different pathway for each of us. We seldom control the timing, which remains part of the mystery of healing. A healing journey comes about suddenly or gradually, and may include physical, mental, emotional, and spiritual aspects. The process can take you to great heights of joy and triumph, as well as great depths of sorrow and despair, when life as you knew it is forever changed. You may struggle with learning to trust your individual timing, inner wisdom, and the unique ways your heart and authentic Self guide you. Each of these becomes a compass for your journey. You may also encounter passages through which you travel alone, "places as narrow as a razor's edge," as described in the *Katha Upanishad*.[1]

When you enter the realm of healing, you may find yourself in new and unfamiliar territory. Many clients described it like being on Mars without a road map. These places of solo passage are an essential part of your journey home to who and what you are in your authentic Self. I also refer to this as your *core being* or your true nature. I believe our soul, or essential life force, exists within our authentic Self, as does our link with the Divine. I believe connection to each of these can stimulate healing.

Coming home to your heart and soul is vital to healing. It occurs each time you consciously reconnect with your authentic Self. The process strengthens your resilience and helps you create a sustained response when you face challenges to your health and well-being. During each return visit home you will learn to transcend conditioning, roles, personality, attitudes, beliefs, and ego. When clients came home during sessions, it showed on their faces and in their bodies. Many had lost touch with their hearts and authentic Self. Coming-home tears often flowed as their minds and bodies relaxed and as they opened to and released into a process of deep healing.

In this chapter you will learn more about the healing journey. Two stories will highlight uniquely different paths taken, and how the wise-hearted spiritual warrior was awakened in each of these individuals as they encountered passages and triumphs. This enhanced their response ability and helped them integrate wholeness and their fullest potential during their Self-healing journeys.

Seeking Wholeness

As you seek wholeness on your healing journeys, you will be challenged to develop your ability to be strong and soft; open and cloistered; active and still; and have the discernment to know when each best serves you and your journey. On the healing path you will be strengthened and empowered as you learn and develop characteristics, skills, and powers of the wise-hearted spiritual warrior.

Carl Jung sought to better understand human motivation and behavior. He believed there are instinctual, unconscious forces within us that have deep, primitive origins. Jung termed these forces **archetypes**. He defined archetypes as universally observed patterns of thought and behavior that represent positive and negative qualities within each of us. Archetypes can be recognized through images and emotions that arise.[2] Jung believed that awareness of our archetypes could enlighten us about unconscious behaviors and our shadow – the unexpressed or undeveloped aspects of our personalities. He concluded that behavior, emotions, and life could change through looking within, weeding out negativity, and planting seeds from which new archetypes can grow. Jung felt this process enables us to embody wisdom, **grace**, and beauty through our life experiences and relationships.

Today we see archetypes in art, myths, and even advertising. You may identify with thought and behavior patterns of archetypes such as the hero, heroine, magician, guru, healer, lover, teacher, visionary, father, mother, child, warrior; or unconscious shadow aspects, such as the victim, martyr, servant, egotist, silent child, and actor/actress. Awareness of your current archetypal behavior patterns can help you identify ones that serve and ones that block you from your true nature. You will pass through stages of development and transcend behavioral patterns as healing and transformation occurs. When you understand, embody, and tend to who you are in your authentic Self, you will become your own wise-hearted spiritual warrior. You will flourish in creative ways, gain access to higher spiritual awareness, and free up vital energy.

My early understanding and heart opening relative to the warrior archetype began as I read *Way of the Peaceful Warrior*, by Aikido master, world-champion athlete, and teacher Dan Millman. I realized that heroes and heroines from myths and history were noble warriors who battled tyrants and monsters. David fought Goliath, Luke Skywalker fought Darth Vader, Mother Teresa fought for the poorest in India, and King Arthur's knights protected the kingdom and its inhabitants. Each rescued others as well as themselves.

I also participated in an Empowerment Workshop with authors and human potential trainers Gail Straub and David Gershon. These wise leaders described and modeled the qualities and practices of a spiritual warrior. I realized that wise-hearted spiritual warriors are not macho men or women who fight for superiority and power over others. They stand up to unjust or corrupt external and/or internal authority and often confront their own demons. As I studied the teachings of American author and medical intuitive Carolyn Myss, I realized the healing power within archetypal awareness. I recognized my orphaned child and my magical child. Each needed parenting, self-expression, and healing through the Divine Mother/Father within me. I saw my saboteur using self-destructive behaviors when I feared Self-empowerment and the changes it could bring into my life. Each realization made me more aware of options and choices relative to my thinking and behavior. Each enhanced my spiritual awareness and taught me how to give and receive what we are each worthy of – respect, compassion, and love.

Through Process Acupressure bodywork sessions I discovered that my persona, who and how I presented myself to the world, was different from who and how I was in my authentic Self. My wise-hearted spiritual warrior also began to awaken as I recognized archetypal patterns that had shaped my thoughts, emotions, and behavior: the good girl, good mother, earth mother, seeker, teacher, martyr, prostitute, victim, perfectionist, orphaned child, playful child, jester, caregiver, and warrior. Do you recognize these or other patterns in yourself or others? You, too, will uncover more about your unique archetypes in exercises at the end of this chapter and through the resources in the Bibliography and Appendix B.

The Passage to Healing

For some people I worked with, the passage to healing was short and uncomplicated. They quickly returned to full daily activities. For others it was frustrating and confusing, because they could no longer return to the activities and life they once enjoyed. Many embarked on endless journeys, seeking answers to their "problem" and ways to "fix" it. Their continuous search for answers led them to multiple consultations with medical doctors, surgeons, physical and occupational therapists, pain management specialists, counselors, nutritionists, and complementary medicine practitioners.

For these people, the journey became long and arduous. Their choices for care were often costly and limited in approach. They gathered information and tried alternative or complementary therapies, but they were often unaware and unadvised as to how to combine these with inner knowing, wisdom, and internal and external resources during healing. I found it confusing and frustrating when comprehensive care plans did not take into account the mental, emotional, and spiritual aspects that affect physical healing. This is apparent today as veterans return from war and receive treatment for their broken bodies. The post-traumatic stress disorder (PTSD) that too many come home with is not sufficiently recognized and attended to when their plans of care are established and reviewed.

For many clients I worked with, the healing journey enhanced their response ability. Necessity became the mother of invention, and I observed that whatever brought heart and meaning into their lives – pets, grandchildren, family, friends, favorite songs or types of music, gardening, art, or nature – also stimulated their ability to respond. These experiences reminded them of what was still alive within. This touched their authentic Self and activated their wise-hearted spiritual warrior, as well as their will to live.

For individuals who sustained acute injury through sports or trauma, interventions involved repairing their bodies. They were strongly motivated to heal so they could return to full daily activities. Theirs was a passage of summoning determination. Other clients faced recurrent or chronic conditions such as spinal, head, neck, and facial pain; chronic pain; or the diagnosis of a life-changing illness such as Parkinson's, multiple sclerosis, or fibromyalgia. Their physical, mental, and emotional response ability drastically changed. They needed to summon new capabilities and strengths. Not everyone was able to meet the challenges that pain and dis-ease deposited on their doorstep. Some became addicted to drugs, alcohol, food, or work in order to numb the physical, mental, emotional, or spiritual pain they could no longer tolerate.

Lab work became part of all my clients' physical therapy "homework" and healing process; it included therapeutic exercise, *acupressure*, breathing, mindfulness, journaling, reading, and Self-care practices. Lab work stimulated awareness and helped integrate learning. It was essential that clients learned how to enhance their response ability. There was no automatic pilot on this journey. Learning and participation was the way. Backpacks for the journey needed to be filled with patience, Self-trust, Self-compassion, courage, and persistence, along with faith in themselves, their health-care team, and a force greater than themselves.

Clients who faced chronic pain or life-threatening illness were greatly challenged by this approach. However, I learned to assist in bringing forth their response ability at these times through a combination of listening to and following their body signals, emotions, and words, versus leading with my agenda. Doing and being were incorporated into their healing process. This involved active listening, waiting with compassionate presence, and providing space for silence and/or deep rest during hands-on therapy sessions. We listened and honored whatever emerged as grist for the mill: tears and laughter; chaos and confusion; feeling lost and alone; and sacred moments of silence and peace. Everything served the journey. Following and trusting the process was especially challenging when individuals faced the end stages of life.

Life-threatening illness ushers us into a new landscape with slippery slopes and unfamiliar, frequently changing terrain. A struggle often begins when death becomes the enemy to be defeated at all costs versus recognizing this time as a sacred passage. This passage requires unconditional positive regard, listening, and support on many levels for the individual, family, significant others, and the health-care practitioners who serve them. Pioneers in the field of death and dying, such as Dr. Elisabeth Kübler-Ross, Dr. Bernie Siegel, and Stephen Levine have helped many to map out this territory. It is here that fear and anger often become our close companions.

The prospect of death is a stark reality, frequently filled with overwhelming situations and emotions. As a new therapist I was inexperienced in regard to death and dying. As I worked with patients facing terminal illness, I realized death is a mysterious passage that we face many times before our final physical passing. Throughout life we experience the loss of hopes and dreams, loved ones, financial security, and moments when life falls apart. Each death can help to prepare us for the ultimate letting go at the end of life when we again encounter the challenges of acceptance and surrender. Author Norman Cousins broadens our perspective on death, reminding us that "death is not the greatest loss in life. The greatest loss is what dies inside us while we live."[3]

Individuals, families, and significant others who walked through the dying process showed me that death does not always indicate the absence of healing. For some people, dying was a time of struggle, as they faced what remained unsaid or undone in their life and relationships. Fear, pride, anger, and old habits, attitudes, and beliefs shaped their world. They encountered unpredictable steps and unstable bridges over huge chasms as they moved closer to death and the ultimate unknown. The wise-hearted spiritual warrior within helped them touch upon peace during moments of acceptance and surrender. I, too, met these passages as my mother was dying. It was here I learned how necessary it is for our soul to be midwifed as part of the dying process.

We are all terminal. Some of us know it sooner than others. When end stages of life are faced, I am reminded that dogs get fixed, fish get cured, and people heal. However healing manifests, we find ourselves seeking greater physical, mental, emotional, and/or spiritual balance and harmony on our journey to the heart of healing. From our first to our last steps, we are guided home and supported as we discover what has heart and meaning in our life and relationships.

Mom's Story

The healing journey may take you on detours with unexpected side trips or discouraging impasses. When I walked through Pick's dis-ease (a type of dementia) with my mother before her passing, I was also separated from my husband. Each situation took me on a healing odyssey. I learned much about compassion in the face of suffering and separation – my mother's and my own – during the harsh reality of dementia and the seemingly endless days she lived at a nursing home. The wise-hearted spiritual warrior was awakened in the process for each of us.

To know my mother was to love her. Within the innate goodness of every action and step she took, every word she spoke, even amidst her faults and limitations, was the grace of a woman of valor. Mom began her final, solo voyage home when dementia took her from our family while she was still here. After my father retired, my parents lived in Florida during the winters and came back to New Jersey for the summer/fall seasons. I became concerned about changes in my mother's health status during several phone conversations with her, but I was not physically present to observe these changes while they were in Florida. The information I received from my father was confusing, and his comments often contained mixed messages. At his breaking point, Dad admitted Mom to a nursing home, informing my siblings and me about this after the fact.

I brought Mom back to New Jersey with the help of my husband, Stanley. He remained a heart-centered, grounding influence through Mom's passing, during a time when we were still separated. Stanley often spoke of how much he loved my mother, whose presence brought him what he never received from his own mother. The light that beamed out from his heart was like a lighthouse. It kept me aware of home shores as I traveled unfamiliar waters in my role as Mom's caretaker. About four weeks after we brought Mom back to New Jersey she was admitted to a facility for evaluation. She was eventually diagnosed with Pick's dis-ease. During her stay, the fog, confusion, and bewilderment of dementia lifted during a few rare moments. My mother shared precious, poignant, and fleeting seconds with my siblings and me, which we recorded in a small pad by her bedside so that we could update one another. The recordings grew fewer and farther apart as we encountered the shell that my mother formerly inhabited.

Within two months Mom was transferred to a nursing home, something I initially swore I would never do. As seasons changed and fall approached that year I went through the motions of preparing for Thanksgiving. I arranged to take Mom out of the nursing home on that day and bring her to our family gathering, her first outing. We filled moments with laughter and song when nothing seemed funny, as our voices met Mom's silence and withdrawal. She was in a place we could not go to with her, a place where she seemed to remain alone and confused. We filled our bellies with food, as our unnourished, empty hearts and souls ached with separation. Mom picked at her food as her eyes stared vacantly. She looked around the room as if she were asking, "Where am I? What is going on?"

Dread filled me when it was time to take Mom back to the nursing home. I felt I had failed her. I had sworn I would never put my mother in a nursing home, as my father had done. We walked down the long hallway taking us to the Alzheimer's unit, stopping to ring the bell by the door, which was locked for the safety of residents who wandered. Mom glared like a cornered rat, a riveting and piercing stare on her face as her floating mind captured the realization that she was back in this foreign territory. I wrapped my arms around her. "I'm here, Mom," I said. "I'll stay with you and keep you safe until you fall asleep. I'll be back tomorrow and every day, I promise." I desperately scrambled to surround her with protection, as if she were one of my children who had awakened from a nightmare. Mom looked at me, looked back at the door, and again looked at me. Her angst was palpable.

That moment is forever etched on my heart. Only in retrospect, many years later, have I been able to appreciate how it brought insight and wisdom to me through my wise-hearted spiritual warrior. Like sand within an oyster, this once incomprehensible experience created a pearl of compassion in me for my mother's solitary journey and suffering, and for my own journey and challenges alongside her.

As my mother's journey took her through dementia, I put my emotions on the back burner. As her primary caretaker and guardian, it was my job to act and make decisions objectively. I had learned and developed this skill during training and work as a physical therapist. Denial served me at times during my mother's illness, when it helped me function effectively on my mother's behalf. However, I paid a price and disconnected from my heart each time I went into my thinking mind without also connecting with and consulting my heart.

Years later, through counseling and bodywork sessions, I became aware of and began to process emotions I had separated from during this time. I left these emotions untended in order to cope and survive, but they remained behind a closed, locked door to my heart, awaiting my compassionate presence. Each of us needs to honor times when we need to stay objective and put our emotions on a back burner. However, when we do not revisit and process these emotions we betray and abandon these parts of ourselves. Our issues become stuck in our tissues. Healing is promoted as we journey home to our heart and authentic Self, through listening to, witnessing, and processing body-mind signals and emotions. This awakens the wise-hearted spiritual warrior within and enables us to grow wholehearted again on our healing journeys.

Being together with my mother during her passing was a gift she gave our family at the end of her life. She showed me, through our shared journey, how to gracefully support and be with others at the conclusion of life. My mother lived her life as a wise-hearted spiritual warrior without fanfare, in her own quiet way. Mom taught me firsthand about life and death. Through her courageous example and journey, she demonstrated how vital it is to be midwifed in our passing from this world, just as our birthing and entry are midwifed, with heart-centered presence.

Response Ability and Participation: Charles's Story

Time after time I watched people become tenacious, persistent, and mindful as healing journeys took them into deeper passages within themselves. Layers of conditioning unraveled and brought forth enhanced awareness, insight, and enlightenment. Healing journeys limed and tilled their interior soil, and enriched their connection with their heart and authentic Self. This helped them live wholeheartedly through phoenix-rising experiences. Their unique gifts, talents, and contributions emerged, and they came into new, unimagined ways of being.

Of all the clients who have graced me with their individual healing journeys, I will always remember Charles. I met him when he was nineteen and in the early stages of his healing journey.

Charles was at an age where he was becoming independent when a car in which he was a passenger went out of control. The car crashed into a tree, leaving him with a spinal cord injury that left him paralyzed and wheelchair-bound with only limited use of his arms and upper body. Charles's healing journey began at the moment of impact, during those irrevocable minutes that took him from independence to dependence. Charles and I started a new course of physical therapy, and a long, arduous process of physical healing, eighteen months after he had completed extensive rehabilitation. His story reveals a real-life re-enactment of the phoenix-rising myth. Charles's wise-hearted spiritual warrior courageously guided him through rebirth, regeneration, and rising from the ashes of a former life into a new one.

Physical therapy sessions with Charles centered on relieving and reducing recurrent muscle pain and spasms in his neck and shoulders. When we first met, I was struck by his indomitable spirit, sense of humor, and his presence. This immediately brought a sense of ease and collaboration to our work. Charles never perceived his physical, mental, or emotional healing as anything special, merely something he did with the help of his family. "I had no choice," he said, sharing poignant moments about how the love of his family brought him through early challenges.

I grew to learn from and respect Charles's motivation, perceptions, beliefs, vision, and journey, which was one of victory and joy versus victimization. We became heart-and-soul friends during physical therapy sessions, as well as during off-the-table conversations about life and healing. Charles rose above limitations. He graduated with a bachelor's degree and started his own business. He now coaches school-aged children about the dangers of drinking and driving, how to prevent head and spinal cord injuries, and the importance of using seatbelts. Charles also understands how vital recreation and sports activities are to a happy lifestyle. He continues to share his passion, positive attitude, and information during speaking engagements and through Beyond Wheels, Inc., his nonprofit organization. Charles has participated with friends in activities such as white-water rafting, skydiving, bi-skiing, and climbing pyramids in Mexico. He continues to demonstrate his beliefs, motivation, and visions for people with disabilities; he shows how to make the impossible possible using inner resources, power, and strength, along with external resources and support. Charles lives the path of a wise-hearted spiritual warrior daily.

Your Relationships on the Journey

A healing journey is like an odyssey, an epic voyage home to our authentic Self and a life lived "on purpose." My healing odyssey began with miscarriages and marital separations. I faced the loss of a dream and my personal identity, an inability to create union with a life partner, and the loss of what held heart and meaning in my life – being a mother and having a family. Your journey may begin with physical pain that dominates your daily life and becomes your entire identity, limiting how you stand up and walk through your life. Or it may begin with an emotional crisis that overwhelms and forever crushes the heart of everything that matters in your life. Perhaps a financial crisis bankrupts you and calls into question all you have put your faith in, especially confidence in others and your coping and life-management skills. And you may also face the raw challenge of sudden or unfathomable loss, perhaps of a child, which may set in place a rift with G-d and the spiritual beliefs that once provided a foundation for meeting life's challenges.

No matter how you arrive there, your healing odyssey will lead you, again and again, to awareness of one of the most important relationships you will have – with yourself. As this relationship grows and deepens, you will understand the value of integrating your experiences physically, mentally, emotionally, and spiritually. This may involve deep rest after stress and exhaustion; Self-compassion and forgiveness; the development of curiosity and creative ways to walk through these times; and play and laughter. Though it may seem unthinkable, play and laughter can ease your journey when grief or strong emotions feel all consuming.

As I consciously engaged with healing and experienced the tears and the pain, I kept coming back to this relationship with myself. The more patience, Self-compassion, and awareness I brought to the process, the more I was able to embody and apply insights gained during the healing journey. Acceptance did not come easily or all at once, but through repeated application of three principles:

- Witness and gain insight from all aspects of life: the good, the bad, and the ugly.

- Remain compassionately present versus going into judgment, drama, or reaction.

- Honestly acknowledge the truth of what is as you seek insight and understanding.

Of equal importance to me was having a relationship with a force greater than myself. Being an independent woman, I needed to continuously remind myself to connect with and honor G-d's relationship with me, along with my relationship with G-d. I was humbled each step of the way, but as I committed to both relationships many paths opened. I became willing and able to manifest my creative gifts, talents, and life potential more often. This proved invaluable during the writing and publishing of *The Heart of Healing*. Both relationships needed conscious tending daily to help me steer through stormy, dark passageways as well as peaceful waters.

My healing journey occurred through the grace of everyday angels, helpers, and messengers who walked beside me to support and enrich my experiences. They came in the form of teachers, mentors, friends, books, pets, music, art, and especially Mother Earth. Some chose to remain invisible and anonymous. These angels guided my enlightenment, deepened my faith and trust, and taught me how to walk the mystical path with practical feet.

Between Heaven and Earth

In Chinese medicine, human beings are considered the bridge between heaven and Earth. As such, we need to develop roots for grounding and wings that allow our visions and dreams to take flight. Our hearts contain the "glue" or cohesiveness that grounds heaven on Earth. Heart connection transforms our entire being as we reconnect with a force greater than ourselves.

Every step of your journey will serve and support healing for yourself and others. Your body will provide the vessel for embodying learning. Healing will stretch you beyond your physical body, perhaps on the mat during yoga *asanas* or off the mat when beliefs, perceptions, relationships, and life situations shift. When your reach exceeds your grasp, you will also be reminded not to stretch yourself too thin. Pain and suffering will sit alongside Self-compassion and Self-love. Each will help you develop the strength and courage of a wise-hearted spiritual warrior. Rather than becoming stoic and resigned to life's trials, this warrior lives resiliently through your heart and authentic Self.

Awareness, mindfulness, and Self-care practices are your empowerment tools for your healing journeys. Heart connection provides the key that opens doorways to healing and soul wisdom. As you heal, you, too, become part of a transformational process that brings heaven to Earth. Initially, when unanticipated processes and events arise, this may feel like opening Pandora's box. However, at the bottom of Pandora's box was hope – a hope that will aid our struggling individual and collective humanities.

Tools and Reflections

Knowing others is wisdom,
Knowing yourself is enlightenment.
–Lao-tzu

Congratulations on your commitment to continuing your Awareness Journal and willingness to use physical, mental, emotional, and spiritual insights and Self-care practices to support your healing journeys. Please continue this journal and use it for all end-of-chapter exercises.

Many of us look externally for cues, clues, and resources. You will now begin to also look for these within. Please remember to use professional resources as needed – physicians, therapists, counselors, and bodyworkers – with credentials and experience. None of us is meant to go this route totally alone.

Tool #3, Your Autobiography, involves taking a journey from birth to present time. You will explore this process during three separate sessions. Witness what you recall as you honestly and nonjudgmentally review your life. Notice what lights up and comes forward. I encourage you to learn from and use the past to serve your life and healing today. This will anchor your individual journey and enhance relationships with Self and others. Above all, remain gentle and compassionate with yourself as your journey unfolds.

Begin this session with several breaths to center and ground you. Feel each inhalation and exhalation as they move into, through, and out of your body. Sense the sacred sanctuary within you, which sets you and this time apart from the rest of your day and world. Light a candle, say a prayer, and if you desire, play soft music. Create a space that serves your inward journey. Have a pen and your Awareness Journal nearby.

Tool 3: Your Autobiography

Session One:

While in the sacred space you have now created, begin to review your life in chronological intervals by decades (birth to age ten, ten to twenty, and so on). In your Awareness Journal draw a horizontal time line, on which you will now list significant relationships and events you recall (family, siblings, friends, relatives, teachers, mentors, lovers, colleagues, pets, school, work, vacations, ceremonies, graduations, sports, books, music, art, and so on). As you do so, explore the following:

- What were the major experiences, highlights, crossroads, and transition points?

- What events and individuals touched your heart and influenced who you are today?

- When and how were you physically, mentally, emotionally, and/or spiritually present, or not, from your heart space? How did this impact you during times of transition?

Session Two:

Create a collage with photos or pictures from magazines that depict your life. Give it a title. Take a few moments, in silence, and be with this overview of your life. Notice where and with whom you traveled on journeys to the heart of healing.

Session Three:

Explore, reflect, and respond to the following in your Awareness Journal as you review your autobiography:

- How did conditioning and roles you took on affect how you presented yourself to the world? How did this serve you, or not?

- What specific thoughts, beliefs, and behaviors developed from roles and conditioning? How were these impacted by your heart connection? Which still serve you, and which do not?

- Explore Table 2 below, which contains a partial list of archetypes. Carolyn Myss's website can also be used to assist you further.* Which archetypal patterns or roles do you wish you embodied more or less of? Who or how were these demonstrated to you?

Table 2: Archetypes

addict	father/mother	monk	seeker
alchemist	fool	mystic	seer
artist	gambler	nature girl/boy	servant
avenger	goddess	olympian	shaman
beggar	healer	politician	slave
bully	hermit	prince/ princess	storyteller
caregiver	hero/heroine	prophet	student
child	innovator	prostitute	teacher
clown	judge	puritan	trickster
crone	lover	rebel	vampire
dictator	magician	saboteur	victim
diva	martyr	sage	visionary
dreamer	masochist	scapegoat	warrior
earth mother	matriarch	scribe	witch

- When and how did your wise-hearted spiritual warrior show up? What internal cues or signals (sensations, images, Self-talk) announced this? What enhanced or prevented your warrior from emerging?

---

* www.myss.com/library/contracts/determine.asp

Take a few moments to return to center within your inner sanctuary. Bring your awareness to your heart space, and let the stillness embrace and restore you. Welcome home!

CHAPTER THREE
Recovering Reverence for Life

*There is only one valid way to partake of the universe
– whether the partaking is of food and water, the love of
another, or, indeed a pill. That way is characterized by
reverence–a reverence born of a felt sense of participation
in the universe, a kinship with all and with all matter.*
–Larry Dossey, M.D.

Watching the night sky as a child became the first of many experiences that filled me with awe and connected me with universal life force. I took in these priceless moments like a sponge filling up with water, not having or needing words to ground them in my heart and soul. As an adult I discovered and more fully comprehended the riches deposited there. These memories became gold mines to revisit and explore, personally and professionally. They helped me unearth my authentic Self and took me to the heart of healing. Here I rediscovered reverence for life through Self-care practices that encompassed ancient wisdom and the natural world.

This reverence, at the heart of my childhood fascination with the universe, established an inner pathway to my heart and soul early on. It enabled me to recognize a core element within healing experiences – heart-and-soul connection. This alliance is a wellspring; a source that provides insight, wisdom, and guidance; a port in a storm; and a lighthouse beacon that reminds me where home is. This partnership is a source of comfort and safety when healing and life challenges feel overwhelming. Healing involves a process of rediscovering this core connection, and with it reverence for life.

In my mid-thirties, while I was searching for what brought heart and meaning to my life, I began to process awe-filled childhood memories during bodywork sessions. Through practices that originated in ancient ways, I tapped into my body's natural wisdom. A startling, unexpected revelation arose: Everything that existed in the external universe also existed within my internal universe. I discovered that, as Ralph Waldo Emerson wrote, "what lies behind us and what lies before us are tiny matters compared to what lies within us."[1] During sessions I uncovered realms and routes of healing throughout my being, which I began to travel and investigate: the **meridians** of **acupuncture**; the arteries and veins, which circulate nutrients and cleanse the organs; the lymphatic system, which protects and restores. Organs became planets to explore, and I discovered they often housed unprocessed emotions – anger within my liver, fear within my kidneys, grief within my lungs, and joy within my heart. My heart's wisdom provided sustenance, support, and guidance, which kept me on target during these sessions. I found myself again in awe of the life force I was discovering within me and the built-in mechanisms and resources for healing that we are graced with.

My intuition and insight deepened as I participated in Self-care practices on a regular, consistent basis. They became tools with which to meet the unknown. My intuition was not grounded in my analytical, rational mind. During bodywork and counseling sessions, my intuition tapped into conscious and unconscious memories stored in my body. As I began to use and trust my intuition, I encountered the defensive stronghold my ego and rational mind had erected. I needed to differentiate and disengage from this – not an easy proposition. I discovered what Albert Einstein described: "The intuitive mind is a sacred gift and the rational mind is a faithful servant. We have created a society that honors the servant and has forgotten the gift."[2] Trusting my process became easier when intuition and soul guidance came forth as I groped in the darkness on unfamiliar pathways.

I was like an astronaut going from outer space to inner space, using meditation, prayer, bodywork, and counseling to access and explore my inner worlds. Some journeys were beautiful and filled with awe. Some were scary and filled with erupting emotions, and many provided way stations along the route. T. S. Eliot wrote, "We shall not cease from exploration. And the end of all our exploring will be to arrive where we started and know the place for the first time."[3] Thus began a journey of healing experiences that led me home to my authentic Self and reverence for life.

Obstacles on the Path

In the busy, highly technological world I inhabited, it was easy to consciously or unconsciously disconnect from nature, my authentic nature, my life path, and reverence for life. During precious moments spent alone in nature I touched upon the interconnectedness within everything and everyone. However, each time I returned to my everyday world I experienced an internal tug of war. I desperately craved the stillness I found in solitude while in nature, yet I was repeatedly drawn more to external commitments than to commitments to my life and well-being.

I found it hard to be patient and compassionate with myself when life stood still and I wasn't busy. This was the case after two miscarriages, two lost babies. I was afraid. I was angry. These feelings built up within me over time. I felt ashamed, angry, and confused about my inability to bear a child. It felt like punishment.

When I became pregnant for the third time, my doctor suggested I stop working as a high school teacher, strongly recommending bed rest for the first trimester. It was late autumn, when nature was giving up life, and the long, dark days of winter approached. I spent months at home in bed. There was extensive, seemingly endless time to reflect and be present with my life – the new life growing within me and the memory of two lives my body miscarried. My fear of miscarrying resurfaced. I brooded incessantly. I felt overwhelmed.

One day, as I again faced my brooding, something snapped inside me. I was no longer willing to be held captive by my fears. I needed to uncover and consider other possibilities. An unconditional attitudinal shift occurred, like a seismic vibration shaking up everything within me. I vowed to myself that if this pregnancy did miscarry my husband and I would immediately look into adoption. This decision strengthened my willpower and commitment to go the distance instead of becoming morbid, stoic, and resigned.

That winter I came to respect how, during stillness, much was occurring beneath my conscious awareness. During those months nature provided many insights. Within winter's profound silences, and long periods of hibernation, new life and beginnings awaited opportune moments to birth in the spring. I learned the importance of slowing down and centering myself through my breath. I learned to be present with my changing physical body through gentle yoga, mindfulness, and other grounding practices. I began focusing inward to commune with new life germinating within me. As I participated in my healing first-hand, I discovered a transformational process of living from the inside out, in addition to the outside in. As I integrated inner knowing and guidance with external medical care, I made more informed, discerning choices about my health and well-being.

During the snowstorms, I watched as gusts of wind tore through trees, bending their trunks into almost inconceivable positions without breaking. Winter storms came and went, depositing icicles on bowed branches, which glistened during rare moments of sunlight. Much-needed beauty came to my world – a world that previously seemed dark and unknown. The natural world now taught me about developing flexibility; weathering change and storms with grace, and finding beauty amidst the cold, biting winters of my life. In retrospect, I now realize how everything in my life has been interconnected. Each situation and relationship enhanced my return to reverence for life. Seasonal changes have occurred in nature, and my human nature has changed as well during the seasons of my life. Endings have always been followed by new beginnings. Everything has served the grand design, or larger plan, often beyond human understanding and my rational mind.

Challenging situations left priceless insights for me to discover during subsequent bodywork and process sessions, such as great appreciation for our two children born after two miscarriages. After two separations I was more inclined to let go of Cinderella beliefs about being rescued by a handsome prince. I learned that blaming my husband shifted my being responsible for my life to him, serving no one, especially me. I grew to appreciate that heart connection and love, like bread, needs to be made fresh daily through open and honest communication with our Self and significant others.

My challenge has been to remember that my individual healing is connected to and part of the grand design, which I initially witnessed as an innocent child. When expanded awareness returns me to this place, I am reminded that I do not need to control life. At these times my process tends to unfold easefully and organically, like the change of seasons.

At various crossroads on my journey, I understood the truth in what Albert Einstein stated, "The significant problems we face cannot be solved at the same level of thinking we were at when we created them."[4] I had accumulated a heavy backpack of conditioning over the years, filled with attitudes, beliefs, and "shoulds." Emptying the backpack required honest, astute awareness and discernment, made possible through guidance from my heart and my authentic Self.

In order to change my thinking and expand my awareness, I began to explore my resistance to change. This took many forms: procrastination, busyness, and lack of commitment to and accountability for daily Self-care practices. Making life changes required giving up resistance, setting clear intentions and goals, and implementing a plan for practically applying learning and insights. You, too, will explore this in Chapter Seven.

I was afraid of change. I wanted to keep things as they were, which often led to denial and self-deception. When I separated from my husband, I married my physical therapy practice. Staying busy was easier than facing betrayal and loss of a dream. Problem solving for others was easier than touching on the immense pain, grief, and rage in my heart. It was easier to help clients solve their problems than face my own. All this led to more pain and suffering. Unexpressed rage and fear consumed me. Soon my lower back was in great pain and spasms. I gained weight. I was depressed.

As my awareness expanded, I realized that while I brought my car in for regular servicing I often left the vehicle I traveled through life in unattended – until a healing challenge, pain, or a crisis arose. To change this pattern, I reached out to others and created a health-care team, taking responsibility for guiding my healing process. Bodywork and counseling sessions became ways to support my whole being through regular and consistent checkups. These provided opportunities to oil, grease, and restore my body; reconnect with my authentic Self as I cleared and refreshed my mind; balance my emotions; and renew my spiritual connection via spiritual "tune-ups."

I became more accepting and less judgmental of myself as I awakened and healed. Checkup sessions showed me that shadow aspects within my personality were places needing the light of awareness and the touch of compassion from myself as well as others. I continue to appreciate how this process unfolds and evolves in its own way and time. It is something I cannot rush or superimpose my will and ego upon, though at times I still try.

Each time I committed to remaining awake and mindfully present through Self-care practices, I appreciated how they expanded and strengthened Self-awareness. Each practice helped me cross uncharted waters toward healing. They revealed and clarified several aspects that occur on healing journeys:

- returning home to our heart and our authentic Self
- embracing our response ability through commitment to our healing process
- developing our wise-hearted spiritual warrior
- recovering reverence for life

Walking the path of healing is often vigorous for me. It requires that I choose conscious presence over going back to sleep; stark honesty over denial and self-deception; patience over impatience; Self-compassion over self-judgment, and living *with* versus *from* my emotions. This unfolding series of choices builds and empowers my response ability, discernment, and acceptance of what I cannot change. I have realized that resistance and what I termed my ignorance frequently stemmed from lack of awareness and feeling extremely vulnerable.

The Path of Reverence

The more I enhanced my ability to respond, the more Self-acceptance, forgiveness, and healing flourished. Today, when I observe clients pushing themselves beyond limits, judging themselves harshly, or going through life at breakneck speed, I am reminded of how conditioned and vulnerable we all are. I also realize how similar we are in our pain and suffering. Through our interconnectedness we support healing for one another during every heart-centered encounter.

Each of us is being called to awaken to our own power and wholeness now. Answers to questions that arise during healing and during the reading of this book must be sought within. No one knows better than you what serves your highest good in any situation. Unfortunately, this is the last place we look, or have been taught to look, as a patient/client or health-care practitioner.

Our ancestors understood and used Mother Earth and the elements to devise formulas and a natural pharmacy. Though not yet fully destroyed, nature's resources are frequently devalued, cut down, or overlooked as our civilization advances. We have evolved into a highly mechanized culture, governed by our heads first and foremost. As a result, less priority is given to heart-and-soul wisdom, so vital to health, healing, and our quality of life as human beings.

The practice of seeking answers from within is not new. Mothers, grandmothers, shamans, healers, and indigenous cultures have followed this for centuries. Through lessons passed down from elders, rituals, connection with nature, and silence, we can reclaim inner pathways to enlightenment. These authentic paths teach us about strength, trust, patience, hope, grace, and honesty, as well as how to combine these with love and prayer during healing. You will begin this process of connecting with inner wisdom and guidance through the seven theme chapters and Self-care practices that follow.

The path to reverence is not the easy or obvious way. However, I have experienced that this is the way to flourish wholly, in body, mind, emotions, and soul. I have come to believe it is the deepest and most abiding way to uncover what awaits us at the heart of healing.

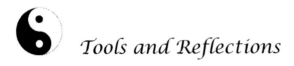

Tools and Reflections

The heart has reasons that reason does not understand.
–Jacques Benigne Bossuel

Before you journey into the seven theme chapters, it will be beneficial for you to explore additional ways to use mindfulness practices in daily life. These practices will open and soften your heart. They will pave the way to developing compassion for yourself and others, and will help you realize the beauty and reverence in both pleasant and unpleasant aspects of your life. Before you begin, reaffirm your commitment to participate in honest Self-reflection, journaling, and Self-care practices as you journey through this book and your life.

Author Michael Nolan reminds us: "There are many things in life that will catch your eye, but only a few will catch your heart . . . pursue those."[5] The Self-care practice of tracking will develop your ability to observe and interact consciously with your four-chambered heart. This will strengthen your wise-hearted spiritual warrior's ability to recognize who and what brings heart, meaning, and reverence for life to your healing journey.

Tool 4: Mindfulness Practices in Daily Life

Mindfulness practices bring us into the present moment. They help us gain perspective and reduce anxiety. These practices provide a break from stressful thoughts, experiences, and relationships, and enhance our ability to manage life. You will now take your mindfulness practice from sitting meditation to daily activities, such as eating.

Begin to breathe slowly, mindfully, and deeply as you enter your sanctuary. Notice how your chest expands and contracts with each breath and how your body settles in or has difficulty with this. Be compassionately present with any distractions and concerns. Bring your attention back to your breath when your mind wanders. Count each inhalation and exhalation to help you focus, making your exhalations slightly longer than your inhalations. Take time to read the following practices, and decide when and how you will implement them this week.

1. Mindfulness and Eating

Thoughts occupy much of our time, especially when we are eating. As a result, exploring, savoring, tasting, and taking pleasure from food and eating is missed. In this practice, you will apply mindfulness to your senses as you prepare and eat a meal.

Begin with several mindful breaths as you sense and listen to your whole being and your internal and external environments. As you prepare your meal, notice and become present with the color, feel, and aromas of your food. As you begin to eat, slowly bring food to your mouth. *Before* any food enters your mouth, take in the sight and aroma of what will bring you nourishment and pleasure. Chew slowly. Enjoy the different flavors and textures. Listen to any sounds. Notice when you feel hungry and when you feel satisfied. What foods please you? What foods don't please you? Do memories, aromas, tastes, and textures stimulate your awareness while you eat? Write your discoveries in your Awareness Journal.

2. Daily Mindfulness Practices

Now that you have experienced mindfulness relative to eating, you can apply this to other daily activities such as walking, showering, shopping, cleaning, gardening, listening to music, doing crafts, and spending time with pets. As you walk, bring your awareness to what you see, hear, feel, and sense internally and externally. Notice how you move throughout your whole being. What draws your attention during these activities? When you shower or bathe, feel your whole being connect with water, and listen to the sounds around you, including your breath. Feel and become present with the warm, soapy water as you wash dishes; take in the warmth of laundry just out of the dryer; and enjoy releasing clutter as you give things away. Bring mindfulness to any activity, and notice how your whole being responds in the now. Write about your discoveries in your Awareness Journal.

3. Mindfulness in Relationships

How can you bring mindfulness to your relationships over the next few weeks? Bring your hand to your heart at these times as a physical reminder of your intention. Start by becoming aware of what you notice in friends and family when you listen to them – gestures, facial expressions, words. Notice your own body-mind responses, gestures, and emotions. How does mindfulness impact you and your relationships? Write about your discoveries in your Awareness Journal.

Tool 5: Tracking

Bring your attention to your breath, and move your hands to your heart. Embrace the amazing life force contained there, which circulates throughout your being. What does your heart look and/or feel like? Do any emotions or images surface as you connect with your heart? Breathe into whatever arises as you compassionately witness this world within you. Slowly enter your heart's realm, where you will gather insights as you see and hear through the eyes and ears of your heart. Great wisdom resides there and eagerly awaits your presence.

Take as much time as you need, perhaps several sessions, to explore and reflect on the questions that follow. Each inquires about a different aspect of your four-chambered heart, described by Angeles Arrien and referenced in the Introduction. Remain open and nonjudgmental. Let your heart reveal honest answers and insights, versus mentally trying to grasp for them. Trust your process as it unfolds and as it stimulates reverence for your life and the universe in which it manifests. Write your responses in your Awareness Journal.

- Where in my life am I, or have I been, open-hearted versus closed-hearted?

- Where in my life am I, or have I been, full-hearted versus half-hearted?

- Where in my life am I, or have I been, clear-hearted versus doubtful within my heart?

- Where in my life am I, or have I been, strong-hearted versus weak-hearted?

As you conclude each tracking session with the above questions, take time to return to center in your sanctuary. Give gratitude for all that has come forth from within and for what is yet to be discovered. Listen for wisdom that emerges from your wise-hearted spiritual warrior during Self-care practices. This will strengthen healing and your body-mind connection with your authentic Self.

CHAPTER FOUR
The Heartbeat of Healing

Theme One: Healing Involves Showing Up and Being Present

> *There is no need to run outside*
> *For better seeing,*
> *Nor to peer from a window.*
> *Rather abide*
> *At the center of your being ...*
> *Search your heart and see ...*
> *The way to do is to be.*[1]
> *–Lao-tzu*

To show up and be present, to consciously inhabit our body and being, is a challenge we meet throughout life. Are challenges stumbling blocks or portals to new healing? Consciousness makes all the difference. When we seek healing, we are called to be more mindful of how our conditioning and perceptions influence us, how our beliefs shape our actions, how our attitudes serve or do not serve us. We are called to show up and be present.

Like Sleeping Beauty, we may remain asleep during early stages of our healing processes, waiting for something or someone else to awaken us. In this chapter you will read stories about awakenings. Healing evolves as we become aware of and embody our whole being. We also come upon another challenge, caring and seeing from our heart along with accumulating knowledge. As part of showing up, we need to discover what has heart and meaning.

Showing up during healing is not easy. It involves facing painful experiences and unconscious parts of yourself and recognizing hidden possibilities that lie within. A healing crisis can become a turning point as Self-awareness expands. Dante Alighieri referred to turning points in *The Divine Comedy*: "Midway upon the journey of my life, I found myself in a dark wood, where the right way was lost."[2] Showing up and being present involves courage, especially when we need to bring the light of awareness to internal and external dark places – places where we are, as yet, unconscious and feel lost. It is here that we encounter the paradox of pain or distress, and possibility.

I initially explored this paradox with Lawrence Phillips, a Guild Certified Feldenkrais Practitioner.[CM] Lawrence quoted Moshe Feldenkrais as he described the **Feldenkrais Method**® to me, "making the impossible possible, the possible easy, and the easy elegant." I was fascinated by this approach to movement awareness, but stymied that as a physical therapist I was still not embodying my whole being. Healing, at times, manifests like that as we uncover ways to show up and embody our whole being – body, mind, emotions, and soul. Inner guidance and wisdom arose during our lessons and brought well-grounded possibilities to my distress and lack of movement awareness. You will read more about this in Chapter Eight.

Before beginning any journey of awakening, it will be helpful to center and ground yourself, consciously bringing awareness to your whole being. Prior to reading further, please take time now to review and practice Tool 6: Breathing for Stress Reduction and General Relaxation at the end of this chapter. If you have breathing practices you prefer, select whichever serves you best and use that practice now. When you consistently practice breath awareness upon arising in the morning, during the day, and before retiring at night, the quality of your life and sleep will improve, and your body will more easily center and ground. Your ability to show up, deepen connection with your authentic Self, and use internal and external resources will strengthen with these practices.

The Journey from Our Head to Our Heart

We are each on a healing journey from the moment we are born. We meet risks, detours, and rites of passage along the way. When we are not present, we mindlessly drag our bodies through "war zones" of shock and stress. We find no solutions using everyday mind and frequently become disembodied heads in the process. Rarely are we taught how to be present through regular check-ins with our Self, which help us monitor the pulse of our healing. We become like racehorses panting at the starting gate, our minds whipping us toward an imagined finish line. We may win, but at what cost? We often lose sight of the most precious breed in the race, our sacred, authentic Self. The first theme relative to healing involves the journey home to our heart, which occurs through the action of awakening consciousness.

No one escapes the call to heal. Challenging experiences usher us into new or different ways of being present and living our lives. Each step along the way we may choose to go back to sleep and remain unconscious, or we may choose to awaken. I remained asleep through constant busyness and denying my emotions. I ate too much, and I worked too much. These actions were like narcotics and kept me in a fog of unconsciousness.

When my body showed symptoms of "something wrong," I sought out therapeutic bodywork techniques to "fix things," treating myself as a body, an object to be manipulated, rather than a human being with a heart and soul, deserving of compassion and care. I allowed external distractions to draw my attention away from what was happening in my body, mind, emotions, and soul. This limited my ability to be present and truthful with myself about what I experienced. It disconnected me from my body's signals and internal resources. Mental powers alone – mind over matter, mind over heart – brought no solutions, only frustration. I felt like a gerbil running on a wheel, expending extensive effort and getting nowhere. My learning would come through experiencing the wisdom from an African proverb, "When there is no enemy within, the enemies outside cannot hurt you."

What I sought was way beyond my conscious mind. Access to answers, I was to discover, came through being present. Yoga balance poses and inward versus outward focus during meditation helped me reconnect with my core being – my heart and soul, my *psyche*, and my essential Self – which waited for my presence and listening. To become more present within the physical, mental, emotional, and spiritual aspects of my being, I began to receive bodywork sessions with two *somatic therapies* I had studied, the *Trager Approach*® and Process Acupressure. I craved feeling at home through touch during these sessions, but vulnerable places arose, which frightened me. Safe touch brought me to my heart. Defenseless places needed to be safely wrapped in blankets of compassion, by myself and talented bodyworkers and therapists, during our sessions. This created unanticipated heart openings. The most important life journey I would take called me – the journey from my head to my heart. I began to listen.

Call to Action: Awakening
Early Beginnings and Conditioning

Like you, I didn't become unconscious overnight. This came about as a result of conditioning and the particular dynamics of the family and culture in which I was raised. As I became attentive to these factors, I uncovered my authentic Self and saw that I could learn a new way of being present through my heart, higher mind, and soul. This awareness deepened through Self-care practices.

I was raised in a post-World War II home with a mother who lived for her children and a father who worked two jobs to support his family. Children of immigrants, they both lived according to their upbringing and conditioning. They took on typical roles for that time – the male being the financial provider supporting the family, the female maintaining the household and raising the children. My dad worked days, nights, and many weekends. He was seldom free to attend school events, take my siblings and me to the movies, or just play and spend time with us. When he was home, chores became the place where we met, weeding the garden or repairing our house. Saying no to helping Dad was never an option. After witnessing his spontaneous bouts of rage, usually directed at my mother, silence became golden.

My mother was the glue that held our family together. As with many women of her era, she learned through conditioning to play what seemed a subservient role. Though my father was clearly the outwardly dominant personality, Mom's warm and strong-hearted presence was the core of our family and values. She contributed endless patience and kindness. Sundays were special in our home. In our small dining room at least twenty-five relatives and friends would gather to share time and meals with us. Mom's huge heart and cooking were renowned. Friends often jokingly asked her if the kitchen sink was attached to her apron. Everyone loved my mother for who she was. I grew up wanting to be just like her.

Living with a volatile father and a silent mother, I chose silence and denying my emotions as my modus operandi. I realize now that I feared losing control. I was afraid my anger would erupt and harm others, as I had experienced with my father. I feared others would not like me if I exploded, and I would be rejected. When I lost my temper, I harshly judged myself and felt ashamed. My mother's warning "Someday your temper will get you in trouble" reinforced this. I now realize that keeping my anger under wraps also held my fears at bay. Silence became how I showed up.

I learned about showing up with an open heart from my mother's example. Mom's love filled a room. It brought great joy and healing. However, when I showed up in adulthood with an open heart and experienced fear, grief, and/or anger, things changed. I became aware that keeping my heart open also involved learning to set clear boundaries relative to my heart's concerns, especially in relationships. My mother didn't set boundaries. This was not part of how she showed up. Her example was a gift that revealed where I needed to grow, beyond her example, through Self-healing. This also taught me how to remain clear, objective, and strong-hearted with clients when their emotions surfaced, aspects of our four-chambered heart mentioned in the introduction.

Showing up with clear boundaries required me to:

- be aware of unrealistic expectations, my own or others

- grow beyond emotional and psychological dependency, or *co-dependency*, in my relationships

- be present from my authentic Self, beyond my ego and personality

- be clear about intention(s) during interactions with others

- be mindful of service versus sacrifice when giving and receiving love to myself and others

Being silent and hiding began for me during the innocence of childhood. Fantasy and play with invisible friends and angels provided a respite when I felt frightened and alone. I, too, then became invisible, untouchable, and safe. Underneath my cloak of invisibility was an uninhabited shell to which I occasionally returned. I carried unprocessed emotions, stuffed unconsciously into my body for years, like a weighted backpack.

This backpack has been opened many times in adulthood. When muscle spasms limited movement in my trunk and low back, and severe pain limited my function, I needed to explore the contents of that backpack. Massage, Process Acupressure, and acupuncture sessions gradually brought relief and revealed connections between current symptoms and *cell memories* within these walled-off areas. During psychotherapy and Process Acupressure sessions, my now-wise adult and wise-hearted spiritual warrior helped me develop boundaries. Each brought safety to the young, vulnerable, and unhealed places in barricaded regions of my body. This helped restore the flow of vital life energy within these regions. As I healed, became stronger, and reconnected with my authentic Self, I was again at home in my whole being.

Call to Action: Awakening Angels in Disguise

We all experience and are affected by conditioning. However, other people show up along the way to provide healing, illuminate our path, and keep our hearts open. As we become more conscious and awake in our lives, we appreciate how these people were present to serve us.

When I felt unsafe in childhood, I disappeared. I lost trust in others, life, and myself. I was unaware of the power and healing available if I reached out and talked to someone, until I met Aunt Lilly. "Aunt Lilly," a woman with sparkling ice-blue eyes, was a neighbor who lived in the apartment above us in the Bronx. She was Mom's best friend, and my "other mother." Aunt Lilly was the one person who throughout her life saw, respected, and made it safe for the real me to show up. Aunt Lilly was tough and gentle. She spoke her mind to my father when he yelled at my mother, my siblings, or me in her presence. Aunt Lilly was my mother's voice, no longer hidden behind a veil of silence.

Aunt Lilly and her husband, Uncle Al, had no children of their own. Without question, my siblings and I were their adopted children. Their love was visible and palpable, as was Aunt Lilly's undisputed honesty. She always had a broad, mysterious, and beckoning grin when she greeted me, sealed with a loving pinch on my behind. Aunt Lilly was heart-and-soul centered. Charity work was a significant part of how she showed up, and it was her full-time "occupation." Giving and receiving love and service was the salary she received. Cooking and knitting gifts for friends and family were Aunt Lilly's meditation practices. I relive her presence today whenever I make Aunt Lilly's cookies. I touch her again as I knit gifts for family and friends with her "magic wands," her knitting needles. My niece, who lived near Aunt Lilly, passed on these knitting needles to me, along with their precious legacy. Her life, too, was touched by Aunt Lilly.

Our soul friendship was sealed the day I went to Aunt Lilly's for lunch during kindergarten. I began eating vegetables in my soup with my fingers, at which point Aunt Lilly gently smacked the back of my hand. "We eat soup with a spoon, not our hands." Mortified, I defiantly stood up with my hands on my hips, telling Aunt Lilly, "You are not allowed to hit other people's children. I'm going to take you to court!" That moment was one of the few times during childhood I was able to honestly, directly, and fully speak my truth to another person, without fear of repercussions. "Taking Aunt Lilly to court" was a special memory our family shared with laughter through the years. Whenever this memory was recalled, it echoed the love shared between Aunt Lilly and me.

When I felt frightened, abandoned, and alone in childhood, Aunt Lilly was there. She provided magical moments, safety, and healing every time she was present. Her unconditional listening and always-available lap was a giant cocoon of safety. With Aunt Lilly I was out of harm's way and able to be my spunky, bubbly, authentic Self. Aunt Lilly provided security, a place to which I could retreat from the chaos in my family.

Years later, during a Process Acupressure class meditation, I recalled my childhood relationship with Aunt Lilly. During brief, poignant moments, I again experienced how her unconditional love was a lifeline for me growing up. Aunt Lilly was a significant teacher and role model. She demonstrated how to show up and be present as a woman who spoke her truth no matter what, who set boundaries, and who made life safe in an unsafe world. Aunt Lilly showed me firsthand how to give and receive unconditional love.

Call to Action: Awakening Adolescence and Early Adulthood

We all meet universal challenges during adolescence and early adulthood. Like many of you, I tried to fit in and be approved but felt like a square peg in a round hole. When I didn't measure up to others, I felt ashamed, believing I was not good enough and something was wrong with me. Guilt, shame, self-doubt, and self-judgment became part of my self-talk, burying my authentic Self. When I began dating, got married, and started my career as a teacher, showing up became exciting. I felt loved, seen, and alive. I became busy making a living, unaware of the need to also create a vibrant, animated human life. I was yet to develop into an independent woman in my life and marriage.

I wore *masks* to cover up vulnerable aspects of myself: the clown; the good student; the good wife; the knowledgeable and competent individual. Unprocessed issues and emotions went into my tissues, ignored or denied for years. These surfaced at times when I became engulfed by my emotions and the stories and drama that surrounded them. I needed to learn how to use my emotions to gain access to shadow places within, as part of the process of embodying my authentic Self.

Hiding from myself and the world continued to work, until life was no longer funny and masks no longer fit. I needed to understand the difference between belonging at any cost and my longing for heart-and-soul connections with others, as I had experienced with Aunt Lilly. I came to appreciate that showing up and Self-healing are facilitated through love, compassion, and listening – from others as well as from ourselves.

Showing Up and Embodying Experiences

The body is vital to the experience of showing up and being present. We know that infants deprived of physical contact tend to withdraw, become sickly, and even die. People who encounter abuse during childhood, adolescence, and/or adulthood endure unhealthy, destructive contact. They withdraw into silence or escape behind masks or behaviors that keep vulnerable places hidden and safe, under wraps, inside their body and being.

After any kind shock or trauma, we can facilitate the reinhabiting of our physical vessel through sessions with well-trained and discerning therapists. These sessions may include **body-oriented psychotherapies, movement therapies**, yoga, and various forms of bodywork. These sessions and experiences provide entry points for healing, which help us show up and be present again.

In my mid-thirties, I began studying and practicing hatha yoga and meditation. Showing up during meditation, breathing practices, and yoga postures (asanas) was rejuvenating and restorative. Breath practices took me to quiet spaces within, some days quickly and other days slowly, as my "monkey mind," with its frenetic activity, ceased to intrude. My body-mind awareness was enhanced as sensations, emotions, images, and movement brought me alive, and I again began to consciously embody my physical vessel.

I learned and practiced the Zen concept of "don't know mind," or "beginner's mind." Though challenging, this practice still remains a way for me to meet life experiences without preconceived beliefs, interpretations, judgments, or the need to act. My everyday thinking mind began to experience moments of rest as compared to continuous activity. Retaining a beginner's mind greatly challenged my need to know, to have an explanation or answer to life situations, and challenged my habit of doing versus being. Yoga practices helped me sense when I was fragmented and not present, as well as when I felt balanced, strong, and powerful. Yoga and meditation helped me manage stress while raising a family, as well as when I returned to physical therapy school. Yoga studies, practices, and classes I taught revealed the benefits of combining healing, psychology, and spirituality. Yoga and meditation continually enhanced my journey from my head to my heart and soul. I learned how to connect with inner wisdom and joyfully embody my whole being.

Self-healing requires a container to hold the challenges and gifts that arise for our attention. Our physical body provides this container. It is an alive and authentic built-in laboratory, one that we can consult and creatively explore at any time. Yoga and meditation showed me that everything needed for my healing process was already present within. To access this, I needed to slow down, notice, and listen. Step by step, I began to practically apply experiences and insights. Showing up involved integrating being with doing.

Physical therapy school also brought lessons about showing up and embodying experiences. While taking two prerequisite physics classes, my mind and emotions revisited my math anxiety from junior high school days. When I failed every weekly physics quiz, I felt insecure and afraid I would not get into physical therapy school. I felt unnerved and intimidated. A tutor helped me get back on track. After admission to physical therapy school, I failed my first anatomy lab practical by two percentage points. It took weeks to calm my fears and refocus. As a result, I discovered that my self-worth needed to be as strong as, or stronger than, my self-doubt. I also learned that a strong desire and persistence fueled my intention to become a physical therapist.

Learning About Showing Up

As a physical therapist, it has been eye opening for me to watch individuals challenged by pain shatter their old attitudes and beliefs. Through their pain and experiences they taught me stark, unadulterated truths about the realities of showing up. These individuals spoke volumes about meeting loss, uncertainty, overwhelming emotions, and seemingly insurmountable odds. They demonstrated strength and courage in the face of despair and their will to live. They honestly shared their struggle to keep their hearts and minds open. They summoned their wise-hearted spiritual warrior by tapping into their whole heart and authentic Self. These spiritual warriors fought battles and found peace and acceptance in the face of death, physical death as well as the loss of beliefs, ideals, hopes, and relationships.

Fight-or-flight survival, volcanic on every level, stirred these awakenings. When individuals dealt with overwhelming issues at the heart of their healing process, they broke through protective walls, which could no longer keep them barricaded and isolated. Some individuals began addressing their life meaning and purpose. Others began a roller-coaster ride through stages of grief, anger, depression, and bargaining. Everything impacted how they chose to show up, consciously or otherwise.

There was much to learn and unlearn on my part as a physical therapist, including the differences between helping, fixing, and serving. I had two archetypal reminders that guided my immigrant passages during work in the field of healing: Mother Teresa, a strong, disciplined, wise-hearted spiritual warrior; and the words at the base of the Statue of Liberty, "Give me your tired, your poor, your huddled masses, yearning to breathe free."

If I helped clients but did not assist them with helping themselves, I created codependent relationships instead of empowering ones. This stroked my ego but did little to enhance a client's growth and healing. With this revelation, my role began to shift to that of a facilitator and educator. I was there to support healing and advance clients' participation and collaboration with their health-care teams. My professional journey to the heart of healing was now guided by the clients with whom I worked.

Call to Action: Awakening
John's Story – A Test of Courage

Making the link between chronic physical pain and psychological pain is often vital for patients. That certainly was the case for John, a highly intelligent businessman who had chronic migraine headaches. In physical therapy, he mentioned that as a young child his mother frequently banged his head into the wall when he misbehaved. He asked if I thought this had any connection to his current headaches. Although I sensed they did, John needed to realize any connection himself. As a result, body-mind centered psychotherapy was added to his plan.

I used bodywork during our physical therapy sessions, integrating hands-on manual therapies such as ***craniosacral therapy, myofascial release, neural mobilization, strain-counterstrain***, and ***visceral mobilization***. During one craniosacral session, I discovered ***energy cysts*** in John's body, brain, and spinal cord. Energy cysts are places in the body where physical, mental, and/or emotional trauma has occurred. Imprints from John's childhood trauma had been retained in his body. Over time his body encapsulated and adapted to these events. His body's ability to compensate diminished with repeated exposure to intense life stresses at work and home, which went unmanaged. Neck pain and migraine headaches demanded attention. Our sessions helped John relax and raised his ability to experience his body-mind connection.

In psychotherapy, John gained insight into the way early conditioning and trauma had prevented him from developing cognitive and emotional processing skills. Without support or role modeling in his childhood, John grew up lacking self-trust and self-confidence. He realized that rage had been held in his body for years, bottled up in his tissues until he "could no longer hold it all together," as he described it. During our bodywork and process sessions, John discovered that as a young, frightened child he felt overwhelmed by his very unstable mother. He also desperately sought her approval. John coped and survived by dissociating from his body, denying his emotions, avoiding conflict, and going into his head.

Over a six-month course of physical therapy, John experienced a renewed sense of well-being. He felt as if a weight had been lifted off his shoulders. Indeed it had! The results of his courageous, active participation in physical therapy and psychotherapy sessions were tangible. Pain and headaches lessened, John's posture and sleep improved, his mobility increased, and muscles throughout his face, neck, and shoulders were more relaxed. Shackles that surrounded the issues in his tissues were unlocked as John became conscious of when and how they were created for protection. Patience, compassion, and tenacious courage were vital ingredients in the healing balm John applied through Self-care practices he learned during sessions. Through **Gestalt psychotherapy**, John also learned how to re-parent himself as an adult. As healing strategies became more integrated and automatic, the frequency and intensity of headaches diminished.

John felt empowered each time he showed up and was fully present in his life. As he spoke more honestly to himself and others, his communication and listening skills became stronger. His Self-trust and ability to take risks also grew each time he remained awake to keeping his heart full, open, clear, and strong.

Call to Action: Awakening
Alec's Story and Being Present

Alec had been diagnosed with autism, a diagnosis neither his mother nor I was willing to let define who and how he would be present in the world. I began working with Alec when he was nine years old. Alec played many roles during our work together – client, teacher, and friend. He mentored my understanding of a world where heart-and-soul presence alone brought about human interaction, healing, and wholeness. I believe each of us was healed through our collaborative sessions.

While on a sabbatical, I spent time with Alec at his home, as part of a program his mother was trained in through the Son-Rise Program at the Option Institute. The program is based on an attitude of love and acceptance, is profoundly gentle, non-judgmental and respectful of the child's world, and creates maximum opportunity for growth. Mutual change and growth are essential aspects of the program, which Alec and his family began to apply. During sessions Alec and I connected and communicated with each other through eye contact, music, movement, play, and noninvasive touch, which included acupressure. I also incorporated sound healing, using a folk harp and tuning forks. The ticket to Alec's world was purchased through playful, loving, unconditional positive exchanges, and tickles, which he loved and encouraged. Tickles became the secret password that opened our hearts to each other. They also relaxed me and my unspoken expectations. Alec's laughter and wide-eyed excitement as we played this game were infectious. He showed me that love is contagious – we get it from each other.

Sometimes, though, sessions with Alec were challenging. After learning about **Tachyon crystals** for **energetic healing**, I purchased two crystal bars, eagerly awaiting our explorations with them. When I handed them to Alec, I explained the need to be careful with them because they were expensive. Alec touched them, smelled them, licked them, put them over his ears, skull, and body, and finally took them to his heart. To my horror, Alec then threw them across the room. Aghast, I saw each crystal shatter upon impact. In a single instant, my compassion and love for Alec were now sharing space with horror, anger, and disbelief.

I sat motionless. I was mortified and overcome with emotions. Alec looked at me. He got up and moved to the door. As his hand touched the doorknob, he turned toward me for one final glance. Our eyes met, and in that moment I came face-to-face with a turning point: How would I remain present with Alec? In this moment of choice, how would I resolve love and fear, love and anger, love and loss? Unexpectedly I heard a voice within: *There is no choice other than Alec. Love needs to be stronger than anything.*

But what about my anger? What about my loss? Self-judgment arose, followed by Self-compassion. I heard myself telling Alec we did not have to stop playing. I explained that I felt angry and upset about what had happened and needed a few minutes to just be with myself. As Alec and I met, eye-to-eye and heart-to-heart, healing and forgiveness began. I was learning how to remain present during a challenging situation and extreme emotions. Alec turned to face the door again and let go of the doorknob. He walked away from the door toward me. Very slowly he sat down next to me. Alec was testing the waters, and rightfully so. In an instant, I realized that this child and our relationship were more valuable than any material possession. Material possessions could be replaced; Alec could not.

As I allowed myself time to honestly witness and be present with this experience, I gained insights. Alec had helped me embrace versus deny my emotions. The heart of this child taught me about my response ability and choice to fully and honestly show up and be present, with myself and another human being, in a heart-and-soul-centered way.

Transformative Healing: Demons As Allies

As you gain insight and integrate your feelings and experiences, aspects of your core Self will come forth and begin to transform your demons and challenges into powerful allies. You will also notice when early life experiences continue to impact how and when you show up. Developing compassionate, nonjudgmental presence with yourself is a necessity for wholeness, empowering your life, and being your authentic Self. When you feel confused and vulnerable, turn to the wise-hearted spiritual warrior within you, who will highlight inner strength, courage, resources, and untapped potential in your authentic Self. Feelings and unprocessed experiences and relationships buried alive never die. They can, however, bring you insights, guidance, and a way into Self-healing through compassionate listening and presence from others. With time you will also learn to give this gift to yourself.

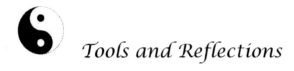

Tools and Reflections

Life is not measured by the number of breaths we take, but by the moments that take our breath away.
–Anonymous

Life begins and ends with breath. Breath is the bridge between body and mind. Self-care breath practices provide a direct connection to the vital life force within you, whatever you name this: soul; Higher Power; G-d; universal consciousness; etc. There is endless power in this connection, which will sustain you and enhance your journey from your head to your heart.

Yoga breathing practices support health and well-being. They enhance healing as they carry oxygen-rich blood throughout your body. During stress our **sympathetic nervous system** is activated, and breathing often becomes shallow. You can stimulate your **parasympathetic nervous system** and promote relaxation through breath practices that regulate blood pressure, heart rate, circulation, and digestion. Self-care breath practices awaken and connect your body-mind and enhance homeostasis throughout your being.

Tool 6: Breathing for Stress Reduction and General Relaxation

Begin this Self-care breath practice seated comfortably with your back and legs supported. Practice it twice daily for fifteen minutes over a seven to ten day period of time. You will recognize a response in your body and/or whole being between the fifth and seventh day (i.e. feeling of letting go throughout your body;

deeper inhalations; increased yawning during the practice; and a sense of mental and/or emotional calm during and/or after the practice). After the initial seven to ten day period of time repeat the cycle once daily for fifteen minutes. The KEY is remembering to do the breathing exercise once daily after the initial seven to ten days.

Here are the steps to follow to complete one full cycle.

Step 1:   Inhale to a silent count of 1-2-3.

Step 2:   Hold your breath for a silent count of 1-2.

Step 3:   Exhale to a silent count of 1-2-3-4, silently adding the word "relax" to end the step and one full cycle.

Repeat the cycle for fifteen minutes. You may want to describe what you witness, experience, and discover in your Awareness Journal.

Tool 7: Tracking Events and Angels in Disguise

Countless stories have been told of events or people who intervened in individuals' lives and prevented disasters and/or forever changed their paths. These events and people help us to show up and be present from our heart space.

Look back on your life – childhood, teenage years, and adulthood. Recall events and/or people who impacted you and the course of your life, especially at times when you felt protected. Who were the spiritual warriors/angels who watched over you? What feelings arose? What lessons did you learn about life, yourself, and others as a result? Bring mindfulness and heart-centered awareness to your recollections. Describe your feelings and discoveries in your Awareness Journal.

Conclude this practice, as in prior exercises, in your inner sanctuary. Rest here for a few moments and become aware of your internal and external environments. Notice the breath of life that enables you to show up during life and healing. Sense what surrounds and protects you, and the ways you are touched by the Great Mystery.

CHAPTER FIVE

The Heart's Pathway

Theme Two: Healing Is a Journey versus a Single Event

Even though you're on the right track,
you'll get run over if you just sit there.
–Will Rogers

Though we are each on an individual journey of healing, a common human journey is shared: Healing, as a process, unfolds over time and is not a single event. Common to this process is our search for a sense of connection, wholeness, well-being, harmony, and inner peace. When we feel alone in the depths of trauma we want a map, guidance, and some idea of when, where, and how healing will be complete. How do we find that map for healing when it is a process that is always unfolding, a map that is always changing?

Where do we look for guidance? It takes time, patience, awareness, and a journey of Self-discovery.

As you excavate your life and examine past routes to healing you have taken, you will uncover insights from the places you've been and the relationships and situations you've encountered. This will assist you with creating a new map for your current healing journey. Looking within becomes your way of consulting your compass, connecting you with internal guidance and resources that you can combine with external sources and support. This will help you explore pathways to healing and will deepen Self-trust and inner resolve.

Illness, pain, and anguish that beleaguer us have value. The process of learning their unspoken language and discovering what may be unconsciously present under the surface is gradual. As we shine the light of awareness on dark or dimly lit places within us, our journey and learning unfold. We uncover meaning and insight within illness, change, or conflicts we experience. As we learn to use our process to facilitate change and empowerment, we embody qualities of the wise-hearted spiritual warrior. This process reveals the heart's pathway and becomes our individual map to healing.

You will read about healing as a process in this chapter, journeys that brought individuals face-to-face with pain and possibility. You will witness Tom's challenges learning to adapt, in his daunting journey with Parkinson's. You will also read about what I unexpectedly uncovered through my process of Self-healing when I faced the threat of uterine cancer. More importantly, these examples will help you begin to uncover and understand your own Self-healing as a process and enable you to find ways to embody it consciously.

The Tools and Reflections section in this chapter includes a valuable Feldenkrais Awareness Through Movement® breathing lesson, as taught to me by Lawrence Phillips, a Guild Certified Feldenkrais Practitioner[CM]. This lesson will give you an opportunity to expand use of your Awareness Journal. Self-care practices will enhance your lab work and ability to relax and ground your whole being as you deepen your body-mind connection.

Living in Process

To understand healing and living as a process, let's go to the dictionary. Merriam-Webster's dictionary defines *process* as: "continuing development involving many changes; a method of doing something, generally involving a number of steps or operations." Healing in our Western world is typically facilitated through external steps and resources – physicians and therapists, books, videos, classes, and support groups. However, the process of Self-healing asks us to also take steps to empower internal resources: mindfulness; heart-centered awareness; higher mind; intuition or inner wisdom; and ***soul guidance/ wisdom***. Like Miriam's well from the Old Testament, which nourished the Israelites as they wandered through the desert, these resources are a continuous source for Self-reflection, regeneration, and healing.

American psychologist Carl Rogers reminds us that "The good life is a process . . . It is a direction not a destination."[1] In Chapter Four, you learned that Self-healing begins the moment you show up. I have described the process of Self-healing as a noun, a journey. Process is also a verb, involving action steps. In this chapter, you will become aware of action steps involved with process work.

Your journey will require a fully equipped vehicle for travel and exploration. As awareness grows and you more consciously inhabit your whole being, you will recognize that your physical body is the vehicle in which you travel through life. Your heart will provide you with fuel and nourishment along the way, and soul wisdom will reconnect you with reverence for life. These will be the spark plugs that ignite your motor during healing journeys. Inner knowing will bring guidance and insights and help you navigate through challenging yet empowering lessons. Plan time accordingly for lab work. Plant seeds of Self-compassion and grow patience to use when you face change, chaos, and confusion during your process of Self-healing. Now let's learn more to help you map your journey.

Experiences with Process Acupressure

I was introduced to process work in the early 1990s when I met and began to study Process Acupressure, the life work of author and transpersonal psychologist Aminah Raheem, Ph.D. Aminah's approach to individual and world healing uses acupressure, psychological processing skills, and bodywork with energy pathways and centers (meridians and *chakras*) to facilitate *soul actualization* and guidance. It is not my intention to go into depth about Process Acupressure and process work in this book. However, I want you to appreciate how this approach facilitates Self-healing and connecting with internal guidance and your life force, or soul. Please consult Appendix B for additional resources regarding Process Acupressure.

Aminah Raheem emphasizes that the client and therapist need to engage with the flow of information, which arises during bodywork sessions, from whole-being awareness (body, mind, emotions, and soul). This challenged me early on. It was familiar and easy for me to show up with my mind and intellect, in life and as a therapist. It was simple to be present with clients and help them process their emotions. Being present with and processing what arose in my body and being was another story! It took years and my becoming a certified practitioner of Process Acupressure to gently take down the walls of protection my intellect afforded me. This work helped me to compassionately embrace and grow with the edges I encountered during bodywork sessions and life situations. It strengthened my ability to move with and through edges using unconditional positive regard and easier, softer ways. Process Acupressure helped me recognize and release unconscious patterns that no longer served. It also showed me internal resources that ground and sustain Self-healing, soul guidance, and Divine connection.

In my sessions, I experienced profound letting go throughout my whole being. Experienced practitioners provided safety when unprocessed emotional pain poured through my body like a torrent, seeking to be heard and healed. The unleashed power in these emotions frightened me, and I ran away through intellectual discussions about what was happening. I knew how to do this well. However, this kept my body, mind, and emotions separated, like a family whose members no longer spoke to each other.

Not every session involved process work. Many times my body needed deep rest, in which my whole being could relax, and through that, a sense of safety and trust was established. As practitioners listened unconditionally to my body language and signals during sessions, their presence strengthened my own. This established a clear, strong field in which my healing and soul guidance could emerge. As sessions progressed, I discovered that the map for the wisest path forward already existed within my core being.

The warmth of compassion I experienced during sessions defrosted frozen places in my body and being. Long-suppressed tears flowed. My soul connection grew stronger; I learned that I have a history, but I am more than and not limited to my history. A much wiser aspect of my being was now showing up and overseeing my Self-healing process, my wise-hearted spiritual warrior.

Recognizing and Developing Your Wise-Hearted Spiritual Warrior

Self-healing asks you to develop a warrior spirit and a strong, peaceful heart. Dan Millman, spiritual teacher and author, states that many individuals have a warrior spirit but lack a peaceful heart, and many individuals have a peaceful heart but lack a warrior spirit. Combining both is a gradual and continuous life process. It involves embodying courage, honesty, loyalty, strength, and wisdom. Part of the process is meeting shadow or unconscious aspects of your warrior – places where you abandon your ideals, where truths may have been distorted through self-righteousness, and where power plays have been fueled by your fears and ego-driven behavior. Self-healing will occur as you allow both light and shadow aspects within to bring insight. Helen Keller stated, "I do not want the peace that passeth understanding. I want the understanding which bringeth peace."[2] As you evolve during wise-hearted spiritual warrior journeys, you will uncover and be empowered by this peace.

Lab work strengthens your heart's pathway and your wise-hearted spiritual warrior. Everything serves learning and helps you develop a warrior who guides, protects, and empowers your life purpose and what has heart and meaning. Through Self-discovery and living in process, this warrior will be your navigator and help you make heroic choices and commitments. In the stories that follow, you will read how others evolved during their spiritual warrior journeys.

Call to Action: Processing
Self-Healing Opens a Deep Process

Two years ago, I faced the threat of uterine cancer when my doctor detected a cyst in my uterus. This meant surgery and a biopsy to determine if it was malignant. As usual, I ushered in a rush of activity and arranged for diagnostic tests and admission to the hospital. However, I committed to an intention to remain present and bear witness to my process and inner dialogue: *What if it's malignant? What if this is life-threatening? What if I die?*

The more my self-talk centered on fear, the unknown, and my story, the worse I felt. I did not anticipate that prior trauma in my unconscious would surface to be healed. Process Acupressure showed me how unprocessed early trauma often acts like a magnet, drawing new situations and relationships to it to bring them into our awareness. This new challenge in my life turned up the volume on original trauma, which was only a whisper in my unconscious. My attention was drawn to this trauma, once again, for healing. When this occurred, and I connected with internal resources for healing, new possibilities arose.

Some of my presurgery fear was reality based. During a prior surgery, I became conscious before the anesthesia wore off. I felt the tube in my throat, there to prevent choking, still in place. Because of the anesthesia, I was unable to move even a finger or scream out for help. I panicked. I struggled to breathe. An immense battle arose as I wrestled silently within myself. Suddenly I recalled yoga breathing. I dropped into meditation and sensed a deep letting go occur. Moments later, a nurse abruptly pulled the tube out.

This memory of unprocessed fear and trauma was magnetically drawing my attention. My physician assured me the same thing would not recur and suggested I talk with the anesthesiologist, too. To calm my fears, I investigated the anesthesia device that would be used. I was calmer in my head, but the emotional trauma remained unprocessed. The root trauma was yet to be revealed.

My lab work surfaced immediately. Every time I looked at the picture and description of the anesthesia mask, severe nausea and an overwhelming need to vomit overtook me. I searched my mind: *Was I was getting sick? What had I eaten?* Nothing I tried helped, and my symptoms continued. I began Self-care practices and journaling, sometimes several times a day, and spent silent time in nature. These practices took my focus inward, amidst physical and emotional distractions, and opened the pathway for soul guidance to surface.

My soul sent messages as I journaled, like a lighthouse beam in the darkness that revealed home and safety. I wrote:

In midair . . . I am catapulted across a giant chasm,
unsure when, where, and how I will land. I grasp for
anything to bring me to the opposite side. There's
nothing to hold on to. I'm in free fall . . . my body is
stiff as a board . . . fear is running wild . . . my mind
is a cyclone out of control.

One recurrent childhood fantasy emerged. I repeatedly felt myself soar, joyously and freely above the earth like a bird. I became Jonathan Livingston Seagull, living the fable about flight and self-perfection. Soul guidance emerged in my journal without effort:

Fly above this situation . . . get a bird's-eye view . . . be
in it but not of it . . . notice possibilities . . . surrender,
listen, and let go of your need to control events.

I watched my ego still struggle to remain in charge. However, an inner resource was emerging – my wise-hearted spiritual warrior.

After attaining this bird's-eye-view, my commitment to regular Self-care practices was sealed. I began daily meditation, journaling, acupressure self-treatment, **Qigong, Chakra Tai Chi** movement practices, and weekly counseling. One powerful flashback from childhood emerged next under more layers of armoring. This showed the original root trauma and drew my attention. I realized that what needed to be thrown up was not the current anesthesia device but what had been shoved down my throat as a child: the stipulation to behave and be a good girl; the demand that I remain silent and not express emotions; the requirement to stifle fear, rage, or talking back that challenged my father's authority; the pressure to be seen and not heard. My wise-hearted spiritual warrior, guided by soul wisdom, was helping me be the victor in my life, not the victim of my father's behavior and actions. Self-care practices opened the doorway to fully showing up and discovering other possibilities.

Healing spins us into such memories. Emotional wounds from our past spiral up and out into our awareness. When this happens, greet it. Bear witness to it. You will now get to see more clearly how your conditioning has shaped you. Opportunities will present themselves to you and bring further insight and guidance. Be patient. Self-healing is a process.

Call to Action: Processing Self-Healing and the Unwinding

A cocoon of conditioning began to unwind as my process continued. During a self-treatment Process Acupressure session, an image arose. I saw myself covered by a dark burka, with only my eyes showing. I realized this was my authentic Self, concealed. The image of the burka and my process continued to unravel during this session as I gently created safety and compassionate presence with myself.

A kaleidoscope of images from childhood burst forth as I continued this self-treatment session. Places where I separated from my authentic Self were revealed. I was constantly on guard as a child, never knowing when my father's erratic and explosive behavior would erupt. When I left the scene in my mind, and buried its memory in my unconscious to survive, I did not realize I was abandoning myself. My process was now leading me back to myself.

One memory that arose was of coming home from public school to my father ranting and screaming. He stalked the house like a tiger. My mother stood motionless and frozen, her eyes downcast, like mine in the burka. Mortal fear overtook me, and I suddenly heard someone screaming at my father – me. "Stop yelling at her! She's not your boss from work." How I had the courage to confront him remains a mystery. I'm sure Aunt Lilly's modeling had paved the way.

I fled and hid in the basement afterward; afraid my father would come after me. He never did. I remained in hiding until it got dark and then ran to my bedroom. This young child within me waited in vain for an adult to take her to safety. She remained frozen and stuck there for many years. I was now bringing her to safety. I recognized parallels between my mother's conditioning and my own. I also realized that my wise-hearted spiritual warrior momentarily surfaced when I stood up to my father during that incident. A lifelong process of Self-healing, which broke ancestral chains my mother could not, was being highlighted in my consciousness.

This frightened child emerged again during sessions at a Process Acupressure *inner child healing* class. When I initially approached her during a session, she recoiled like a frightened animal. She still did not know she was fully out of danger. She needed me, as an adult, to take her to safety. She also needed reassurance I would not leave her again. As I subsequently grew kinder and less judgmental toward myself, I became able to extend this to her and this once-abandoned place within me.

Inner child healing became a vital part of my healing process and lab work. I was now providing a place out of harm's way for my young, frightened inner child, as Aunt Lilly had done for me.

Self-Healing As a Personal Process: The Unfolding

My discoveries did not end there. It was only the beginning, as you will discover, too, when you start unearthing early conditioning that may be hidden in cell memory. Often, people feel immense grief for the beauty and innocence they lost in childhood. As you surround such vulnerable parts of yourself with compassion, safety and trust will grow and support your return journey home. You always hold the key to the door, but not through fixing, planning, or mindless repetition of your story. It is through unconditional presence, forgiveness, and heart-and-soul connection that Self-healing occurs. The process will evolve in its own natural way and timing. Your inner child will provide you with guidance about whom, when, and what to trust, including yourself. My inner child revealed that safety and Self-trust were precursors to my healing and development of the skills of a wise-hearted spiritual warrior.

You, too, will find that each inner aspect of your being that surfaces will support your return to wholeness. Parts of yourself abandoned in childhood will come forth and lead you to an aspect of yourself that is strong, creative, and courageous, your wise-hearted spiritual warrior. As I continued my journey, other inner aspects surfaced and challenged me to grow – the perfectionist and the workaholic. I again met pain and possibility, vulnerability and strength, shadow and light, victim and victor. I became the heroine in my own life story.

I am grateful that my wise-hearted spiritual warrior now provides grounding, instruction, compassion, strength, and security in a snug harbor. My inner child is now my muse, teacher, playmate, and honest companion. Each acts in service with and for the other. Wise and magical aspects within my inner child create moments of joy, curiosity, creative exploration, and deep healing.

Your Safe Place

Yesterday is history. Tomorrow is a mystery.
Today is a gift. That's why they call it the present.
–Alice Morse Earle

You, too, need to provide safe places for yourself during your healing journeys. Where would they be and what would they look like? Would they be indoors? Outdoors? A combination of both? What season(s) would you incorporate into this place? Who else would you like there with you? In your life has there been someone like Aunt Lilly, who protected and empowered you to grow and develop into all that you are, who gave you roots and wings? What characteristics do they demonstrate that you admire and seek to embody? What experiences have challenged you to bring forth the wise-hearted spiritual warrior within you? Who or what enhanced your process? Who or what blocked your process?

Your safe place will change. Be open to changes, and redesign it to serve your changing needs. Enjoy your process!

My friend Kathleen recently spoke about becoming more conscious of her fears and her need to feel safe amidst them. The paradox that bridged these feelings together became apparent as she spoke. "I didn't know there was a scary place inside me until there was a safe place to be scared." The silence between us was profound. Strong emotions led her to insights and opened doorways to deeper healing.

Before reading further, please find a comfortable place for reflection. Have your Awareness Journal handy. You may want to light a candle or play soothing music. Keep water nearby as well. Water nourishes your brain and body, and is a vital element needed for all body functions. Water, like breath, also helps to flush out toxins and remnants of trauma.

The courageous questions then become: Can you bear to go for what is deeper and more lasting amidst the pain and suffering in yourself and/or others? Can you explore pain and possibility? Can you love and trust yourself enough to at least test the waters before you begin any Self-healing process?

Let your *soul wisdom* guide you as you answer these or other questions that arise. Allow yourself to respond freely, without judgment. Remember there are no right or wrong answers. Draw or write your responses in your journal. What surfaces within as you read and listen is more important than anything I am writing.

Call to Action: Processing Tom's Story and Adaptability

Tom was referred to me for balance, gait training, and a home exercise program after being diagnosed with Parkinson's dis-ease in his fifties. He was a quiet businessman whose early symptoms included: stiffness and difficulty walking; mild tremors; intermittent loss of balance; and limited mobility in his trunk and arms. With his first courses of treatment, he became independent in a home program, increased his walking pace and speed, improved his upper body mobility, and felt he was better able to manage balance issues as movement improved. Tom's wife was his advocate. She adapted his diet, identified supplements recommended for Parkinson's, and found a local support group. She also kept him on track with his home exercise program.

Over several years his symptoms gradually worsened, and he became less active, less mobile, and more withdrawn. Tom's wife arranged for him to be seen at a large teaching hospital, at a clinic specializing in Parkinson's, where he was chosen to participate in a study using a deep brain stimulator. This surgically implanted, battery-operated device was used to treat neurological symptoms such as tremor, rigidity, stiffness, and problems with movement and walking. Everyone was amazed watching Tom's ease, speed, and agility of movement improve with this device.

Sometimes when Tom returned for physical therapy it took him forty-five minutes to move from the parking lot to a treatment room. Tom responded well to collaborating with me on his treatment. When he left sessions, he frequently walked out to the car with ease in less than five minutes. Because his follow-up at home with exercises was vital, I had Tom document this in an exercise journal we created. This allowed him to track changes and his progress for himself.

As Parkinson's progressed, Tom's process changed. He became less mobile, and cognitive changes began to occur.

His relationships with his family changed as well. His wife and children became frustrated with his reduced participation and tendency to be passive. Tom had retired several years before this and now spent many long days at home in front of the television. It was a challenge to determine which changes were simply the progression of the dis-ease and which changes were due to lack of activity and stimulation.

After he participated in individual and family counseling, Tom occasionally shared his emotions and difficulties adapting, as well as his frustration about family expectations. Tom's process gradually became more inward, and he shared it with me and his wife only on rare occasions. I have fond memories of pinching his behind, to change his mood and encourage him to speed up his walking. This was accomplished, but only for a moment. Watching Tom laugh and come alive was poignant. Watching Tom fall back into silence and inactivity was difficult.

I learned to be patient with Tom's process. Everyone involved needed to remember that Tom's life, healing process, and choices were his to make. We were also responsible for how we chose to respond to Tom's choices. When I look back, it is clear that he adapted in his own way, in his own time.

My experience with Tom reminded me of a quote from British naturalist Charles Darwin: "It is not the strongest of the species that survives, nor the most intelligent that survives. It is the one that is the most adaptable to change."[3] We may not be able to control what happens to us. We can, however, control how we choose to respond to our life and healing process over time. I have learned through clients such as Tom that whether we choose to change or not, a process emerges. Our challenge is to hold compassion, unconditional positive regard, and love for ourselves and each other, no matter how our journeys unfold.

Living in Process: Why We Need to Process Our Life and Healing

An old Chinese proverb states, "What I hear, I forget. What I see, I remember; and what I experience, I understand." As we process our healing journeys, we gather understanding and empower our growth. Process work can occur through various means – talk-based or body-mind-oriented psychotherapies, and bodywork-oriented somatic therapies such as Process Acupressure, *Zero Balancing*®, CranioSacral therapy, Trager®, and the Feldenkrais Method®. The heart of healing in all these approaches involves showing up, being present, connecting with your heart's pathway, and understanding that this can bring you into a larger process that is beyond a single event. Living in process will help you to:

- bring unconscious aspects within you to the surface
- gain insight into persistent, chronic symptoms and/or recurrent injuries
- release physical, mental, and emotional patterns that no longer serve
- balance and harmonize energy pathways and centers (meridians and chakras) in the body
- gain deeper access to Self-healing and wholeness
- use insights and understanding to reclaim your authentic Self
- connect with and use your inner compass – that is, your soul guidance and wisdom

Our life is always in process: consciously and unconsciously; with and without words; outwardly and inwardly. We can see this in the changing of the seasons and the passing of time. Living in process keeps you awake and connected with your authentic Self, your heart's pathway, and your dynamic life force, or soul, which taps into reverence for life.

To deepen my understanding about living in process, I investigated what prevented me from honestly and compassionately living in process beyond the treatment tables and therapists' offices. I discovered that living in drama and mindlessly retelling my story kept me stuck and avoided my processing of it. Although drama fueled a false sense of aliveness, it never provided safety and a sense of home within, only brief adrenaline rushes and diversions. I realized that my thoughts fed my emotions, shaped my perceptions, and either blocked or enhanced the flow of my creative expression and insights.

My true feelings were denied when I lived with illusions that prevented me from hearing the truth when I told myself: *Things really aren't that bad. This too shall pass. Others have it worse than me* or *When I achieve or attain _____ life will be better.* Self-judgment, comparing myself to others, and playing roles prevented me from being my authentic Self in daily living. When I lost my sense of humor, play, and spontaneity, this was a clue I had taken myself and life too seriously. Living in process kept me awake and connected with my authentic Self, my heart's pathway, and my life force, or soul.

What Enhances Living in Process

Living in process helped me to meet internal and external disturbance without disturbance. During Process Acupressure and Jungian pyschotherapy sessions, I came to deeper realizations and explored ways to practically integrate the insights I gained. I also learned the language of my authentic Self as expressed through my whole being – body, mind, emotions, and soul. My wise-hearted spiritual warrior was empowered through soul connection and wisdom. Living in process brought challenges along with possibilities and great joy.

Self-healing is dynamic, not static. It is an unpredictable process that evolves over time with many paradigm shifts.

Action steps you choose will be based on timing, situations, relationships, resources, and what supports your heart's pathway. Journaling, breath work, meditation, movement practices, and so on will help ground you. They will bring clarity and insight into the tedious process of unraveling tangled ends and twisted parts of your life and Self-healing process. What you can track and name you can interact with versus remaining in a cycle of conditioning and reactivity. You can create a beautiful tapestry out of the once-tangled heap in front of you. Your life tapestry will be enhanced through:

1) *Alone time with clear intentions*: A dear friend used this practice during her journey with breast cancer. She scheduled one full day each month, on the day of her birthday, for a silent, solitary vision quest. This provided time for her to rest, listen, receive, and bring forth inner guidance, wisdom, and Self-trust. Solitude with clear intentions brings harmony and integration to your whole being and healing process.

2) *Meditation*: Many options are available. The works of Jon Kabat-Zinn and Thich Nhat Hanh have brought simplicity and grace to my practice. David Richo's book, *The Five Things We Cannot Change, and the Happiness We Find by Embracing Them* helped me remain mindful of my internal CIA, my Critic, Interpreter, and Adviser, who seek to rule.[4] Meditation guides you to portals that lead you home and connect you with the vast oneness we all are part of.

3) *Self-care body-mind practices*: These provide direct learning about remaining centered, grounded, and awake in your process. When grounded you inhabit your body, your mind becomes clear and focused, your emotions bring greater harmony to your whole being, and soul guidance is available. Pain and suffering become signals that indicate you are off center. Self-care practices support your return home and maximize well-being.

Healing and Time

Living Self-healing as a process over time is a direction you take your life in, rather than a destination you arrive at on a single journey. Life will not necessarily be easier. However, your journey will be less chaotic, more potent, and definitely less stressful. We must each stand in our courageous place and be part of the Great Mystery within life and healing. Each "now" moment and the Self-awareness insight discovered there is filled with precious, nourishing gifts – when you take time to awaken, receive, be present with your healing process, and return home.

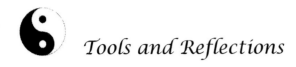

Tools and Reflections

*We are explorers, and the most compelling frontier of our time
is human consciousness. Our quest is the integration of science
and spirituality, a vision that reminds us of our connectedness
to the inner self, to each other, and to the earth.*[5]
–Edgar Mitchell, Astronaut

I learned the following Self-care breath practice during a
Feldenkrais Awareness Through Movement® lesson. I have used
it with countless people who also found it extremely helpful.
I now pass it along to you. Use the diagrams that follow for
additional guidance regarding hand placement for each step.

Although I have found it best to practice this lying down,
it can be done seated. Used prior to sleep, this practice will
enhance sleep quality, reduce anxiety, and calm and center your
body-mind. Begin with approximately five to seven repetitions
of each step that follows before moving on to the next one.
Let your breath be like a lullaby that whispers in your ear and
reminds you of who and what you really are in your heart, soul,
and authentic Self.

Remember to draw upon various channels of perception
to deepen your experience and awareness – images that arise,
sounds you hear, sensations you feel, and movements you
experience.

Tool 8: Feldenkrais Awareness Through Movement® Breathing Lesson

Step 1. Place your right palm over your right collarbone, and your left palm over your left collarbone. Breathe and notice through your hands how your chest rises and falls with each inhalation and exhalation. Notice any differences in ease or quality of movement, or depth of breathing, from right to left, top to bottom, front to back. Repeat for three to five breaths.

Step 2. Place your right palm on the bottom and side of your right rib cage, and your left palm on the bottom and side of your left rib cage. Breathe and notice how your rib cage expands and contracts, side-to-side and front to back, with each inhalation and exhalation. Notice any differences in ease or quality of movement, or depth of breathing, from right to left, top to bottom, front to back. Repeat for three to five breaths.

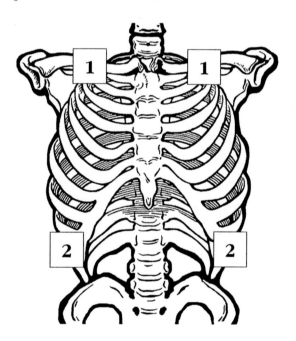

Diagram 1: Hand Positions (Steps 1 & 2)

Step 3. Place your left palm over your right collarbone, and your right palm over the bottom and side of your right rib cage. Inhale: imagine and feel your right lung filling with oxygen, like a vase of water being filled from bottom to top. Exhale: imagine and feel your right lung deflating, like a vase of water being emptied from top to bottom. Repeat for three to five breaths.

Step 4. Follow step 3 for your left lung. Place your right palm over your left collarbone, and your left palm over the bottom and side of your left rib cage. Inhale: imagine and feel your left lung filling with oxygen, like a vase of water being filled from bottom to top. Exhale: imagine and feel your left lung deflating, like a vase of water being emptied from top to bottom. In steps 3 and 4 compare the right and left side for any differences in ease or quality of movement, or for depth of breathing from right to left, top to bottom, front to back. Repeat for three to five breaths.

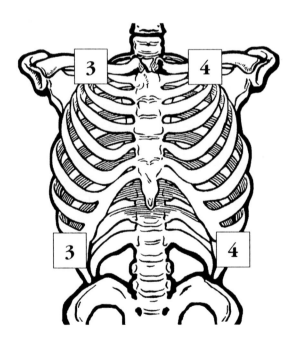

Diagram 2: Hand Positions (Steps 3 & 4)

Step 5. Place your right palm over your right collarbone and your left palm over the bottom and side of your left rib cage. Inhale in a diagonal manner, from bottom left to top right, as your breath fills your left, then right lung. Sense this movement through your palms. Exhale in a diagonal pattern, sensing the movement with your palms as your lungs empty from top right to bottom left. Compare the right and left side for differences in ease or quality of movement and depth of breathing from right to left, top to bottom, front to back. Repeat for three to five breaths.

Step 6. Follow step 5, in the opposite direction. Place your left palm over your left collarbone, and your right palm over the bottom and side of your right rib cage. Inhale from the bottom right lung to the top left lung, and exhale from the top left lung to the bottom right lung. Compare right and left side for differences in ease or quality of movement and depth of breathing from right to left, top to bottom, front to back. Repeat for three to five breaths.

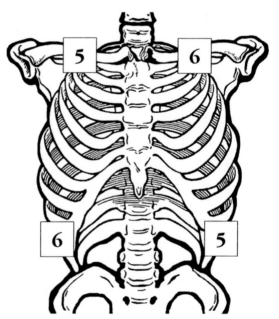

Diagram 3: Hand Positions (Steps 5 & 6)

Tool 9: Advanced Awareness Journal – Living in Process

The Awareness Journal helps you use your sensations, emotions, thoughts, and soul messages to be more consciously present with your whole being and life. As you review the daily and weekly entries, insights and conclusions will arise that impact the choices and changes you make. Living in process involves regular time alone for listening and Self-care. It will also ask you to embody and integrate the insights, adaptations, and choices you make to reclaim your authentic Self. Soul guidance, at the core of your internal GPS system, will help you process and navigate beyond prior conditioning, perceptions, roles, and beliefs.

Continue with your Awareness Journal a minimum of three or four days each week. The following reflections for Self-discovery will help you gain clarity and bring new healing options to current pain, confusion, and/or suffering. As American journalist, feminist, and activist Gloria Steinem states, "It is never too late to have a happy childhood."[6]

Review your Awareness Journal, and with Self-compassion, honesty, courage, and heart-and-soul guidance, respond to the following as each pertains to your physical, mental, emotional, and spiritual well-being:

1) What beliefs, attitudes, perceptions, judgments, illusions, roles, losses, emotions, etc., prevent you from honestly and compassionately living in process? What enhances living in process?

2) What Self-care practices enhance your healing, and how? Think about the practice of establishing your safe place, which was referred to earlier in this chapter. Describe aspects of this place that establish trust and safety, or if this is a new concept for you, describe how you would design it.

3) What practices connect you with soul guidance and your wise-hearted spiritual warrior when you need insight?

Slowly bring your awareness back to your breath and your inner sanctuary before returning to the outside world. As you breathe in, become aware of all you take in that nourishes and supports you. As you breathe out, become aware of what is released that no longer serves you. In each "now" moment, receive insights that support Self-healing.

CHAPTER SIX

Coming Home to Your Heart

Theme Three: Healing Involves Self-Healing and Coming Home to Your Heart and Your Authentic Self

I wish I could show you, when you are lonely or in darkness, the astonishing light of your own being.
–Hafiz

The process of Self-healing goes beyond the elimination of pain or dis-ease, to an ongoing life journey of growth and reclaiming our authentic Self as we come home to our hearts. On this journey, we evolve and come alive to the intricate and mysterious puzzle pieces that combine to make up our dynamic wholeness as human beings. Self-healing brings continuous inner work of gathering and bringing home the unique pieces that create who we are: our gifts and limitations; light and shadow; pain and possibilities; and wounds and healing. Coming home involves welcoming and honoring each piece. As you embrace paradoxes within, your original Divine spark within your authentic Self will shed light that guides you home.

Coming home will resemble a series of archaeological digs, in which you recover priceless, hidden artifacts and parts of yourself. Some of these will be in the form of archetypal patterns or aspects of personality mentioned in Chapter Two, your inner child and wise-hearted spiritual warrior. As you begin your journeys home, these symbolic patterns will challenge you to grow. You may experience this when the victim or saboteur within you surfaces. These parts of yourself hold great value. They provide stepping-stones to your heart-and-soul wisdom. As you honor and utilize insights they bring, you will be reminded of what you have forgotten, your authentic Self. All this awaits you, at the heart of your healing process.

When you accept a call to return home, you are summoned to meet it with loving, patient, gentle presence, through reconnection with your heart. In addition to archetypes, you will also discover lost and abandoned parts of yourself, forgotten aspects still held within cell memory. These memories contain pieces of yourself from the past, longing to heal and come home. Some will provide keys that open doorways to your authentic Self, helping you evolve and more easily move through change and growth. They may lead you to parts of yourself that house fears, doubts, dark shadow places, and wounds. Seeds of healing are also contained within these places, waiting to grow and flourish. At junctures where surrender and acceptance are your only option, what brings heart and meaning to your life will carry you through. Each part you welcome home will bring authenticity and wholeness to transformative healing experiences.

Coming home to your authentic Self is a gradual process, whereby you discover and learn to trust the healer and healing forces within your whole being. You will become your own health-care advocate and help create healing partnerships between your authentic Self, wise-hearted spiritual warrior, and members of your health-care team. At this juncture, you will be challenged to balance independence and asking for help.

Like many of you, I had trouble asking for help, accepting what was offered, and trusting who and what was given. I needed to learn how to balance giving and receiving. I needed to understand the difference between service and sacrifice. This was brought home on several occasions when I was late for personal appointments after work because I had not adequately monitored my time with clients that day. The Awareness Journal and Self-care movement practices heightened my awareness and reminded me to serve my Self as well as others.

The big picture reveals that any change, trauma, shock, or small separation in life will trigger a fight-or-flight response that challenges us to remain present in our physical bodies. There are many ways available to us for escape at these times: detachment, addiction, numbing ourselves, overworking, replaying our stories and getting lost in them, and drama. When we partake in any of these, we not only flee the situation or the relationship, but we leave ourselves behind as well. We abandon ourselves and leave home.

In this chapter, you will read about my return home from shock after a car accident. During my recovery, I experienced firsthand how valuable and necessary touch and bodywork are for coming back into our bodies after shock. You will also read about Linda and Marion, two former clients who bravely shared their journeys home with me after diagnoses of breast and advanced colon cancer respectively. Both of these courageous women honored and respected their life cycles – growth and decay, celebration and loss, birth and death. Linda and Marion were women of valor. They met personal, family, and professional challenges with grace and determination. Each revealed true courage in the face of the unknown and helped me realize that even thorns have roses.

You will also learn about options you can consider when you or someone you know experiences shock or stress. At the end of this chater you will again use tracking skills. Tracking will help you read and respond to body-mind signals during stressful times, such as when you are in unfamiliar territory. Tracking will enable you to make healthy deposits into your energy bank accounts. Self-care practices will support you between office visits to therapists and other health-care professionals. They will lift you out of victimization and dependency and empower your response ability.

Coming home is a process that cultivates and develops heart-centered wisdom, wise discernment, and the ability to surrender and let go. Regular doses of Self-compassion will help you embrace your process with open arms, especially as you reflect on the questions at the end of this chapter.

Call to Action: Returning
A Shock to the System

Many clients who went through the trauma of a car accident were challenged to remain present afterward. They walked around in an ungrounded state of shock, with perpetual anxiety, sleeplessness, hypervigilance, and constant fear. Some confessed to being terrified of traveling in a car again. Prior shock and trauma, which had unconsciously remained beneath surface awareness in their bodies, became apparent during our sessions. This was due to a phenomenon known as cell memory. Healing brought the light of awareness to these areas and activated memories. Chronically tight muscles, which barricaded repressed shock and fear, began to relax. We gained insight into physical issues, but emotional, mental, and spiritual issues surfaced, too, in search of healing.

Bodywork with experienced therapists, whose presence and touch encourage trust, is vital for coming home to our body after shock. This became clear to me during my recovery from shock after a car accident. As a society, we face tremendous stress daily.

Our immune systems become challenged and compromised as a result. Self-care practices will enhance your stress mastery skills. They will also strengthen your physical, emotional, mental, and spiritual immunity in the process.

I was in an internal tug of war when I approached Self-healing and coming home. Initially full of self-doubt, I lived in a fortress of defensive ego self-talk. I was like Alice protesting to the Red Queen in *Alice's Adventures in Wonderland*, "There's no use trying . . . one can't believe impossible things." In contrast, my soul guidance resembled the Queen's response: "I daresay you haven't had much practice. When I was your age, I always did it for half-an-hour a day . . . sometimes I've believed as many as six impossible things before breakfast."[1]

Call to Action: Returning Self-Healing and Coming Home

On a rainy day in 2004, when hurricane Jeanne roared up the East Coast, I was involved in a car accident. When the car crashed, I found myself amidst an uncanny silence. I heard every raindrop, smelled burning rubber, and saw smoke around me. I felt a strange numbness and pinched my arms and legs to determine if I was still alive. My body was rigid and hyper-extended, like a board, in the driver's seat. I called my therapist, Lydia, from the car to cancel the appointment I had been driving to. She responded slowly and emphatically, "Okay, Gina, feel your buttocks and legs, ground yourself, and breathe!" I followed her instructions and felt like a bellows suddenly reinflated my lungs and kick-started my breathing.

When police and a tow truck arrived, I needed to exit my car and climb up the steep embankment my car had gone down. The ground beneath my feet was invisible to my eye as it was covered with underbrush and broken branches. Chills raced through me as I looked up to where I needed to go. My legs felt like rubber as I exited my car. I was not centered or grounded.

Every step up was like crossing a rickety bridge that traversed a gorge. My entire body felt jumpy crossing the unstable terrain. I could barely feel my feet. I heard branches breaking underfoot as I swayed and regained my balance several times. Prior Feldenkrais Awareness Through Movement® lessons jogged my memory. I was transported back to those sessions and the kinesthetic memory of feeling centered, balanced, and elongated. My feet now felt magnetized to the ground. My head, neck, trunk, and spine elongated. I was mindful and physically present with each step.

After I reached the top of the embankment, I climbed into the tow truck to go to the auto-body shop. I strapped myself in. The seat belt felt like a baby's receiving blanket wrapped around me, creating safety for my physical body. It also calmed my emotional body, which remained anxious and unaware I was out of danger. When the driver started the engine, my body jolted and became rigid. The movement of this vehicle had reactivated the shock. My breathing was shallow. Lydia's words echoed, "Breathe!" My chest felt encased in a tight, heavy suit of armor. I struggled for air with each inhalation as my chest pushed against the unyielding metal frame.

I met my husband at the auto-body shop. His arms and loving presence embraced me and reminded me that I was safe. We remained silent during a long hug. I wanted to let go and collapse into his arms, but curiously I was unable to release the rigidity in my legs and body. As we left the auto-body shop, my entire body felt ice cold. I couldn't stop shaking. All I wanted was a hot bowl of homemade chicken soup. This memory from childhood, of my mother's cooking, grounded me as I began my return home journey. It seemed miraculous that I survived without any apparent physical scrapes or bruises. I was to learn much about the shock and detachment that occurs when we unconsciously leave the scene during trauma.

After the accident my chest, neck, and head were stiff and achy. I had a low-grade headache day and night. I felt like a robot, empty inside my physical shell and inexplicably numb to physical touch, though I craved it. During an acupuncture session the next day I first sensed that I was not present in my body. I was still dazed and out of it. I was in shock, though I was not yet aware of this. Bodywork became a major way for me to reconnect with myself again through touch. Whenever my skin was touched, sensations began to awaken my physical body.

I continued feeling here and not here throughout each day. I did not understand that parts of me were still in shock. I went through the motions of living, emotionless. I cried for the first time three days after the accident, reading an e-mail my daughter sent to a local radio station. She asked them to publicly thank the three men who stopped to help her mother. Her heartfelt words opened the floodgates that had kept my heart under lock and key. Held-in emotions poured out. The warmth and caring I received from my husband, family, friends, and health-care team nourished and helped ground my mental and emotional coming home process. My frozen heart and life force began to defrost. These people provided a container of kindness and love, in which I felt safe. Hypervigilance lessened, and a sense of peace intermittently returned.

The first week after the accident I slept continuously. Although my body needed rest I pushed myself to be active, which was a conditioned way of being. I judged myself for not getting back to "normal" quick enough, especially with no outwardly apparent signs of injury. Months later this provided insight into clients' behavior when they, too, pushed themselves too far after accidents. I understood their experiences as a result of embodying my own.

I returned to see Lydia one week later. As our session began, my breathing became shallow and difficult. My chest felt like it was in a straitjacket. I felt deep, achy pain within my heart. Huge fear arose. It encased my entire being. A stitch occurred in each lung at the end of full breaths, not unlike stitches I felt when running. A deep sigh and yawn emerged after the stitch.

A long, full breath followed. Lydia reminded me to stay present with each stitch and any feelings, sensations, movement, or images that emerged with them. Each stitch felt like a tight scar. Suddenly I was transported back to the accident, where in shock I had stopped breathing. My arms and chest felt like cold, hard stone. Lydia's words were my map: "Breathe in, take in the life force. Breathe out, release bits and pieces of shock and stress." I followed her instructions. Pieces of me began to come home.

During another session my attention was drawn to an image that surfaced in my heart. An injured, frightened, and alone animal cowered there. This vulnerable animal was me, in shock, untouched, and untended. Lydia reminded me to ground my body and establish compassionate presence with this vulnerable place within me. "Call upon your strong, wise woman to surround you with safety."

My chest and heart felt as if they were breaking open during painful and frightening moments. Time seemed endless. I suddenly felt myself being drawn up and out of a deep, narrow well. With one final breath I broke through to the surface. Bright daylight surrounded me, and fresh air filled my lungs. Coming-home tears of relief emerged. I was home. I was safe. I was grounded as I began to embody my whole being.

The gifted hands of Maxine, a bodyworker and certified practitioner of the Trager Approach®, helped me rediscover my physical boundaries. I felt as though my vacant interior was being filled in. I was in a safe cradle during our sessions, as Maxine gently rocked and stroked my body and being. After one session, I became the scarecrow from the *Wizard of Oz*, who received a brain; the tin man, who received a heart; and the lion, who received c-c-c-courage. Maxine's hands were like mirrors that reflected me back to me. I felt deeply present within my body – fuller, longer, lighter, and aware of my body's weight on the table.

The very gifted hands of Bill – a chiropractor, healer, and soul friend – further grounded me. Bill told me, "The accident knocked you out of your body." His words reverberated through me. Everything began to shift and come together differently. With physical healing, something initially spurs a healing crisis – infection, inflammation, trauma, and so on. The angst, confusion, and frustration I felt after the accident stimulated my body-mind awareness and healing. I was now consciously receptive to my process.

During a Zero Balancing® session I again felt comforted and grounded when Leah, a colleague and Zero Balancing® practitioner, solidly placed her hands on my legs and ankles. I again sensed my physical boundaries. Parts of my body, once numb and in shock, were now coming alive. At one point during this session I noticed I was not fully in my body. A turning point arose. My life passed before me, and I realized my life's work was not yet done. I felt angry and very hesitant the moment I knew I would need to leave the peaceful place I had inhabited while I was in shock. Almost instantaneously I crash landed back into my body with that thought.

Weeks later, during additional bodywork sessions, I began to process my need to remain busy. I was frustrated with myself and impatient with the slowness of my recovery. I realized that keeping busy, focused, and on task was a familiar way I knew how to ground myself – through my mind. I hid in keeping busy, and I avoided touching upon shock, the unknown, and vulnerable places within. I needed to balance my busyness with downtime and physical rest. My challenge was to remain compassionately present with vulnerable parts of myself that left the scene of the accident – too shocked to remain on board. It was during downtime that they sent me SOS signals.

When I remained busy, I unconsciously abandoned fright-ened parts of myself. I avoided communication with what was unfamiliar. I avoided what I knew nothing about. I avoided trusting my body's truths and my authentic Self. I was unaware of the need to establish safety and trust within myself, which would invite and beckon vulnerable places home. I gradually became aware of how out of sync I was internally and externally. Healing evolved and became a place for listening versus controlling the process.

Through yoga, *pranayama*, and the bodywork I have mentioned, along with Jungian, Gestalt, and body-mind therapies, I realized firsthand that traumatic memories hold seeds and roots for healing. The seeds need to be nourished by compassionate presence and the warmth of our hearts, in order to emerge and grow.

Self-care practices were invaluable tools and brought moments of safety to the recurrent storms that arose. As my emotional healing continued, I had spontaneous and frequent nightmares. I awoke to my body shaking. I was filled with fear each time I revisited the accident during dreams. These moments pushed me to apply insights gained from Self-care practices and strategies.

I gradually realized that shock had served me. It provided a safety valve. Shock prevented me from experiencing more than I could handle during and after the accident. The numbness and detachment from shock was a buffer. Self-healing now entailed allowing shock to surface. Areas of shock still present in my being needed to feel embraced and tended to – without blame or judgment. As I processed shock over time, it transformed and sought exit pathways through tears, angry outbursts, and unanticipated trembling throughout my body. Therapists helped me listen and be present with these messages. In retrospect, I can see the unique and synchronistic timing, ways, and means through which my process evolved. I needed to return home to my heart through the same compassion I had brought to clients.

With time, patience, willingness, and gentle reminders, I discovered the still, small voice within me – when I was willing to surrender and listen. I heard this voice express deep love to my children when I held and rocked them to sleep as infants. I also heard this voice when I was hiking in nature, as the wind whistled through my ears and gently stroked my face, and the sun warmed my being. The sound and feel of each l-o-n-g, full breath renewed and reconnected me with my authentic Self. Through this still, small voice I reconnected with my heart. As my process continued to evolve, layers of shock and stress peeled away. Self-healing and coming home opened, stretched, and enlarged my heart's capacity to feel and give and receive, beyond what I ever conceived possible.

Call to Action: Returning Linda and Reconnecting with Lost Parts of Ourselves

I initially met Linda when she was referred to me for physical therapy for neck and arm pain, and numbness in her hand. We had much in common: our ages; our return to school in our late thirties after starting a family; our love of learning; and our desire to make a difference in the world through our families and careers. The initial course of therapy was beneficial to Linda. When it concluded, she returned to working full time and going to graduate school. Linda completed her master's degree and began working as a licensed clinical social worker.

Linda and I again met five years later when she came to therapy to relieve post-mastectomy pain and swelling. We began from where we left off years ago as if no time had elapsed. She brought me up to date on family, work, and her personal and family struggles after being diagnosed with breast cancer. Linda returned to work after her mastectomy surgery and began personal counseling, primarily Gestalt oriented. Through her professional experiences with Gestalt therapy practices, she realized their value with clients who needed to integrate body-mind awareness. Linda was now challenged to integrate difficult and frightening body-mind experiences as part of her own Self-healing process.

We began with post-mastectomy exercises and Qigong to support physical healing and reestablish flow in meridian pathways after surgery. Linda journaled after our sessions. Writing became a portal into deeper aspects of her being. She brought unconditional presence to feelings, images, sensations, and body language that surfaced during and after our sessions. She gained access to deeper insights beneath her awareness of loss and grief. Linda explored her process and insights further during counseling sessions. With her permission, Linda's counselor and I spoke every two weeks to exchange insights and further support her healing process.

During our third session Linda began to process a significant aspect of her Self-healing journey. Linda's body became very relaxed and still during the session. I was familiar with this phenomenon from my own bodywork sessions and meditation. We continued with craniosacral therapy and Process Acupressure. Linda's breathing suddenly changed. It became very rapid and labored as she recalled the day of her surgery. Linda commented that she felt as if a tight towel surrounded and twisted her spine. She felt fear mount throughout her body, like a volcano about to erupt. She brought awareness to her breath to ground and center herself. Her breathing became difficult. Linda's hands wrapped around her chest, "to form a protective shield," she said. We remained with this, in silence, for close to five minutes. I had observed that when it seems as if nothing is happening on the surface with clients, much is occurring beneath it.

Linda's eyes were closed, but I noticed rapid eye movements. These occur during sleep and indicate that a person is in a dream state. Linda was in a deeper state of awareness and process. I remained silent so as not to interrupt what was occurring. Her breathing became shallow, almost still, and there were several large sighs. Her hands now softly rested on her chest over the site of her surgery. She gently opened her eyes and spoke, as tears flowed. "I never prepared myself for the loss of my breast. I never made time to say 'thank you' to my breast for how well it served me. There was no goodbye to my breast before surgery!" Linda related that she was so busy with medical preparations before the surgery that she never made time to process her grief and loss. Her arms now moved to embrace and gently hold this vulnerable area as she said, "A part of me was cut away and removed." With tenderness and compassion she cried and stroked the site of her surgery. I had not witnessed this presence before during our sessions.

Linda remained silent and continued to address and integrate her process over the next ten minutes. I continued with bodywork and prepared to close our session. Her process again revealed the value and power in silently holding unconditional presence with clients during sessions. It was vital to trust that Linda knew and could follow her own internal process and guidance. As tears flowed, Linda related that she now needed to create a ritual around this very significant life experience. We began to frame this, and she completed the process during counseling sessions.

In subsequent sessions, as we again returned to the time of surgery, her presence was filled with a newfound courage. She described herself as filled with strength and softness, sadness and gratitude, lightness and darkness. Linda was bringing all aspects of her authentic Self home. She next spoke about what occurred when she entered puberty. She recalled and internally sensed how as a tall girl she slumped her posture to close down her chest. Linda wanted no one to notice her emerging breasts. "Ashamed at such a young age – I can't believe it." she said. Gently, she related that the wise-hearted spiritual warrior within her now needed to come forth and embrace this adolescent part of herself, without words. Her Self-compassion was palpable. Linda's body felt like water gently and quietly flowing. I noticed her rib cage and chest soften and more fully expand with each inhalation. Her trunk and body elongated, her rib cage relaxed, and a deep letting go occurred throughout Linda's body. She appeared to almost melt into the table.

Our sessions concluded about two months later. They were especially poignant for me, because my mother and sister were both breast cancer survivors. When these family memories unexpectedly arose with Linda, I was reminded of the need to keep clear boundaries between myself and Linda during sessions. Classes in Zero Balancing® and Process Acupressure had taught me about *interface*, the clear space that exists when a practitioner's hands meet and touch the structure and energy of a client during bodywork. In this space there is no blending and boundaries are clear. I know where I end and the client begins, and we meet and interact there. Interface is also the place where we meet in relationship off the table. Trust, intimacy, and communication are greatly enhanced when interface establishes respectful boundaries in relationships.

Sessions with Linda taught me how to practically apply the concept of interface. When issues surfaced during client sessions, and I became aware that interface was lost or unclear, boundaries needed to be clarified. This clarification helped me avoid blending with and/or taking on clients' issues and energy. It was also necessary to keep personal issues outside the treatment environment, separate and apart from client sessions. When my process arose during sessions, I took time to reestablish interface by momentarily lifting my hands and then replacing them on the client's body with clear intent. I also needed to honor my commitment to Self-healing at these times by making time afterward for Self-treatment or sessions with practitioners.

Call to Action: Returning Marion and the Final Journey Home

One of the most inspiring clients I shared coming home and Self-healing with was Marion. An occupational therapist and mother of three children under twelve, she was referred to me for physical therapy. Marion sought alternative approaches to support her healing process after being diagnosed with recurrent colon cancer, which had advanced to her liver and bones. She was dearly loved by friends and colleagues, and highly respected for her years of dedicated professional work in her county, advocating for children and families with special needs.

Marion's colleagues and I joined her during her final year on Earth. We combined integrative manual therapy protocols, craniosacral therapy, music, and prayer as part of her therapy process and healing-circle sessions. Marion, her friends, family, and I encircled one another during our gatherings. Many times ripples of laughter emanated from us, filling the room and gracing our hearts with the joy of simple heart-to-heart presence.

We laughed, cried, touched, and were touched as we shared priceless and profound healing time together. We recalled memories as we all sang "Kum-Ba-Yah" and "Ain't No Mountain High Enough." We took advantage of multiple listening hands during sessions to create a loving, safe, and supportive cocoon for Marion as she met pain, anxiety, and the unknown – physically, mentally, emotionally, and spiritually.

As Marion's journey progressed, she made the decision to receive hospice care at home. She wanted to remain in a familiar and loving environment, especially through her dying process – a courageous choice in light of her having a young family. Sessions with Marion up to and including her passing were filled with sacred, poignant moments that I still recall and treasure.

Marion's authentic Self and wise-hearted spiritual warrior showed up as she journeyed through her final days. Those of us present were graced being in the presence of her full, open, clear, and strong heart. Her smile embraced us and brought a sense of wholeness to the entire process. She created an environment of love while she was conscious, and we reverently held it for her when she lapsed in and out of awareness. The angst I had sensed in the past when I worked with other people in hospice care was surprisingly absent. Marion taught us how to say goodbye with laughter as well as tears, with song as well as silence, with faith as well as fear.

During her passing, Marion spoke with us about her going-home journey into a different reality. Her words and presence touched our souls and helped us return to our hearts as we midwifed her soul during her passing. She demonstrated how to die with dignity, surrounded by love. Marion lived her life from courageous personal choice and actions. She always had a twinkle in her eye, a song on her lips, and love in her heart. A friend and colleague related to me that she was at home with Marion one day and observed her reach her arms upward while in bed. When she questioned Marion about what she was reaching for, Marion simply replied, "G-d."

Marion was a visionary, a true alchemist who showed us how to spin straw into gold by adding the magical elixir – love and laughter. They transformed her and those blessed to be in her presence. Marion demonstrated how to live outside the ordinary rules of life, which impacted all of us present with her during those sacred moments.

From Birth to Death

Self-healing and coming home to our heart and our authentic Self is a process that occurs from the beginning of our life through to our passing. In my twenties and thirties I looked and found support for healing externally, discovering only half the process. Healing will not only be found outside yourself. What you will often tap into, through your own process and inner work, is an endless source of Self-healing and support within. This gold mine will surface each time you become aware of it, as in Sleeping Beauty's awakening or Dorothy's homecoming in *The Wizard of Oz*. You, too, can awaken to a magical elixir present at the heart of healing. Once recognized and embodied, it will invigorate and strengthen what brings joy and meaning into your life. Stay present and remain awake. You will find it in the last place you tend to look, within yourself.

Tools and Reflections

*Your pain is the breaking of the shell that encloses
your understanding. It is the bitter potion by which
the physician within you heals your sick self, so
therefore, trust the physician and drink his remedy
in silence and tranquility.*
–Kahlil Gibran

On our Earth journey we live, love, learn, and evolve through our heart, authentic Self, and wise guidance received from our indestructible Divine soul. Self-care practices, such as mindful breathing, create a bridge for enlightened communion to occur between our human self and our Divine Self.

Tool 10: Circular Breathing

Begin this practice lying down or comfortably seated with your legs and arms supported. If seated, be sure your neck and lower back are supported. Allow your shoulders, jaw, and facial muscles to gently relax, and your lips to part slightly. Bring your awareness to your spine and posture. Imagine your spine as a string of pearls. Notice and feel a connection at your tailbone that draws and anchors you and this string of pearls deeply into Mother Earth. Notice and feel a connection at the crown of your head that draws and lifts you and this string of pearls up to the heavens. Imagine the string of pearls running through your spine, from top to bottom, between these two points.

Become aware of your breath as you gently inhale and exhale three or four times through your nose (or mouth if this is not possible). Draw your next breath in through the front of your body from the area below your navel. Allow the inhalation to move up your spine to the crown of your head. Begin your exhalation from there, and allow the exhalation to move down the center front of your body, back to the spot below your navel where you began. This completes one cycle. Repeat this cycle, inhaling up from your lower pelvis and tail to your crown, and returning through an exhalation back from your crown to your lower pelvis. Sense your breath as a wave that moves through your body.

Use your breath to connect with and draw in Earth, or yin, energy during inhalation and to draw heavenly, or yang, energy through the core of your being during exhalation.

Tool 11: Awareness Journal – Recovering and Healing Lost Parts of Yourself

The Zen concept of "don't know mind" provides a way to place mind and ego aside, allowing them to serve, versus run the show. It also helps disengage your constantly active "monkey mind." When you adopt a "don't know mind" during meditation or journaling, you will be guided to a place within, beyond blame, judgment, and attachment to outcome. This will help you listen from your heart and soul as you begin to recover, process, and heal unfinished aspects from your past. Use patience and Self-compassion as you open to and welcome unconscious, vulnerable places within. I encourage you to seek professional support, as needed, in addition to using reflective Self-care practices.

For this Self-care reflective practice set aside thirty to sixty minutes to go within, in silence. You may need to plan several sessions.

While seated comfortably, begin circular breathing or any mindful breath practice you use to center and ground you. Surround yourself with whatever you need to set a safe, sacred space. Remember to ask for support and higher guidance. Keep your Awareness Journal nearby.

Slowly and gently go back in time. Notice or ask to be shown a situation in which shock and trauma occurred. Hold unconditional presence with any images, emotions, sensations, and memories that arise, and remember to breathe as you encounter body-mind signals. Use your breath and heart-and-soul presence to establish trust as your process unfolds. Ask your wise-hearted spiritual warrior to be present with you. When parts of you that seek healing emerge, surround them with your breath, patience, and unconditional positive regard. Let writing or drawing provide a voice for them. Establish a dialogue over time, versus a full-court press all at once. Be present from your heart, and approach these tender, unguarded places gently. When it feels right, ask if they wish to speak, what is needed for healing, and how you can support them. Above all, provide safe space. Trust that this process will unfold in its unique time and way. Here are some guidelines:

- Notice how you respond and from where, your head or your heart.

- What enhances your listening? What blocks your listening?

- As you witness shock and parts of yourself, ask how each served clearing, letting go, and a return to your authentic Self.

- When and how did you lose power through lack of awareness, sacrifice versus service, insufficient Self-care, saying "yes" and meaning "no," and so on?

- How can experiences and insights you have gained empower you now?

- What Self-care practices can you use to reconnect with and strengthen your wise-hearted spiritual warrior?

When you are ready to conclude this session, bring your awareness back to your body-mind with several circular breaths. Create a safe place for what remains unfinished, where you will meet again and continue this homecoming process. Sit quietly and journal about your experience and the insights you gained. You may want to conclude with a favorite prayer, and express gratitude to courageous parts of yourself that surfaced along with everything that supports and reverently guides your journey.

CHAPTER SEVEN
The Heart's Illuminating Wisdom

Theme Four: Healing Is a Lifelong Process of Growth and Development

Ninety percent of the world's woe comes from people not knowing themselves, their abilities, their frailties, and even their real virtues. Most of us go almost all the way through life as complete strangers to ourselves.
–Sydney J. Harris

From the time I was a child I have had a thirst for learning, but I have not always let my heart be the illuminator for learning. I have not always realized that my body and whole being are a storehouse of wisdom, much as the library that so enthralled me as a child was a storehouse of knowledge. From early on, when I touched on mystery gazing up at the night sky, my heart and soul reminded me to reach beyond the mind's learning. It was heart learning that reconnected me with that mystery in the last place I considered looking – within.

As children, our early creative explorations and learning are frequently altered as we enter school and begin formal education. We learn about following rules and regulations, remaining in our seats, raising our hands to speak, coloring within the lines, and taking tests. Our zest for learning and creativity frequently gets squelched along the way. We are taught about the world around us, but lose touch with our hearts and the world within us. This greatly affects our future education and how we integrate our life and world.

Merriam-Webster's dictionary describes education as "a process of training and developing knowledge, skill, mind, and character by formal schooling or study." Growing up in our Western culture, I learned to think according to cause and effect, and to function in linear ways. Consciousness and healing, I believed, was to be sought outside myself and gained through fixing myself and/or trying to control my life.

In my early thirties, hatha yoga and meditation became catalysts that impacted my learning. They introduced me to an intriguing world, where I experienced my body, mind, emotions, and soul in nonlinear ways, beyond my rational mind and left-brain thinking. During pranayama, yoga asanas, and meditation, the intuitive, nonlogical right side of my brain was activated. I felt vibrantly alive as these practices provided moving meditation that expanded awareness throughout my being. I was more present and able to embody the human vessel I was graced with from birth, and I again found myself amidst the wonder I tapped into through the night sky – now within my being.

I was in awe of how my whole being – thinking, feeling, sensing, and moving – automatically worked together. This grand design took little conscious effort on my part. I witnessed this during a yoga session as I stood in tadasana, mountain pose. My mind was steady and attentive. My emotions were calm, like still water. My body felt stable and grounded, and my trunk felt long and lifted. I sensed my spine automatically realigning itself, from tailbone to crown, through gross and subtle muscle movements. Breath moved into and through my body during profound silence. I was immersed in the Great Mystery.

Sometimes, my unsettled mind whirled with endless thoughts during practice. I found respite in *restorative yoga* poses, where I was able to release into deep rest. At other times, emotions stormed through my being. As I breathed Self-compassion into and through emotions, I felt calmer and more accepting of their presence and messages. As my heart opened during yoga, breathing, and meditation, Self-compassion and insight flowed more easily from me into my daily life and relationships. This learning process continues to inform me today regarding who I am, why I am here, and how to integrate my heart with being and doing. As a result I am more conscious of the oasis for learning and rejuvenation within, which I call "home."

Your body is a precious, sacred gift to befriend, instead of a force to be conquered or the bearer of a dis-ease to be eradicated. You can tap into places of wonder and wisdom in yourself, through yoga, dance, movement, walking, bodywork, music, painting, gardening, or whatever resonates with you. Your body and being house fascinating treasures that await your discovery and exploration as you come home with open-hearted presence through Self-care practices.

In this chapter, you will read about the ways heart intelligence and Self-care affect challenges, conflicts, and learning. You will gain understanding about wholehearted learning, which involves:

- shifting from an illness to a wellness model
- exploring the puzzle of pain
- clarifying illusions and misconceptions about healing

- growing through illness, stress, and dis-ease
- enhancing your energy bank accounts
- softening your heart
- nourishing yourself and others through unconditional presence
- making peace with yourself

You will meet eight women who participated in the Chronic Pain Self-Help Class that I taught at my practice for more than three years. Connection with heart-and-soul intelligence was a core element of their education and Self-healing. They learned much about themselves and each other over time. As they explored hard-to-accept places within, they saw that self-judgment created internal wars and smoke screens, which limited access to their heart and authentic Self. Their explorations helped them witness the resulting auto-immune disorder of their soul, which they sensed as emptiness, absence of life purpose and meaning, and the feeling of being anxious, depressed, and/or lost.

You will learn how these women met the challenge of chronic pain and learned to flourish and thrive in spite of it. *Mind-body medicine* and Self-care practices helped them transform two illusions: (1) Someone else is responsible for my life and healing; and (2) I have the power to change others.

Group sessions provided an efficient, cost-effective way for them to strengthen connection with their heart and authentic Self. The interconnections and compassion they shared became an antidote to fear and the unknown, and stimulated learning and Self-healing.

You will also read about learning that occurs during heart-illuminated moments and how Self-healing manifests through reconnection with your authentic Self. Life lessons become initiations into new ways of being and are reminders of how vital it is to recall and listen to your heart song. Self-healing will be illuminated by the light you uncover during these sacred moments.

I have been blessed to experience this illumination through the unconditional love and presence of a spiritual teacher whom I have studied with for more than thirty years. You will read about how her presence and wise insights helped me learn from fear and emotional reactions, and how this guided my growth and Self-healing.

In the Tools and Reflections section, you will be introduced to the four dimensions of wellness. You will explore how each dimension – physical, mental, emotional, and spiritual – currently influences the metaphorical house you reside in as a human being. Your discoveries will help you consciously reinhabit this house and reignite your pilot light at its source, your heart. Lab work will help you envision and organize Self-care practices into a healing curriculum, or action plan, you can use along with your Awareness Journal.

Soak up the times you spend in Self-reflection, mindfulness, and Self-care practices. Each will shed light on your path and help you embody and integrate insights gained. The eyes and ears of your heart will be natural filters that clarify what will bring heart and meaning into your life and healing through your authentic Self.

Your Metaphorical House

The key that will open doorways to inner wisdom is within you, in your heart. The doorways will bring you to rooms within a metaphorical house, which your body and being occupy while you are here on Earth. Use the following to explore rooms in your house, from the basement to the upper levels, through your heart.

The Basement:

The basement of your metaphorical house is where valuable subconscious memories are kept in storage, perhaps hidden and submerged for years. What is your internal basement like? Is it overcrowded with outdated beliefs, perceptions, attitudes, or memories, set aside and forgotten? At times, we may close off what we no longer want to recognize or address within ourselves. Parts of your history and conditioning may also be stored in your basement. These can influence your current house and life. Do you need to bring illumination from your heart into dark places in your basement? Is an overhaul or spring cleanup needed?

The Ground Floor:

The ground floor of your metaphorical house is where you receive nourishment through food, relationships, entertainment, and hobbies, which provide a break from the day's activities. What does this part of your house look and feel like? Who and what nourishes you here during the seasons of your life? When your physical, mental, emotional, and spiritual needs are met, you are strong and vibrantly alive. You will need to consult your heart to meet your minimum daily requirements for nourishment in each area. Anxiety, stress, exhaustion, and burnout can occur when you are too busy or forget to listen. The wiring of your house, your nervous system, is especially impacted by this. How and when do you create sacred, restorative time at home, apart from the rest of your day? Who and what brings nourishment, pleasure, joy, and meaning to you during these times?

The Second Floor:

The second floor of your metaphorical house contains your bedroom, where you rest and can meet your subconscious in dreams. Here you share intimacy, or *into me see*, which deepens compassion, love, and understanding through what may be shared between you, your authentic Self, and significant others. In bathrooms on this level, you cleanse and clear your being. Is this upper floor in your house designed for rest and relaxation? Reflection? Intimacy? Cleansing and clearing? When and how do you create intimate moments with your authentic Self and others here? How is your internal environment enhanced through clearing and heart-and-soul connection? Does anything need clearing and re-visioning?

Your heart is central and at the hearth of your house. Tending to your heart will keep the home fires burning and your passions alive.

Shifting from an Illness to a Wellness Model of Dis-ease

It is far more important to know what person the [dis-ease] has than what [dis-ease] the person has.
–Hippocrates

Health in our country has drastically changed since the early 1900s. We live longer, face more chronic dis-eases, and experience constant stress and anxiety. Extensive advances have occurred in understanding consciousness and the body-mind connection, and how each affects life and healing. Research by biochemist Norman Cousins and scientists in the field of **psychoneuroimmunology** have revealed that our physiology and biochemistry are not separate from our thoughts and feelings. Research by cell biologist, author, and teacher, Dr. Bruce Lipton, led the way for the science of epigenetics, further revealing pathways that connect our mind and body. His work has described how mind-body medicine and spiritual principles and practices fit together.

American inventor Thomas Alva Edison noted the shift in our medical model when he stated, "The doctor of the future will give no medicine, but will interest his patients in the care of the human frame, in diet, and in the cause and prevention of [dis-ease]."[1] Studies on aging reveal that lifestyle changes impact our aging process and well-being as much as genetics.[2] It is never too late to develop healthy lifestyle habits around diet, exercise, yoga, meditation, support, and practices that strengthen and enhance well-being.

Research clearly indicates that our thinking affects our biology. Back in 1981, John W. Travis, M.D., and Regina Sara Ryan described wellness as a "choice . . . a way of life . . . a process . . . an efficient channeling of energy . . . the integration of body, mind, and spirit . . . and loving acceptance of yourself."[3] They paved the way for the shifting of beliefs and actions from an illness to a wellness model. Today we have unlimited ability to affect our biology, physiology, and well-being. We can access it by witnessing and learning about ourselves and our world through mind-body medicine and Self-care practices. When these are combined with heart-and-soul intelligence, transformational shifts and Self-healing occur for us individually, as a collective, and in our world.

Exploring the Puzzle of Pain

Pain is multidimensional in its scope and impact. Pain alerts us and catches our attention but is one of the least understood of all human sensations. Pain doesn't occur in isolation. Our experience of pain, and the meaning and expression we give it, is influenced by our history, culture, conditioning, relationships, attitudes, and beliefs. Pain forces us to stop and consciously look, listen, feel, and process messages that accompany it, messages expressed through physical, mental, and emotional signals. In addition to pain, signals may include fatigue or exhaustion, depression, burnout, loss of interest in life, or a sense of isolation.

We can view pain as a teacher, and through it meet our vulnerabilities and shadow aspects like old friends. When we meet pain through a compassionate and wise heart, unsettled and/or subconscious aspects within us provide signals that help us uncover what may require resolution and healing. Saint Bartholomew described the challenge this way: "Many of us spend our whole lives running from feeling, with the mistaken belief that we cannot bear the pain. But you have already borne the pain. What you have not done is feel all you are beyond that pain."[4]

Eight women, ranging in age from mid-thirties to early sixties, bravely faced challenges as they learned and integrated this wisdom. They attended a Chronic Pain Self-Help Class, which I will now describe.

Clarifying Illusions and Misconceptions About Healing

Crisis often calls upon us to reach for a new level of humanity. Each member of the Chronic Pain Self-Help Class was experiencing crisis through the changes chronic pain had brought to their lives and families. They came from varied backgrounds, beliefs, education, and work experiences, but they had one thing in common: the need to learn how to take charge of their life in spite of chronic pain. During early sessions, we explored personal beliefs and misconceptions about healing. Through shared compassion and heart-and-soul presence, they created a safe place, a cocoon in which they could learn, grow, and transform through Self-healing.

The first misconception we explored was that there was a magic bullet for full healing, which, once discovered, would enable them to return to "normal" again. Each participant had spent extensive time, money, and effort going to countless physicians and therapists in search of such a solution, only to return back to where they started. Relinquishing this mis-conception meant they would have to face the stark reality of living with chronic pain, but this would also lead them to options they could consider.

One group member, Lois, challenged her belief in magic bullets and discovered what had heart and meaning in her life. While looking internally for healing resources, she reconnected with her love of crafts and desire to start her own business. Lois pursued this as part of Self-healing. As her business grew, it became easier for her to give up her belief in a magic formula that existed outside herself. Her creativity, excitement, and sense of aliveness sparked and lit up her healing process, changing Lois's perception of who she was. She no longer considered herself crippled by chronic pain, although it was a factor to be considered. Her activities stimulated her body and being, promoting the release of endorphins – chemicals that dampen and suppress pain signals and enhance the body's and brain's ability to manage and reduce pain and depression. Lois discovered her ability to impact and interact with her internal pharmacy. She connected with an additional wealth of inner resources: self-motivation, self-trust, self-respect, and a desire to share beauty, creativity, and joy with others.

Terri, another group member, experienced renewed self-worth and physical well-being after she returned part time to a former job in the computer industry. She, too, experienced a significant reduction in pain and depression afterward; she was more able to self-manage her daily status when heart intelligence flowed through her life and choices. Terri and Lois discovered that the magic formula they sought externally already existed within.

A second misconception that arose was that physicians and health professionals are the most important members of the health-care team. As a result of this belief, participants gave their power over to others. Susan, a librarian, had lived and worked with chronic pain for more than five years. During our sessions, she learned that no one knew her better than herself, although initially she did not trust this knowing. Self-awareness gained through Self-care practices proved invaluable to her and to her health-care team's decision-making process. This Self-awareness was especially useful when circumstances were beyond anyone's control, as when chronic pain returned and new options needed to be considered.

Susan used a journal to provide feedback to her health-care team about the effect of medical treatments and Self-care practices. She shared Lois's love of crafts. Their evolving friendship taught each of them about how power grows exponentially when heart intelligence and wisdom are shared. As Susan combined mind and heart learning, adaptations she needed to consider became more apparent. As she became empowered, she no longer continued ad infinitum with approaches that did not serve her life and healing. Susan recognized that she could not change others, but she could impact decisions about her care.

A third misconception also became apparent: Healing episodes have a clear beginning and ending. The women realized that healing involves an organic process. Each of their healing episodes unfolded and opened into the next one, like petals of a flower. Each episode involved more than learning through their mind; they learned through their heart, body, and soul as well. Like the petals of a flower, some aspects of healing fell away, while others strongly came forth as the women's process opened to new phases and stages. It was necessary to greet each aspect of healing that surfaced like a rose, receiving the beauty and the thorns and the process of life and death that unfolded as part of a complete life cycle.

Each woman's enhanced ability to respond dismantled a fourth misconception: Emotional healing is only needed when change or crisis arises. On the contrary, the group discovered that touching upon physical, mental, emotional, or spiritual healing was an essential aspect of everyday living. Self-care tools such as journaling, meditation, acupressure, and Qigong composed the lab work that enabled them to meet everyday healing challenges with strength, a sense of humor, self-awareness, and self-trust versus outdated conditioning, fear, and lack of self-confidence.

Two sisters in the class, Kathy and Pat, had lived together for years. They learned about emotional healing as an everyday process when the family unexpectedly needed to move from their home. Two special circumstances added to the challenge they faced: a handicapped teenage daughter still lived at home; an older son had unexpectedly passed away a few months prior; and the family was just settling in to a new way of living and being without him. Both sisters chose to bring laughter, prayer, and love of family to this situation, qualities instilled in them by their mother.

Kathy and Pat used their combined inner strength, patience, humor, and love of family as tools. They could not change their life situation, but they could affect their response ability. Kathy and Pat supported each other when things became tough, and this calmed their whole family's emotions. They felt more in charge of their lives, and their family was held together through love, compassion, laughter, and heart intelligence, which flowed through their process before, during, and after the move.

One final misconception about healing was difficult for the women to accept: Time heals everything. Each woman in the group became aware that in finite time, events and relationships end, whether through death, divorce, moving, separation, or changes in health and life status. Unprocessed emotional and spiritual pain and/or depression frequently does not stop with endings, but lingers as unfinished business. When pain, unrest, and suffering continued to impact their health, hearts, and lives afterward, they recognized the need to address this from within and with appropriate professionals. They realized that healing at times involves painful and often incomplete endings, with loss, suffering, and lack of closure all too frequently part of the process.

With supportive psychotherapy, bodywork, and Self-care practices, wise-hearted spiritual warriors emerged through the life experiences these women shared. Courageous healing journeys transformed their lives. Lois, Susan, Kathy, Pat, and Terri found it easier to be with and grow through stress, change, depression, and dis-ease when education, Self-compassion, and group support were combined. The words of cardiologist Mimi Guarneri highlight the truth they discovered: "The I in illness is isolation, and the crucial letters in wellness are we."[5]

In the Chronic Pain Self-Help Class, heart-illuminated Self-healing was gained through:

- listening and practicing communication skills
- consistently applying Self-care practices
- being actively involved with maximizing physical, mental, emotional, and spiritual fitness and well-being
- using meditation as well as medication

- accepting and working with powerful emotions
- reconnecting with their heart and authentic Self
- eliciting internal and external support and resources
- flexible planning versus letting pain determine their plans

At crossroads, truth tugged at each woman's heart and soul, as they struggled to find meaning and answers amidst unfamiliar terrain, confusion, and chaos. Each discovered, in her own time and way, that she needed to grieve the life she no longer had, while she remained open for whatever followed. Each needed to use internal and external resources and support, to reconnect heart-and-soul intelligence with their new curriculum for living. Just as we see a cultural shift in our society from an illness to a wellness model, they were also shifting to this path. As you, too, listen to your heart during Self-healing, you will become part of your own shift.

Growing Through Illness, Pain, Stress, and Dis-ease

Western culture and technology have brought wonderful advances, but we have paid a high price relative to our humanity. Healing requires time – time for stillness, compassion, Self-care practices, embodying and integrating Self-awareness and heart intelligence that arise during the healing process. This is unnatural in our Western culture and our old medical model of health.

Tuning into heart intelligence will involve a combination of formal and informal study. It may take place in classroom settings with teachers, in a course of therapy or inner work, or in everyday life. Your curriculum will shift each time you integrate different healing paradigms into your unique wellness model – Eastern, Western, or otherwise. Ultimately, your heart and soul will provide the highest forms of guidance, learning, and wisdom.

Theologian, musician, philosopher, and physician Dr. Albert Schweitzer said, "Until he extends his circle of compassion to include all living things, man will not himself find peace."[6] As a medical missionary in West Africa, he noticed that witch doctors succeeded because they connected with the doctor, or healer, each person carries inside. With each step in your Self-healing process, you will grow and learn. Where you once sought *power over pain* and illness, you can *partner with pain*. You will harness your own power to navigate your ship through troubled waters and into safe harbors. Pain will become part of an initiation process, through which change, character development, and transformation occur.

We are all unpolished diamonds, our true beauty and exceptional gifts hidden beneath our personalities and conditioning. We each have great potential to release ourselves from the prison of pain, illness, and dis-ease into freedom. This occurs each time we return home through Self-acceptance and surrender. It happens as we are cut and polished during life events, which brings forth the strength and sparkle of the diamond in our core.

Enhancing Your Energy Bank Accounts

In the late 1970s, research by clinical psychologist Suzanne Kobasa revealed that many executives she studied were highly resistant to stress and better able than others to manage it. She described their "***stress-hardy personality***" traits, which protected them and enhanced the quality of their work life.[7] These traits also benefited their employers financially, through reduced use of sick time, better job satisfaction, increased productivity, and reduced turnover costs. Research suggests these traits can be learned with time and practice. The traits Kobasa described include:

1) *commitment:* having a sense of purpose and meaning in life

2) *control:* having a sense of influence over how stressors affect us

3)   *challenge:* seeing change as part of life, and difficulties as opportunities for growth and learning versus threats

We begin each day with physical, mental, emotional, and spiritual energy bank accounts, not unlike our monetary bank accounts. To maintain reserves in each account requires conscious, consistent management and wise investment choices. Our goal is to always have sufficient funds, rather than depleting our energies or becoming bankrupt through lack of attention to chronic pain, illness, stress, and dis-ease. As you develop and apply strategies and Self-care practices learned through *The Heart of Healing*, your stress hardiness will grow. As you build up your energy reserves and expand your investment options, enhanced response ability will increase deposits made into your energy bank accounts.

We can learn to be bankers and investment advisers for our energy bank accounts. You will have an opportunity to do so at the end of this chapter. Let heart-and-soul intelligence infuse and guide you to meet healing challenges in a confident, enlightened way. This will build up your reserves, and your heart will become your most valued investment adviser.

Call to Action: Illuminating
Softening the Heart

While working in an acute care hospital setting in the early 1980s, I met Cessy. He was in his mid-twenties and had been diagnosed several years prior with scleroderma, a chronic autoimmune rheumatic disorder that can affect external and internal connective tissue throughout the body. Scleroderma stems from the Greek words *sclero*, meaning hard, and *derma*, meaning skin. Cessy's body revealed outwardly visible signs of this disorder. The skin on his curled, rounded fingers had hardened, causing them to look more like hooks; he had lost the tips of several fingers on both hands due to circulatory, skin, and joint changes that accompanied scleroderma; and the fingertips that remained were blackened, lifeless, and numb. Scleroderma had progressed over the past few years and was now affecting his heart and internal organs. Although parts of Cessy's body had hardened, his heart remained soft and open.

Cessy wrote poetry. He had a strong, indomitable spirit and a heroic heart, which was evident through his life and work. His poetry revealed the different life path he chose while living with chronic physical, mental, emotional, and spiritual pain and dis-ease. Self-expression through his writing was essential to Cessy's healing process. I still recall how blessed and alive I felt in his presence, the moments of laughter that erupted spontaneously, and the insights he revealed about life and pain through his heart-and-soul filled words:[8]

> *As death knocks on my door, inside I stand,*
> *with fingers and palms pressed upon the oak wood*
> *door, blood continuing to flow with each new*
> *breath that I take in,*
> *each new moment of silents,*
> *of pain that has been forgotten by right now.*
> *Each new Beautiful moment of life,*
> *I can see the flowers, a humming bird*
> *A bear taking a chance on getting stung, going*
> *After that delicious honey nestled away in a hive*
> *Full of bees . . .*
> *I told death "I see you at my door, you may come*
> *in when you are ready, for I have found my*
> *Peace". . .*
> *Pain can't hurt no greater than it did yesterday.*
> *Because I left death standing in the doorway.*

Poetry was part of Cessy's inner work, and I was blessed to be with him for a short while on his journey. Writing brought Cessy to deeper places of intimacy with himself, his relationships, and life meaning. During solitude, he discovered how to weave together being and doing, creating greater harmony and a sense of sacred wholeness within. Cessy shared many of his journeys with me. He described times when he felt lost and scared walking alone along dark pathways. As he recounted how grateful he felt when sunlight broke through pain, darkness, and suffering, I observed a shift in his entire being, a sense of relief. These moments occurred when he spent time in nature with his own nature, and when he shared intimate and sacred time in special relationships – "like ours," he added. We each received spiritual transfusions during these moments.

Cessy could have chosen to be a victim; instead, he chose Self-determination. Throughout his struggles, he maintained a sense of curiosity, wonder, and awe. He never doubted his right to exist and shape his own life. He looked at the larger picture, along with consciously making daily choices and plans. As a result, he created a safe and warm inner home to inhabit, with a strong foundation and solid walls. Cessy lived and embodied one of Kahlil Gibran's quotes: "The deeper sorrow carves into your being, the more joy you can contain."[9]

Cessy showed me that healing is one of the greatest challenges faced by human beings, and one of the most vital creative processes in which we can be invested. Listening to his words and witnessing his actions revealed how pain and dis-ease present us with opportunities to create deeper intimacy and meaning in our lives, amidst change and chaos. Through his creative writing, Cessy uncovered broader ways of thinking, listening to, and being with pain and dis-ease. Cessy's poetry mirrored his struggles, but it also brought to light the heart-and-soul intelligence and wisdom that resided within him.

Call to Action: Illuminating Unconditional Presence

In my mid-thirties, I sensed a need for greater meaning and direction in my life. I sought something more, yet was unclear about how to find it or what it entailed. A close friend told me about Maria, a healer she had seen for help with physical and spiritual challenges. Something inside pushed me to make an appointment immediately. I felt a sense of inner calm doing this, as if an unclear path ahead was being illuminated in some way. When I entered Maria's home, I knew I was in the right place at the right time. I sensed peace, stillness, and clarity throughout my being. This began a journey that has brought continuous deposits to my energy bank accounts, enhanced my stress hardiness, and taught me much about unconditional presence and Self-healing.

Maria described her nursing background. She had directed a hospital-based cardiac intensive care unit and had worked in hospice, psychiatric, and home-care settings. She did not consider herself a healer. She worked with various approaches to help individuals create balance, wholeness, and well-being within themselves. When Maria asked why I came, I blurted out "I need more balance in my life," and tears unexpectedly flowed.

Maria keenly listened to my description of the hectic, over-scheduled life I was leading: raising children; running a household; being a wife and mother; teaching yoga; maintaining a spiritual practice; being of service; and trying to find greater meaning and purpose in life. The remainder of our session took place in an adjoining room. During the session I felt as if I was floating on water, as Maria completed our session in sacred silence.

Because I was healthy and strong physically, I rarely saw Maria for what I call "horizontal illness" – times when I was horizontal, in a bed or hospital, with health problems. I could also ignore or briefly work through "vertical illness" – times when

I walked upright through my day, with intermittent headaches, low back pain, gastrointestinal problems, or fatigue. However, it was through sessions with Maria that I began to recognize the disconnect from my heart and soul, and how depleted my energy bank accounts were.

Maria's simple, concise words helped me realize how cut off I was from my heart and authentic Self, especially when I came late to sessions and apologized for getting stuck at my office. Her consistent comment was, "Don't apologize to me, apologize to yourself." Her words highlighted the absence of check-in and restorative time with my authentic Self – in nature, during yoga and meditation, or in moments of sacred, loving connection with others.

I have continued with monthly visits to Maria for more than thirty-five years. We have walked side by side through wondrous as well as difficult periods. During my marital separations, physical therapy school, surgeries, and family illness or loss, Maria's insight, presence, and sense of humor supported my ability to move from fear to faith, from disturbance to inner peace, and from blame and judgment to compassion. Maria lives and manifests her spirituality through unconditional, grace-filled presence. She has helped me to recognize and apply the law of attraction: Where attention goes, energy follows. If I want peace and harmony, I must become peaceful and harmonious in my life and being. Maria has helped me understand how to integrate and enlist learning from life events in service to my heart and Self-healing, like spinning straw into gold. Her wisdom and simple presence have taught me about resistance, suffering, resilience, and gratitude for the miracles we are graced with each day.

Call to Action: Illuminating Meeting Challenges in Private Practice

Eight years after graduating physical therapy school, I opened my own physical therapy practice, something I never anticipated. I started small, spurred on by patients, referring physicians, and colleagues with whom I had worked. I felt creative and passionate about the hands-on manual therapy practice that developed, where clients received one-on-one individualized care during hour-long sessions. I was where I was meant to be. Clients did very well in short periods of time, and within a few years, my practice expanded to include three staff therapists, an office manager, and four office assistants.

There were many administrative challenges and growing pains during my first few years in private practice. When staff problems arose, I bent over backward trying to honor staff requests, but I was not clear or direct about accountability on everyone's part. I remained in a dysfunctional tug of war with myself, seeking staff approval and judging myself harshly when I set limits on staff actions or requests.

On-the-job learning began in earnest during my fifth year of practice. I felt overwhelmed, exhausted, and empty, no longer excited about my work. I needed balance to be restored between being, doing, and belonging. I wanted the joy back in my work and life. In hindsight, I see that I was not fully present when I showed up at work. I stayed busy and remained in denial about staff issues. My ego and mind ran the show, separated from my heart and soul. I had not maintained lines of communication between my body, mind, emotions, and soul. Though I helped others, I was not taking care of myself and my life.

I observed two behaviors in myself that provided insight into imbalances that I needed to change: I was not honoring my administrative and personal needs along with the needs of employees; and I was not utilizing healthy detachment in order to remain objective during decision making. These behaviors are frequently defined as codependency, which often has its roots in painful childhood upbringing and conditioning. My healing process now included unfinished business from my past – issues around abandonment, loss, self-acceptance, and self-trust.

Change could only occur when I became honest with myself and my staff. Telling the truth without blame or judgment was a huge challenge for me. My office had grown, but I still felt like a little kid in big-girl shoes. I had to take a risk. I had to be flexible and remain open, not attached, to outcome. I was flying blind and learning to trust my heart's radar. I returned to weekly therapy and bodywork sessions to facilitate heart-and-soul reconnection. It was also at this time that I began active study with Angeles Arrien and her Four-Fold Way™ Program.

Through conscious, mindful, and compassionate presence, the situation turned around in six months. I moved and rented a smaller office, returned to a solo practice, accepted only self-pay clients, and cut down on office staff. I eliminated "administrivia" from my life, and relationships ended naturally or dissolved. This was a courageous leap, as I feared not having sufficient clients to financially continue my practice. My clientele changed, and I now had a waiting list. I was amazed at how motivated individuals were when they elected to pay directly for their services and wait to be reimbursed by their insurance carrier.

I was relieved and excited with the results of downsizing and my heart's new curriculum. Self-trust grew, and I felt empowered as the pace and scope of my practice became more in line with my natural rhythm. I reduced the number of clients I saw daily, and I committed to doing inner work such as yoga, meditation, journaling, exercise, and dance at least three days a week. Today, my life tapestry is enhanced by what I learned. Like Joseph's technicolor dream coat, this tapestry is now a cloak of many colors, which holds my dreams, truths, and much Light from Spirit.

Nourishing Ourselves and One Another

Part of our heart's curriculum and being human involves learning and applying communication and listening skills with ourselves and one another. Communicating from our heart is challenging in today's electronic world, with its vast communication networks. We live in a noisy environment filled with loud music, horns honking, traffic, and active as well as silent screams. We speak and are spoken to via the Internet, text messages, e-mail, and conference calls. These do not even begin to approach the communication that occurs when we genuinely listen to one another and feel heard. Heart-to-heart and face-to-face communication has become a rare and precious commodity. We are psychologically, emotionally, and spiritually malnourished when we receive insufficient listening and understanding through our communication, and as a result we have great difficulty developing intimacy.

According to psychiatrist Daniel Stern, it is critical for young children to have their emotions met with compassion and acceptance. He refers to this as *attunement*.[10] Attunement is also essential for adult health, but is frequently missing because our attention is drawn to e-mail, voice-mail, texting, the Internet, and other electronic formats. Our need for human contact and interaction is vital, though they are not always available to us. I realized how valuable human interaction is during visits with my mother at the nursing home; when I made verbal and touch contact with clients, colleagues, friends, and family and experienced their responses; and when I calmed my inner child and my granddaughters' fears and tears. Human interaction is essential to our survival and vital to our planet's sustenance through our joint care of Mother Earth.

It is essential that we compassionately mirror and are mirrored by one another, in order to build a strong sense of Self and partnership. Who do you interact with, heart to heart, on a consistent basis? This interaction can occur many ways – through touch, words, presence, tone, gestures, and facial expression. Your Self-healing will nourish and be nourished through heart-and-soul relationships you develop.

Making Peace with Yourself

Self-acceptance is often essential to relearning and revising our heart's curriculum. This is discussed in *Healing Your Rift with God*, by teacher, counselor, bodywork therapist, and my Process Acupressure colleague Paul Sibcy.[11] When I read his book I was initially challenged, as I did not believe I had a rift with G-d. Paul states that any place where we judge ourselves, where we do not accept ourselves, is a place we have a rift with G-d, since we are not recognizing and honoring G-d's presence there. I was humbled and challenged to follow his suggestions: Realize and let go of your ego's need to control; become conscious of, and compassionately interact with suffering (your own and others), which can occur when we feel inadequate; awaken to the authority and wisdom in your heart and soul's guidance; and live and practically apply this daily through your unique heroic journey, beyond mind, thought, and ego.

Members of the Chronic Pain Self-Help Class were able to grow and evolve beyond ego and control through acceptance and love. Each step brought new perspectives and renewed their ability to accept and be with what remained unresolved in their life and healing. Self-acceptance was also clarified for me after reading *The Diamond in Your Pocket*, by author and spiritual teacher Gangaji. Her words remind us that due to conditioning and old perceptions we often look externally for the treasures we seek, only to find them existing in a pocket in our hearts – within our true nature.[12]

William Blake gives us a most realistic picture of life, from which to gain insight:[13]

> *"...It is right it should be so*
> *Man was made for Joy & Woe*
> *And when this we rightly know*
> *Thro the World we safely go*

Joy and woe are woven fine
A Clothing for the Soul divine
Under every grief & pine
Runs a joy with silken twine..."

As you open to your heart and authentic Self during Self-healing journeys, you will be asked to stretch and grow. Each time you will learn anew how to bring patience, Self-compassion, unconditional presence, and love to yourself, others, and your lessons. Expect the unexpected, and anticipate insights, guidance, and miracles; they are everywhere, especially within your authentic Self.

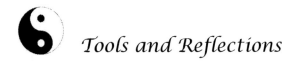

Tools and Reflections

The greater danger for most of us lies not in setting our aim too high and falling short; but in setting our aim too low, and achieving our mark.
–Michelangelo

Self-healing involves lifelong learning in four dimensions of wellness: physical, mental, emotional, and spiritual. Using the tools and reflections in this chapter you will:

1) explore the four dimensions of wellness

2) formulate an action plan for one dimension of wellness in your Awareness Journal

3) learn strategies to build up reserves in your physical, mental, emotional, and spiritual energy bank accounts

Tool 12: Dimensions of Wellness

You are the CEO of your well-being. There are no magic bullets or instant solutions. Pain, stress, and dis-ease are powerful teachers. They will soften, open, and strengthen your heart and highlight inner wisdom, which can carry you through times of adversity. You have the ability to educate yourself and learn how to respond to challenges you encounter in any dimension of wellness. This will enable you to meet and partner with a health-care team that provides support and guidance for your health-care plans and choices. Through this process, an authentic sense of empowerment will grow within your whole being.

Now let's explore the four dimensions of wellness – physical, mental, emotional, and spiritual – to help you determine where you want to make revisions and/or changes. Use Diagram 4 to assist you with responding to the questions that follow regarding each dimension.

Diagram 4: Dimensions of Wellness

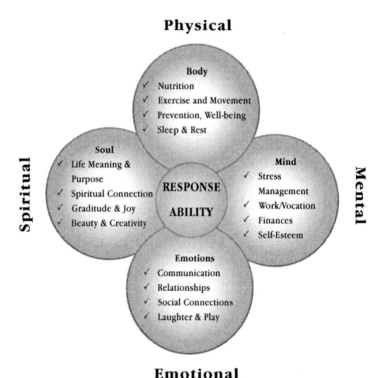

Physical:

Segments in this dimension of wellness relate to your body and include: Nutrition, Exercise and Movement (activities you pursue in addition to exercise), Prevention, Well-being, and Sleep and Rest. What one segment in this dimension would you like to change?

In your Awareness Journal, describe your current beliefs and Self-care practices for that one segment. Do these beliefs and practices serve your current physical well-being, or not? What changes do you need to consider in order to enhance your physical well-being in this segment? What external and internal resources will you incorporate to support and reinforce change?

Mental:

Segments in this dimension of wellness relate to your mind and include: Stress Management, Work/Vocation, Finances, and Self-Esteem. What one segment in this dimension would you like to change?

In your Awareness Journal, describe your current beliefs and Self-care practices for that one segment. Do these beliefs and Self-care practices serve your current mental well-being, or not? What additions and/or revisions do you need to consider in order to enhance your mental well-being in this segment? What external and internal resources will you incorporate to support and reinforce change?

Emotional:

Segments in this dimension of wellness relate to your emotions and include: Communication, Relationships, Social Connections, and Laughter and Play. What one segment in this dimension would you like to change?

In your Awareness Journal, describe your current beliefs and Self-care practices for that one segment. Do these beliefs and Self-care practices serve your current emotional well-being, or not? What additions and/or revisions do you need to consider in order to enhance your emotional well-being in this segment? What external and internal resources will you incorporate to support and reinforce change?

Spiritual:

Segments in this dimension of wellness relate to your soul, or life force, and include: Life Meaning and Purpose, Spiritual Connection, Gratitude and Joy, and Beauty and Creativity. What one segment in this dimension would you like to change?

In your Awareness Journal, describe your current beliefs and Self-care practices for that one segment. Do these beliefs and Self-care practices serve your current spiritual well-being, or not? What additions and/or revisions do you need to consider in order to enhance your spiritual well-being in this segment? What external and internal resources will you incorporate to support and reinforce change?

Tool 13: Your Action Plan

In any dimension of wellness you will need to consider your *intentions* (*what* you want to accomplish) and your *goals* (*how* you accomplish your intentions). Intentions and goals will manifest through action plans that have achievable, believable, controllable and measurable benefits, outcomes, and time frames. The following examples may help clarify this for you.

Your Exercise and Movement intention might be to have a strong, healthy, and flexible body and lifestyle. Your goal might be to establish a fitness program that incorporates flexibility, strength, and aerobic routines, performed five days per week for forty-five to sixty minutes.

Your Stress Management intention might be to enhance your ability to manage stress and to improve your coping skills for greater life balance. Your goal might be to learn and apply stress management skills, strategies, and resources that foster peace and well-being.

Your Laughter and Play intention might be to express and experience more laughter and play in your life. Your goal might be to plan ways to spend time with people and activities that bring laughter and play into your life on a weekly basis.

Your Life Meaning and Purpose intention might be to bring your *values*, dreams, and authentic Self into alignment with your daily life. Your goal might be to spend at least twenty to thirty minutes daily with meditation, teachings, journaling, or other Self-care practices that reconnect you with your authentic Self and your life purpose.

Now it is your turn. Select one dimension of wellness segment that you worked with in Tool 12, which you want to change, strengthen, or one where additional support is needed. Answer the following questions about this segment in your Awareness Journal. This will help you begin to formulate an action plan:

1)   In which dimension of wellness segment do you seek enhanced well-being?

2)   What intention do you want to manifest for that segment? Be as specific as possible.

3)   In order to accomplish your intention, write one goal that is achievable, believable, controllable, and measureable for this segment. How and when will you know your goal is accomplished?

4)   What personal strengths and experiences can you call on to help you reach your goal?

5)   List the internal and external resources you will need to incorporate to accomplish your goal. When will you introduce these into your action plan?

6)   Who will you call upon to assist you in your process? When? How?

7)   When and how will you review and update your action plan?

Keep your action plan specific and simple. Set aside time weekly or biweekly to reassess and update your goals and strategies. In the beginning it will be helpful to pursue one goal at a time, building success gradually. Resources in the Bibliography and Appendix B will assist you further with forming intentions and goals.

Tool 14: Affirmations

Affirmations are personal statements you write, read, picture, and feel now in present time. They are based on what you seek to manifest through the use of conscious awareness and attention. Affirmations use thought energy to reprogram and create new life patterns. They activate and empower intentions and goals. Affirmations begin with "I." They are composed of brief, simple, positive action words that indicate achievement and reflect realistic pictures and emotional excitement about your plans. Written affirmations begin with words such as: I am . . . I have . . . I enjoy . . . I feel . . . I release . . . I accept . . . I am in the process of . . . and so on. Some examples of affirmations are:

- I effectively manage stressful situations and accept needed support.

- I guide my own destiny and am accountable for the results of my decisions and actions.

- I enthusiastically do what I love and experience abundant health, joy, finances, and peace.

Write an affirmation for the action plan you developed for Tool 13. Let your words illustrate ease, joy, optimism, confidence, and positive expectancy. The exact wording may take a few attempts, so hang in there until it feels just right. Post your affirmation in several places to visually reinforce and strengthen your plans. Write it on sticky notes or index cards. Place pictures or photos of your affirmation where you meditate, exercise, work, dress, and/or relax. Use resources from the Bibliography and Appendix B to assist you with developing your affirmation, and update it as needed. Repetition is key when using affirmations. They become stronger each time you write, see, say, and hear them, each time you visualize your desired outcome.

Tool 15: Your Energy Bank Accounts

As a living system, you exchange energy in your relationships and with your environment. Let's explore the ways you allocate your physical, mental, emotional, and spiritual time and energy. As you clarify and adapt your commitments, you will increase the deposits and reserves in your physical, mental, emotional, and spiritual energy bank accounts.

Step 1. Look back at the Dimensions of Wellness diagram in Tool 12. Using the examples that follow to assist you, make two lists for each segment:

<u>**List 1:**</u> people and activities that deposit energy into that segment/energy bank account.

<u>**List 2:**</u> people and activities that withdraw or fail to replenish energy in that dimension's energy bank account.

The examples in Table 3 will assist you further.

Table 3: Examples of Energy Deposits & Withdrawals

Energy Deposits	Energy Withdrawals
Physical	
Meal planning/shopping ahead	Eating on the run, missing meals, too much sugars
Regular attendance at exercise classes	Missing exercise classes – lack of clear priorities/options
Walking outside with my spouse, friend, or significant other	Too busy with work; need bad weather options
Qigong, gardening, hiking, biking	Poor prioritizing and planning for these activities
Mental	
Breathing practices, meditation	Not making self-care practices a priority
Setting and adhering to a budget	Overuse of credit cards, lack of planning, worry
Honoring how I used my time and energy today	Judging how I used my time and energy today
Emotional	
Loving time with spouse, family, friends, significant others	Too busy for relationships and feeling guilty
Time for joy, play, and laughter with significant others	Feeling exhausted, burned out, bored, unloved, alone.
Spiritual	
Time in nature or with crafts, hobbies, art, music, pets	Loss of connection with Spirit and your authentic Self
Daily meditation & prayer time	Unclear, unrealistic, and unfocused life priorities

Step 2. Summarize your discoveries by answering the following:

- What and/or who builds my energy bank accounts?

- What and/or who drains my energy bank accounts?

- What and/or whom do I need to add to my life to increase energy deposits?

- How can I balance and/or lessen the impact of energy withdrawals?

- When I listen to and connect with my heart and soul, what guidance and wisdom comes forth?

Return to the sacred stillness within your sanctuary. Take a few centering breaths before returning to your outer world. Review the intentions, goals, and affirmation(s) written in your Awareness Journal for Tools 12, 13, 14, and 15. Sit quietly with the seeds you are planting. Feel, sense, and experience the magic in your dreams and plans. In stillness, let your heart's illumination bring love and light to your path and evolving process. You've done a great job with new beginnings. Bravo!

CHAPTER EIGHT

The Heart's Voyage Through Change

Theme Five: Healing Involves Change and Movement

*Twenty years from now you will be more disappointed by the
things you didn't do than by the ones you did do.
So throw off the bowlines. Sail away from the safe harbor.
Catch the trade winds in your sails.
Explore. Dream. Discover.
–Mark Twain*

For many years, I have traveled to a pristine, sacred place for renewal, a place that has been transformed over the years. The Anza-Borrego Desert State Park, in southern California, has long been a place that rejuvenates me physically, relaxes me mentally, clears my emotions, and helps me reconnect with my heart. I can count on it to bring me back to my soul. In 2004 floods devastated this wild place, and I had to see it and my healing in a whole new way.

Travel can transport us to new places emotionally and spiritually, providing an opportunity to embrace change and transformation. In this book, I have often referred to healing as a journey, with all that word conveys about moving us beyond the familiar and into new perspectives. The healing journey changes us. It takes us on paths that are deeply entwined with change and movement.

I often look to nature for insight about the healing power of change, because nature is always changing. Nature provides a model of our ability and potential to survive even catastrophic change. Strongly grounded trees, with deep roots, are less vulnerable to heavy winds and downpours. Trees that remain flexible survive storms. Nature continuously cycles through seasonal changes, as do we throughout our life cycle. Movement is continuous in nature. It is also an integral part of healing.

In this chapter, you will read stories about healing journeys. Frank suffered a stroke in his early fifties that left him paralyzed and on a feeding tube. He was told he would never walk or eat normally again. I learned to move home to my physical and sensory bodies through Feldenkrais Awareness Through Movement® lessons. Brody, a ten-year-old boy, was determined to move through challenges he faced with Crohn's dis-ease and hyperactivity. He was empowered as he participated in acupressure and Self-care practices. Each of these healing journeys will show you how we move through change during healing. This is possible in the face of great trauma and loss, as well as during our final journey on Earth when we pass on.

As you move with and through this chapter, I invite you to explore how you have evolved through changes in your life. Your Awareness Journal will greatly assist you with tracking changes. When you approach tracking with curiosity and simple inquiry, you will encounter the mysteries of life that move through us with change.

Call to Action: Changing
The Natural World and Healing Lessons

Angeles Arrien states that we go to four places in nature for healing: the mountains, oceans, forests, and deserts. The desert was the one place I had not gone to for healing until I went to Borrego Springs, a community near San Diego that is surrounded by the 600,000 rustic, scenic acres of Anza-Borrego Desert State Park. From the first time I arrived there I was moved by the towering cloud-capped mountains that shifted colors throughout the day, the majesty of the canyon walls, and the huge boulders that resembled sculptures of prehistoric creatures frozen in time. As I hiked in Palm Canyon amidst the vast washes and rocky cliffs, no one else was visible for as far as my eye could see. In spring, Palm Canyon was an artist's palette, filled with yellow brittlebush, red chuparosa, indigo bush, red-tipped ocotillo, large barrel cacti, and tall yucca spires covered with white flowers.

I traveled to Borrego Springs for many years to study with Aminah Raheem. Each time I went I made it a ritual to walk about forty-five minutes into Palm Canyon, to a grove of endangered California fan palms that surround a natural spring. It was a welcome contrast to the hot desert that surrounded it. The solitude I found there allowed me to center and renew myself. In Palm Canyon the gentle wind brushed across my cheeks, the lofty walls embraced me, and the vibrant sunrises renewed my faith in new beginnings. My authentic Self reemerged.

In 2004 I met a devastated landscape. Floods from the highest rainfall in 100 years had ravaged the landscape, and the trails in Palm Canyon were only partially reconstructed. As I began my hike early one morning, an eerie silence was present throughout the valley. I saw where torrential waters had rushed through the canyon, dislodging mammoth boulders. Colossal fan palms were strewn across the canyon floor. I recognized everything, and nothing, at the same time. This once beautiful, serene landscape had been transformed instantaneously, without notice, much like our lives when a healing crisis arises.

As I continued to hike I was overwhelmed by the destruction, yet astonished by the beauty that remained amidst the devastation. With each step, prayers came forth for the land, for healing, and in gratitude for what prevailed. I left the canyon in silence. I sought out David, a wise Native American friend in his thirties, whom I met on my first visit to Borrego Springs. David, who had lived there his entire life, shared his love of and reverence for this land and place with me many times. He spoke of the heartbreak he felt initially on hearing about the floods and of his reluctance to go to the canyon and witness the destruction. However, he knew he had to go back. When he did, he, too, was overwhelmed yet in awe of the beauty present in the transformed landscape. And when spring blossomed in the desert that year, it was the most abundant spring in 100 years.

After I returned home, the image of Anza-Borrego's vibrant desert blossoms stayed with me. Almost daily I recalled my walk through the agony and the ecstasy of the canyon's transformation. I now had an embodied experience of the balance, integration, and unity within everything and what emerges after transformation. As I returned to my life, what I had witnessed brought forth a new understanding that our healing strongly resembles the transformational and creative processes within Mother Nature.

Growth, Healing, and Taking Risks

As we begin to dream and re-vision our lives during healing, aging, and even dying, we will be asked to go beyond our comfort zones. We will be called upon to take risks as part of growth and development, in much the same way that in order to grow, lobsters molt and shed their shell several times a year through adulthood. In their new soft shells, lobsters are vulnerable. They hide under rocks or bury themselves to avoid being eaten or tossed against coral reefs. Lobsters automatically release what no longer serves them. They risk their lives in order to grow.

We are more likely to take risks and be successful if we do so when our self-confidence is high. To determine where their self-confidence was in any moment, I had clients picture it on a speedometer and asked them if it was above or below fifty miles per hour. If their self-confidence was below fifty, risk taking could be overwhelming and their ability to make heart-and-soul-informed choices would be lessened. If their self-confidence was above fifty, managing risk and making wise, discerning choices were more assured. When we connect with our heart and authentic Self during risk taking, our confidence and sense of empowerment are greatly enhanced.

We face paradoxes and tough questions when we take risks. Our belief systems are challenged as we redefine and revise our life. Since our societal values are strongly based on independence and self-reliance, it can be hard to ask for and accept support when we take risks. If we meet risks from an awake and heart-centered place, our perceptions and beliefs shift as we bridge independence with interdependence and self-reliance with Self-compassion. This helps us walk the slippery slope of taking responsibility as captain of our ship on the one hand and asking for and receiving external support on the other. Although we may be alone at times on our journey, in moments of reflection we realize we are not alone.

Life-Affirming: Mark's Story and Finding a New Self

A carpenter, Mark prided himself on being the primary breadwinner for his wife and three small children. A survivor from day one of his life, he had learned independence growing up in a household in which his father was unable to hold down a job and his mother worked two jobs to support Mark and his younger brother. As a teenager Mark delivered newspapers to provide extra money for his mom, who encouraged him to pursue his dream of a career in journalism. Life went along, though, and he went into carpentry to support his family, his youthful dream set aside.

In his late thirties, Mark had an accident at work while using an electric saw. He lost the tips of his pinky and index fingers, and severed tendons and ligaments in his middle and ring fingers on his dominant right hand. Mark described his physical pain during therapy. However, it was obvious and poignant that it was more painful and worrisome to him that he was unable to work and provide for his family so that his wife could remain home to raise their small children. The accident would change everything about the life he had forged for himself, his wife, and his family.

Mark's pain was intense. It worsened despite therapy. Pain spread up his arm, and his hand became very sensitive to cold weather. He was diagnosed with reflex sympathetic dystrophy (RSD), a complex regional pain syndrome where intense pain is out of proportion to the severity of the injury. Mark learned that there was no cure for RSD. Pain management was his only option.

Mark now faced in himself what he had despised in his father – the inability to work. With ceaseless determination, he continued with intensive therapy to recover movement, strength, and function. All his life Mark swore he would never be like his father. He worked hard to live up to this promise to himself. He was now vulnerable and felt out of control, as he came face-to-face with his worst fears.

Mark possessed a fighting spirit all his life. He began to remember his ability to dream. He had bouts of depression, but his ability to create a new vision arose and was more powerful. During our therapy sessions, he talked about his love for writing. What emerged was a renewed desire to pursue a journalism career. Each time Mark spoke about this, he became animated. The excitement in his voice was palpable. He started to explore this possibility during his free time at home. As his injuries healed, he developed a one-armed hunt-and-peck system at the computer keyboard. Mark hadn't planned for the accident, but creativity and joy for a renewed passion sparked his sense of independence and determination.

Mark was at a turning point. He and his wife talked seriously about their options. He was no longer alone. His support team expanded the moment his wife entered the process. Mark now began to blend independence and self-reliance with inter-dependence and external support. His wife's nursing background and strong compassion reflected Mark's heart-centered qualities, which she loved and respected. He never recognized these as significant in himself.

After lengthy discussions, Mark and his wife decided to exchange roles for a brief period of time. She was thrilled to return to her former job in nursing while he completed a degree in journalism and teaching. Teaching was part of a backup plan to ensure gainful full-time employment upon graduation. Another support also showed up unexpectedly, in the form of a part-time newspaper job that allowed Mark to work from home and be with the children. Because he worked more than thirty hours a week, his employer paid for his schooling. Mark signed a guarantee that he would work full-time for the paper for five years after graduation. This assured Mark that his loan would be taken care of and that he would have a job with growth potential.

Mark completed physical therapy and did well regaining function in his right hand. He called periodically and eighteen months later he returned in person. He had new prosthetic fingers and was overjoyed with them, because they enhanced his fine motor hand function. Mark could now hold a glass, pick up change, and even pinch his wife and children on their cheeks. His schooling was almost completed, and his children were now in school. Mark and his wife had grown tremendously by supporting each other. Although parts of their life were still unknown, they were excited again about their individual and family life plans.

Mark lived his own lobster story. Like a lobster, he needed to shed his former shell and what no longer defined him – outgrown values and former roles as a provider, husband, father, and man – at home and in society. He, too, needed to risk losing his life as he knew it, as part of growth and development. Mark needed to discover, in his words, that his heart's strength was as vital to life support as his physical strength. It was his heart that protected and guided him when he was vulnerable and when fear arose. Mark used time rather than spent time to consciously redefine himself and his life purpose. He created safe places to be alone amidst the shifting emotional currents. In stillness he reallocated his values and inner resources as part of his transformation. Mark participated in Self-care practices such as meditation, journaling, and Qigong to support himself during this transition. He took the road less traveled, spoken of by American poet Robert Frost, and that made all the difference.

As in Mark's story, new patterns of interacting with your life will emerge during healing. The status quo will be disturbed. At these times, you may fall deeper into your own darkness, in search of strength, guidance, and your inner voice. It will help to remember that there are no mistakes, only learning. It is often only in retrospect that we realize this. We often know in our mind that we need to grow and change, but we are not sure how to go about doing so. Heart connection provides the spark that illuminates our path.

Meeting Change: Breakdowns and Breakthroughs

Though we experience change from the moment we enter this world to the moment we leave, we often have difficulty with change. Even the authors of the Declaration of Independence acknowledged this: ". . . experience hath shewn that mankind are more disposed to suffer . . . than to right themselves by abolishing the forms to which they are accustomed."[1]

When we encounter change during healing, it is often a wake-up call. In addition to dealing with the symptoms that prompted our healing crisis, we find ourselves not knowing or being able to do anything. In this situation, we may feel as if we are at the edge of a cliff. Breakthroughs in awareness occur here, and we discover inner strength and courage that enhances our ability to interact with healing and life challenges.

Wake-up calls summon us to break down old beliefs, perceptions, and behaviors that often impact our choice to react or respond. We are challenged to embrace new approaches. In Chapter Seven I related how my codependency habits with employees brought me to an edge, a place of growth and development. At the time, I was studying with Angeles Arrien in her Four-Fold Way™ Program. Angeles spoke about "giving up our shrouds of insufficiency and standing in our gifts and talents" as part of developing the archetypal leader and healer within us. However, when I needed to apply this and change beliefs and behaviors relative to my office, I felt unsure and vulnerable. I was challenged to learn and apply new ways of interacting with employees. This on-the-job training taught me to speak directly to issues and set clear boundaries versus remaining stuck in codependent behaviors. This learning greatly benefited me in subsequent situations and relationships.

In the process, I also reconnected with my authentic Self and soul mission regarding my office. It became clear that I had lost touch with my heart's path when I listened to others' suggestions and expanded my practice to reach more people. When former beliefs and choices broke down I was led back to my original intention, a small, solo practice. Meditation, journaling, movement, intentions, goals, and written affirmations grounded my process. These practices reinforced my new intentions, and a breakthrough occurred in six months. I was back on track and happier than ever. My office and life were again whole, balanced, and integrated. My presence with clients became richer because of this edge work, and I was grateful to be home again within my being.

When breakdowns lead to breakthroughs, we move into greater dimensions of being and living. Our spiritual journey comes alive as we tap into great mysteries that lie within us and our lives. We learn how our bodies function automatically; how we manage to survive stressful times; the synchronicity in events that occur and people we meet. I am touched by this mystery each time I visit Borrego Springs and each time I witness the great mysteries of healing. When you engage the mystery, you may find yourself at an edge. Here you will encounter unfamiliar experiences, may feel unsure and ill at ease, and may have little awareness about how to be or what to do and how to respond.

Being at the Edge

When clients came to an edge, they often felt out of control. Strong emotions arose – quite often fear and/or anger. It was fight-or-flight time. As they stayed awake to their process they developed a third response – flow. It was easier for them to move and flow through change and healing when they processed their emotions and experiences, applied new insights, and pursued Self-care practices to further ground new learning.

Strong emotions will signal you are at an edge and in new territory, your next place of growth and development. We meet what is known, but a greater challenge is meeting the unknown within the mysteries of our healing process. Resistance arises, and is normal, as we approach and move through edges. You may even find yourself automatically going into survival mode when you feel threatened and vulnerable. Our defense mechanisms frequently create protective armoring when we face change. Clients often sensed this as stiffness, tightness, pain, and difficulty with movement and daily activities. They also felt stuck in negative thinking or overwhelming emotions that spiraled out of control. Like a gerbil on a wheel, they repeated many behaviors that kept them stuck. These compensatory behaviors eventually felt "normal."

Healing will challenge you to release your tightly held perceptions and beliefs. This will require persistence and courage. Healing will also require time for rest and renewal. It is here that you will reconnect with and heal your wounded, abandoned, and barricaded heart – the heart you unconsciously left behind as you walked through war zones. With each change you will be called upon to rediscover life meaning and purpose; reach for resources within and beyond you; and keep your heart energy open and flowing to embody healing, reverence for life, and a return to wholeness and your authentic Self.

Use Self-care practices to strengthen, support, guide, and move you through your healing process and new learning. Self-care practices will enhance awareness, which will reduce the chances of your body becoming a garbage dump for what you do not or cannot process at the time. They also alleviate stress, which frequently accompanies change. Self-care practices provide time outs from everyday living. During these moments heart-and-soul wisdom can guide you as to what you can or cannot change and where acceptance may be needed.

As you move through change and release layers of unconscious physical, mental, emotional, and/or spiritual numbness, remember to do so gradually in your unique way, rhythm, and timing. Listen for guidance from your authentic Self. You are in new territory. What signals new territory for you? Early on, you will need to build safety, Self-trust, and Self-respect as part of a foundation for the new home you occupy. Your heart's warmth will enliven and nourish what was once numb, as you bring joy, love, play, creativity, and gratitude to your process. You will read more about this in the next two chapters.

Call to Action: Changing
Frank's Healing, Beyond Medical Expectations

"My life is over," Frank said, with garbled speech. He was lying in bed like a rag doll – limp, pale, curled up in a ball, and withdrawn. He was fifty-two and had lived through a devastating stroke. To meet his every need he now required complete assistance from others, a full-time home health aide and his wife. He was on a feeding tube and unable to sit, stand, or walk. Frank's doctors told him he would never walk or eat normally again.

Our first tasks were to get Frank out of bed and sitting, begin walking, and have him use the bathroom versus a bedpan. This was a tall order for Frank, whose depression squelched any motivation. But Rose, his home health aide, was an angel at his side. She guided him gently yet firmly through a daily home exercise program, which built up his self-confidence, strength, and endurance for walking and daily functioning. Frank grew stronger day by day. He was proving to himself and his doctors that their prognosis was shortsighted, and his life could change.

During our sessions I incorporated singing, to rebuild Frank's vocal muscles. Lollipops and flavored ice cubes were his reward for top-level performances. These also helped retrain his swallowing reflex, which was markedly diminished after the stroke. We roared with laughter when our attempts to remain on key went awry while singing rounds of simple songs. All of us wanted to take our show on the road, with Bruce Springsteen if he would have us.

Laughter and tears were vital aspects of Frank's therapy, healing, and transformation. They oiled Frank's rusty heart, moved stagnant depression through his body, and helped him become a more confident, active participant in his life and healing process. Within three months Frank was walking independently with a cane, was off the feeding tube, and needed only occasional assistance with daily activities. With each step forward, Frank reactivated his vital life force.

Stairs became our next challenge. Frank was frightened about going up and down stairs, as he feared falling. To ease Frank's fears and build his confidence we explored falling during several sessions, initially onto his bed and next onto the floor. Frank gradually regained confidence in his ability to manage and maneuver his body, and his ability to ask for help when needed. As we worked together, Frank taught me the value of having a plan but the need to remain flexible, patient, and open to spontaneous changes and ideas that arose, especially when I didn't know what to do. This simple adaptation provided huge breakthroughs for Frank, and me.

In school, I had learned a simple reminder phrase for retraining stroke patients regarding stairs: "The good guys go to heaven, the bad guys go to hell." This meant that the patient would step first with the strong, uninvolved leg to ascend stairs, then step first with the leg impacted by the stroke to descend. This did not work for Frank. I felt confused, frustrated, and very inadequate. One day, out of sheer frustration, I asked Frank how he wanted to do it. By simply reversing the order I was imposing on him, he became practically independent going up and down stairs. I was speechless. Frank's body wisdom became part of his healing process, and I learned from it, too.

Frank was teaching me something about the *art* of healing. Frank taught me to tap into the resources in each patient's dignity and Self-respect as part of their healing process. We all learned about the power of teamwork sustained by commitment, compassion, laughter, play, and joys shared through well-earned healing victories. Frank's doctors, perplexed by his remarkable improvements, also learned the value of realistic encouragement and the detriment in setting a limited prognosis.

Movement: A Healing Tool

Stop for a moment now. Take in a long, slow breath. Feel your lungs expand within your rib cage. Now exhale, and feel your lungs and rib cage contract. Sense your life force moving through you with each inhalation, and sense the release of what no longer serves with each exhalation. Notice your eyes blinking. See if you can sense or hear the pulse of your human heart beating, as you might when checking your heart rate while exercising. What do all these have in common? They all involve tuning into movement in your body.

Movement can be defined as action or change. In music, movement involves tempo, cadence, and timing, which create flow. Movement is part of our body wisdom. With conscious attention to movement, we can witness the constant flow among body, mind, emotions, and soul. We are served by movement, because it:

- balances and integrates our internal and external being
- gets us from place to place in our external world
- provides ways to creatively explore our life and world
- introduces new possibilities into our body-mind and nervous system
- helps us reach out to satisfy our needs and desires
- brings us pleasure and joy

Our body and being are made to move; beliefs and attitudes move us or keep us from moving; and emotions move us or close down our hearts. Each of these aspects of movement drive our life force. Our spinal cord contains more than half a million nerve fibers, which send and receive messages as we move externally and internally. From conception, we have extensive built-in ways and capacities for moving and sensing ourselves and our environment.

Movement is vital to life. Without movement, our life force diminishes. I have seen this many times when people have long hospitalizations, unresolved loss or depression, or remain stuck in unfinished business through denial or numbing themselves. In each of these situations, they lose their spirit. As adults we tend to move in more fixed, habitual patterns, physically, mentally, and emotionally. If we remain unaware, we miss opportunities that movement, or the lack of movement, provides.

Can you recall dancing "properly" for fear of appearing foolish, or avoiding dancing entirely? How did your beliefs and/ or emotional experiences impact your choice? The end result is a decline in physical movement options and stiff, robot-like postures often seen in the elderly. Sensory and muscle systems in our body end up out of balance and bankrupt, and ease of movement in our whole being is no longer part of our current programming. As I watch the carefree ways my granddaughters move and dance, I am reminded of potential in my own body – what is lost, but also what still remains.

Galileo stated, "You cannot teach a man anything. You can only help him to find it in himself." As a result of trauma, shock, illness, chronic pain, stress, poor habits, and our need to survive, we accumulate postures and movement patterns within our tissues. Our bodies act as shock absorbers. Patterns often lead to armoring, pain, and dysfunction, and prevent free movement and self-expression. After working with Frank, I realized it was possible to interact with these patterns. He demonstrated that when our human drive for dignity and autonomy is encouraged during healing, as well as movement reeducation, our life force is stimulated and we move differently through life. We reinhabit our body-mind each time our hearts touch upon, remember, and move us toward our true nature.

Call to Action: Changing
Making the Impossible Possible

Movement can be used to enhance awareness and healing, especially when mindfulness is brought to daily actions. This can involve stretching in bed when you arise; chewing your food mindfully; recognizing when you are stressed and rushing through your day; practicing yoga or martial arts; or noticing movement, or lack of movement, throughout your day. How do you express your authentic Self through movement? Babies do it automatically as they learn to crawl and walk. We are also moved mentally, emotionally, and spiritually by music, art, dance, pets, nature, and being with friends and loved ones. As you rediscover what still has heart and meaning during your healing process, a change of heart can occur that moves you to consider additional pathways. Insights gained help you develop healing strategies, which affect how you live with stress, pain, and/or disability.

As an adult, I was less connected with the sense of lightness and joy in my being that I knew as a child – until I began to study yoga, Trager®, the Feldenkrais Method®, and Process Acupressure. I discovered places in me that psychotherapy had not touched upon, old beliefs and emotions buried in my tissues. My entire being became a vehicle for exploration, Self-expression, creativity, and the embodying of my life force. I learned to be present with my body from curiosity and Self-compassion, versus my usual self-judgment, blame, and shame. I became informed from within, or "in-formed."

A life-changing breakthrough occurred for me one day during a Feldenkrais Awareness Through Movement® class with Russell Delman, a Guild Certified Feldenkrais Practitioner[CM] and author of the audio series *The Embodied Life*.[TM][2] As he guided our movements, his words brought me into a profound sensory experience with my body. I was consciously connecting with my body's wisdom and deeply sensing my physicality during movement. Each action brought my attention and focus to what occurred in the moment. I was guided to "be here now, listen, receive, release, renew . . . and breathe" as I moved. My feet felt magnetized to the earth; I sensed my spine lengthening and felt taller; and my head and neck felt elongated and drawn upward. My body was aligning itself between heaven and Earth. I now realized how essential it was to embody our lives and experiences to promote healing – something so close to each of us, yet often overlooked.

In the early 1990s, I began to study Feldenkrais Awareness Through Movement® with Lawrence Phillips, a Guild Certified Feldenkrais Practitioner[CM]. At the time, because of a dislocated toe, I had severe pain when walking and was unable to raise myself up onto my toes while standing. I couldn't walk barefoot on the beach or on the Earth's floor, an activity I relished. Although my feet craved this, pain made it impossible. For almost a year I had been treated with orthotics, shoe inserts used to treat foot deformity and improve function. I was able to walk using orthotics, but the sense of connection and grounding with the Earth I felt while walking barefoot – so vital to me – had been taken away.

During early Feldenkrais Awareness Through Movement® lessons, I was appalled at how unconscious I was in my body, and I was a physical therapist! Through movement, I relearned how to listen to and receive from my body's storehouse of wisdom. Lawrence's gentle touch and guidance brought attention to movements and provided reflection. Uproarious laughter and joyous celebration occurred during our sessions, when I finally was able to create simple yet seemingly impossible actions in my body.

As sessions with Lawrence continued, I became very conscious of self-judgment and shame that arose when I didn't get movements "right" or do them perfectly. Angeles Arrien, in a class I took with her, had described how "perfection doesn't tolerate mistakes, excellence incorporates mistakes." My challenge was to apply this. I now understood what Babe Ruth learned from all his strikeouts: One needs to show up and continue playing the game.

Our explorations also brought awareness of a habitual driving pattern that warranted further inquiry. When I turned to look over my shoulder changing lanes, I did so from my head and neck only, and my trunk remained still. Lawrence suggested turning in an upward spiral, beginning with my lower back, followed by my trunk, and then bringing my neck, followed by my head, into the spiral.

As we played with this, I sensed a knot deep within the stiffness and pain I had experienced in my neck over the previous two years. I began to connect with how the protective knot developed. I had literally as well as figuratively stuck my neck out and pushed myself for ten years during physical therapy school and then after opening a private practice. I had moved through these changes with limited awareness of how my efforts impacted my whole being and how much stress my neck, specifically, had absorbed. I moved with this new conscious awareness during several sessions. My body recalled the pressures that arose from returning to school after a ten-year hiatus, and from my strong desire to help others as part of opening a private practice. As I revisited the past and present time, my body went through its process of reintegration as part of healing my neck. When I brought awareness to movement, and Self-compassion to change and healing, I was astonished at how much easier, freer, softer, and more relaxed my neck and body movements became.

Lawrence and I also explored my love for dancing and the freedom, ease, pleasure, and joy that flowed throughout my body with each sway, bounce, glide, wiggle, and twirl. These feelings were absent, by comparison, when I was at work or teaching. My movements there were smaller, more contained and guarded, less joyful, and orchestrated more from my mind than my heart. My sensory and kinesthetic awareness opened doors, but I again met self-judgment. Expanded movement awareness helped me discover how to bring my entire being into work and teaching – dancing and moving more freely when I spoke in front of people. I came out from behind the podium when I taught and faced my fear of not knowing or having all the answers. I was scared beyond belief yet having the time of my life as joy, ease, and newly found freedom came forth. Patience, humor, and gentle nudges from Lawrence helped me realize no movement is right or wrong.

Work and teaching now brought me teachable moments, and I was an eager learner. As I became aware of old patterns, I explored new and creative ways to sense, move, and interact with my environment and myself. Fluid, flexible, conscious interaction replaced fixed habits, and I became content with wherever I was in my body and being. This transformed my experiences, and I sensed the "lightness of being" Dr. Milton Trager, founder of the Trager Approach®, often spoke about.

Movement from unconscious to more conscious presence in my body was worth its weight in gold. I felt lighter, softer, freer, and more open, relaxed, and alive throughout my being. After six weekly sessions with Lawrence I was pain free and able to stop using the orthotics. I was ecstatic being able to walk with ease, without foot pain, for the first time in a year. The ground I craved to walk on was once again available to me. My feet came alive, and with each step, sensory messages engaged and flowed through my being.

Lawrence's example and guidance also altered my presence with clients. My ability to track and integrate movement experiences created paradigm shifts in my role as a therapist. After I learned to be patient with and trust my process, it was easier to do this with clients. As I became more focused and centered, there was less need to talk and "take charge" during client sessions. Silence and open moments during sessions became sacred space for clients. They touched upon and learned to integrate movement and their body wisdom during change and healing. My hands became reflecting mirrors for them, and revealed their own ability to respond to healing challenges.

Touch and the Mystery

We are all affected by touch, or the lack of touch, from the moment of conception. Without touch we may unconsciously armor ourselves to survive threats or assaults to our being. Healing touch includes physical touch as well as energetic touch – kind words, eye contact, tone of voice, gestures, and what we receive from nature or our environment. We may experience healing touch simply when we give or receive a glance across a room when someone or something catches our attention. We learn about ourselves through touch. Touch connects us directly with inner knowing, our gut feelings, and intuitive sensing. These form our built-in GPS guidance system.

The ways and means of healing are mysteriously woven into our tissues, ignited in mystifying ways when our heart-and-soul wisdom enters the process. However, this wisdom is all too often lost in our highly technological world, especially in the field of medicine. When we lose touch with our humanity, it literally hits home. We become numbers and body parts, seeking quick fixes and immediate answers. When we encounter a crying infant, frightened child, or stressed pet, a typical response is to give soothing words and gentle, compassionate touch. Why is it that as frightened and stressed adults, medication often becomes our first option?

Our skin, the largest single body organ, has more than 640,000 sensory receptors, all directly connected with our spinal cord. A quarter-sized piece of skin has more than three million cells, 100 sweat glands, fifty nerve endings, and three feet of blood and lymph vessels. During early fetal development, skin and brain develop from the same cells. From conception, every touch communicates directly with our brains. Through touch, our skin, brain, and nervous systems interact, and many chemical changes occur throughout our body. Safe touch and compassionate presence release chemicals that impact our parasympathetic nervous system, which relaxes our body. Invasive and/or abusive presence and touch release other chemicals, which activate the fight-or-flight response via our sympathetic nervous system. With this alert, we move into action and experience tension, tightness, and guarding in our body, the opposite of relaxation.

On Self-healing journeys, you may want to explore bodywork therapies in conjunction with *allopathic medicine*/ care. Bodywork therapies fit into four categories: mechanical, integrative, energetic, and psychological. They may include craniosacral therapy, visceral mobilization, lymphatic mobilization, the Trager Approach®, the Feldenkrais Method®, Process Acupressure, Zero Balancing®, Integrative Manual Therapy, and massage. Each provides a multidimensional experience in which new patterns can be established in tissue memory and your nervous system. You will need to determine which form(s) are most effective for you, through personal experience and consulting inner guidance. Bodywork therapies have many benefits. They help to:

- reduce stress and balance muscle tension, spasms, and imbalances

- reduce pain, swelling, and inflammation

- increase blood supply and nutrition to tissues

- improve joint circulation and nutrition

- improve posture and alignment

- enhance sensory awareness

- reprogram the nervous system

- open and/or balance energy pathways and *energy centers* (*meridians* and *chakras*)

- release emotions and blocks locked in cell memory

Osteopath and acupuncturist Dr. Fritz Smith, originator of Zero Balancing®, describes *essential touch* as the quality of contact rather than a specific method.[3] This right-brain oriented form of touch helps practitioners contact the energy field and movement of energy within the individual receiving a bodywork session. Essential touch, combined with bodywork therapies, enhances physical, mental, emotional, and spiritual health and well-being. Interface is at the core of essential touch, and is especially necessary when edges arise during bodywork sessions. Refer to Chapter Six, where Dr. Smith's term interface is described relative to touch.

I gained insight about touch and Self-healing during early bodywork sessions with the Trager Approach®. I felt both excitement and fear when I experienced my body as a passionate and sensuous expression of me. This had occurred prior, when I first studied yoga. In both instances, I wanted to run and hide from vulnerable places within, which felt shameful at the time. I was torn between receiving pleasure through my body, and old conditioned beliefs and taboos around sensuality and "being a good girl." Tightness and anxiety, which occurred in my body during these sessions, reflected tensions in my mind around these old beliefs. As I gradually gave myself permission to receive positive experiences around touch and movement, new insights and Self-healing manifested. I realized that my sensual nature, beyond procreation and the birthing of my children, housed the creative energy that also birthed my gifts and talents. It took time to trust my process and insights. This part of my Self-healing journey brought tremendous respect and deeper empathy for anyone facing their vulnerabilities during bodywork sessions. I realized firsthand the need for interface and the continuous establishment of safety and trust during bodywork sessions.

Call to Action: Changing Being Your Own Superhero – Brody's Story

The whole time ten-year-old Brody went through third grade he was in severe pain from recurrent stomachaches and intestinal problems. He also had behavior problems at home and at school related to hyperactivity. His mother, Melissa, a single parent and teacher, had changed his diet, but she was frustrated when it was difficult to enforce the new eating plan. She was also worried because Brody's symptoms affected their family and every area of his life – focus, concentration, school attendance, and behavior.

At our first session, I asked Brody why he came. After he told me his mother brought him, we laughed. Laughter opened the doorway for Brody to tell me about his past year, filled with physical pain, inability to eat as he wanted to, anger, loss of familiar activities, and feeling left out in school after repeated absences. I had Brody draw a picture of how he felt. He described it afterward: "I am angry, stuck, and feel cheated that pain took away my life." He felt and looked overwhelmed and frustrated –

his body a rounded heap, his voice low and slow, the light in his eyes and the power in his spirit lost somewhere inside.

Brody and I easily became friends. He was bright, articulate, inquisitive, and funny, and he was perceptive about himself, his behavior, his environment, and his relationships at home and school. In addition to our acupressure and sound healing sessions, I encouraged Brody to keep a simple journal, with words and pictures, which described one or two moments in his day. He brought his journal to sessions and he talked openly and honestly about his pain and emotions, which he described as a balloon that popped when he was "mad, bad, and feeling upset." The journal and our sessions established a container for Brody, in which he could be present with and learn from what had occurred in his whole being.

Brody continued sessions as he went through diagnostic testing. About four months later, he was diagnosed with Crohn's dis-ease, an inflammatory disorder that may affect any part of the gastrointestinal tract and causes symptoms such as abdominal pain, intestinal bleeding, diarrhea, and weight loss. Brody was facing a chronic dis-ease, one that needed continuous physical and dietary monitoring. Life as he knew it was now drastically changed relative to school, after-school activities, friends, and family. He was enraged.

Brody was stuck in the eye of his internal storm, tossed around and not knowing when or if he would safely land. He no longer had control over everyday life and movement, as pain and relentless anger and confusion took charge. Watching Brody go through this and being unable to prevent it left Melissa and her family feeling helpless, confused, and frightened. Melissa's edge challenge was to make choices daily that held compassion for Brody but that also set limits around his behavior and diet. Everyone involved, at home and at school, was meeting an edge, which changed moment to moment. No one knew when a barrage of symptoms would emerge, or how Brody would react or respond.

Brody's goals centered on managing his pain, reducing stress and spasms, improving his posture, and becoming independent in a home program. He needed to move his energy into productive avenues and behaviors, so I asked Brody what it would be like if he became his own superhero. Brody liked and understood that concept, and we began to explore ways he could do this at home and in school.

We formulated a superhero plan, which contained three easy, simple steps. First, Brody continued with his journal writing two or three times weekly. Second, he began simple breathing exercises to "take superhero energy into his body and let go of excess energy through a dragon's breath." This helped him focus, center, and organize his energy, and manage his emotions. Third, as part of his home program, Brody learned and used the Seva Stress Release Acupressure protocol, developed by teachers from Soul Lightening® International after September 11, 2001.[4] I had used this protocol personally and taught it to many adults, who found it an extremely valuable Self-care practice.

Brody would need to be willing to listen deeply at his edge and consciously choose to transform chaos into freedom. The love in his family greatly supported his choices. Brody's food was cooked with love and nourished not only his body but his heart and soul as well. Meals became a shared adventure, which was later brought to other families through Brody's website. Their family was now giving back and nourishing other hearts and souls.

Brody was the first young child with whom I used the Seva Stress Release Acupressure protocol. His inquisitive nature came alive as he held pictures and a mannequin that showed him acupuncture points he would use in his home program. I described points as "magical windows" that would give Brody an inside view of what was happening in his body, like a submarine probe in reverse. Brody used the protocol on himself two to three mornings a week before going to school. It took him ten minutes to complete. Brody's behavior and ability to manage his day dramatically improved, and he was thrilled he could calm and center his body, mind, and emotions on his own. Brody's superhero was strong and now took charge.

Brody's status has gone through ups and downs. His pain was a wake-up call that affected Brody and his entire family. They learned to meet fear head-on when going through a storm and to stay strong, individually and together. Brody learned to trust his inner guidance and stay in touch with himself through Self-care, which included journaling and acupressure. He was now captain of his ship and learning to use his inner compass. Today, Brody and his family sponsor a yearly fundraising event to increase awareness about Crohn's. Their lives have touched others, and they are living Gandhi's words "Be the change you want to see in the world."[5]

Change and Healing: Know Thyself

When we come to an edge during life or healing, our biggest challenge is to move into deeper knowing and understanding of our true Self. This occurs beyond diagnostic codes and therapeutic techniques, in a realm often beyond words. The journey involves a paradigm shift, in which we engage the mysteries of healing and move toward greater freedom.

Frank became a wise-hearted spiritual warrior, shifting his allegiance from fear to tenacious courage. He took greater responsibility as he developed Self-trust, and he found new meaning and soul purpose in every day. Brody took on a huge challenge and brought his entire family to a place where they developed strengths that supported change and healing for each of them and others.

I am continually reminded, through these courageous individuals and their stories, that everything – the barren, cold depths of despair that overtake us and the passions that arise in our bellies, which change our perceptions and move us out of old patterns – serves our highest healing. Anaïs Nin eloquently described this: "And the day came when the risk to remain tight in a bud was more painful than the risk it took to blossom."[6]

Looking back, I see that change can bring welcome bursts of spring, which reflect new insights and possibilities for healing. It is often during times of change that I return to nature and recall Anne Frank's words "The best remedy for those who are afraid, lonely, or unhappy is to go outside, somewhere where they can be quiet, alone with the heavens, nature, and God. Because only then does one feel that all is as it should be."[7]

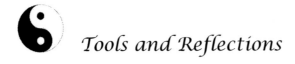

Tools and Reflections

There is a way of being
Which is lighter
Which is freer
A way in which work
As well as play
Becomes a dance
And living a song
We can learn this way.
–Milton Trager, M.D.

Change is a universal phenomenon. To manage change you will need information, skills, commitment, and support. You may find yourself caught up in the "small stuff" when conditioned beliefs and behaviors become the only way you interact with change. New insights and possibilities manifest when you incorporate Self-care, awareness, tracking, and journaling into your response to change. As you do so, remember you are a work of art in progress.

Tool 16: Awareness Journal – Tracking Conditioning and Creating Change

God grant us grace to accept with serenity the things
that cannot be changed, courage to change the
things that should be changed, and the wisdom
to distinguish the one from the other.[8]
–Reinhold Niebuhr

In your Awareness Journal, locate the autobiography you completed in the Tools and Reflections section in Chapter

Two. Review the time line and describe the following in your Awareness Journal:

- What conditioned thoughts, habits, emotions, and decisions shaped your life?

- As a result, what stories did you tell yourself that entailed limited beliefs (for example, "I'll never do _____," "I'll never be able to _____," "I can't _____," "I'm not good at _____")?

- Select from your autobiography an event during which conditioning impacted you. What happened? When? With whom? How did this impact your perceptions, beliefs, and actions?

- When seen through the eyes of your wise-hearted spiritual warrior, how will insights gained now affect your current perceptions, beliefs, and actions?

Tool 17: Awareness Journal – At the Edge

Strong emotions, such as fear, signal you are at an edge and facing unfamiliar territory. Journaling, as a Self-care practice, will support you when you encounter and explore edges.

Recall a time when you encountered an edge. In your Awareness Journal describe the following:

- What did you experience in your body, mind, emotions, and soul that signaled you were at an edge?

- What brought you to your heart space or prevented you from being there?

- How did you manage this edge? What would you do the same? What would you do differently?

- What Self-care practices can assist you before, during, and after edge experiences?

Tool 18: Self-Care Dates and Moving Through Change

Self-care is never a selfish act — it is simply good
stewardship of the only gift I have, the gift I was put
on earth to offer to others. . .
Anytime we can listen to true self, and give it the care
it requires, we do so not only for ourselves, but for the
many others whose lives we touch.[9]
–Parker Palmer

Breath and movement are internal resources that move and vibrate through your being and help you when change occurs. As Self-care options, you can use breath and movement to adjust the tempo, rhythm, pitch, and harmonics of change. They will guide you through indecision, confusion, and frustration, into new vision and possibilities.

To move through change you will need to set aside time to experience options beyond your current mindfulness, movement, and bodywork practices. Use the Bibliography and Appendix B, the Internet, your local library, and community centers to guide you to additional resources. Answer the following to help you plan and organize Self-care dates over the next six months:

- What signals indicate tension in your body, mind, emotions, and/or soul?

- What movement and Self-care patterns have you discovered that need revision or change?

- What misconceptions do you have about movement that need to be revised? Examples include: "No pain, no gain," "I don't need exercise as I get older," and "It takes too long to make a difference."

- Search the Internet and newspapers for movement classes offered at nearby community centers, houses of worship, and so on. What yoga, tai chi, Qigong, or movement/ dance classes are available that will add joy and pleasure to your Self-care practices and healing? Who can you ask for recommendations or invite to join you?

- Take a trip to your local bookstore and library. What DVDs can you purchase or borrow to expand Self-care movement practices at home?

- What health-care practitioners are in your community for bodywork sessions? Who can you ask for recommendations, and what do they like best about their sessions and their practitioner?

Once you have selected options for Self-care dates, commit to two or three monthly dates over the next six months. Put them on your calendar. Describe your experiences in your Awareness Journal.

As the speed of life increases, it is essential to reconnect with your heart, soul, and authentic Self through Self-care practices. This will guide you to truths and insights that optimize your sense of wholeness and well-being.

Take a few moments to return, in silence, to your inner sanctuary. Bring your awareness from your head to your heart, and sense a lighter, freer way of being, which you can always access. Breathe in peace and well-being and let this circulate throughout your being. Exhale easefully and peacefully as you return to the outer world with newly grounded presence and enlightened insights.

CHAPTER NINE
The Joyful Heart

Theme Six: Healing is Stimulated by Life-Affirming Qualities of the Joyful Heart

In the depth of winter, I finally learned that there was in me an invincible summer.
–Albert Camus

O ne of the childhood memories I treasure most was going with my parents to see the musical *South Pacific* on Broadway in New York City. It was an unforgettable experience. I was magically transported to an exotic tropical paradise, immersed in scenes with turquoise seas, swaying palm trees, abundant coconuts and mangoes, and vivid costumes. As Rodgers and Hammerstein's musical score resonated throughout the theater, I was enchanted. My imagination opened to nature, to dreams, to joy, to beauty, and to love. As I began writing this chapter, the merry and triumphant song "Cockeyed Optimist" from this musical played in my head.

Being an optimist during healing may seem cockeyed, but what we are doing is remaining present with vision and possibilities amidst the challenges, uncertainties, and paradoxes we face.

This chapter is about remaining open to a joyful heart during healing. It is a tremendous challenge, but one worth taking. You will read about people who sought inner peace, beauty, and joy amidst their pain and struggles – light in the face of darkness. During these times they summoned life-affirming qualities of the joyful heart: creativity, laughter, play, joy, beauty, and gratitude. Sometimes they succeeded, and life became easier. The qualities they summoned equipped them for times when they struggled to remain afloat and present.

Life-affirming qualities of the joyful heart helped individuals I worked with make tremendous shifts in perception during healing. As I completed this chapter I, too, was challenged to rediscover and integrate these qualities. The pain within my family reached a point where it was overwhelming, and despair engulfed me. I was called to explore and discover what was at the heart of my healing process. Stories in this chapter describe how clients and I journeyed through darkness. Being present with life-affirming qualities of the joyful heart was at the core of our healing. Journey with us and read about what we learned along the way. It is my prayer that what is shared will stimulate the light within you and facilitate your travels through healing's passageways.

Many bridges are encountered as you travel through life transitions and times of change. Each one spans a vast unknown. You may not yet see the new territory awaiting you on the other side, only the depths of uncertainty ahead. As you embark on these great crossings, you will need to pack your bags consciously and wisely.

When obstacles are met during healing, it is vital to remember what still has heart and meaning in your life. You can do so by engaging life-affirming qualities of the joyful heart.

These qualities will ground and guide you as you travel through uncertainty and fear. The joyful heart will also help you bridge paradoxes often repeatedly faced: life and death; joy and sorrow; pleasure and pain; and laughter and tears. The challenge is to remain awake, heart centered, clear, and open as you encounter these paradoxes and the unknown.

Insight for the journey can be found in writings from those who have examined transition periods in people's lives, such as aging. In *Aging Well*, Harvard Medical School professor Dr. George Vaillant says successful aging is influenced less by genetics and more by lifestyle choices, especially the choice to seek what brings joy. I believe this is also true for healing. The comments of one study participant, noted by Vaillant, bring us clarity and relevant insight: "When considering successful aging, think joy . . . the heart speaks with so much more vitality than the head."[1] Life-affirming qualities of the joyful heart create balance during difficult healing transitions. Whenever we return to our heart during healing we also bring energy and buoyancy to our life force. This literally lifts our spirits. Rich deposits are also made into our energy bank accounts when we invest our time and energy in the joyful heart.

Dr. Gene Cohen, author of *The Creative Age*, emphasizes the need for creativity and dreaming throughout our life cycles, instead of subscribing to myths about aging that paint it as a process of dis-ease, decline, despair, and death.[2] You will enter new life cycles during healing. With each cycle your conditioning, personal myths, and beliefs will be challenged. This will free you to move into Self-empowerment versus remaining stuck in victimization, self-judgment, inaction, depression, and despair. When you engage your heart through creativity, joy, play, laughter, beauty, and gratitude, you will come alive. You will also develop courage, feel stronger, and have an enhanced sense of harmony and well-being. When you face the agony and the ecstasy in healing, you will need the discipline and insight of your wise-hearted spiritual warrior to come forth.

Values and the Joyful Heart

Values are challenged during healing. When you reestablish your core values as part of healing, you will touch upon the "invincible summer" within you. As you allow your joyful heart to nourish and guide you, the entire process will clarify and help you reinvest life energy in your core values. You will become clear about what brings meaning to your life.

When values shift, you will need to develop strategies that integrate these changes. You can do so by engaging life-affirming qualities of the joyful heart: joy, creativity, laughter, play, beauty, and gratitude. What personal values have motivated and guided your life? What values have changed and caused you to engage life differently? At the end of this chapter you will have an opportunity to clarify and prioritize your current personal values. This will assist you with making decisions during healing that help you wisely realign your life with your current values.

Call to Action: Life-Affirming
Digging Deep to Find Our Joyful Heart

My spirit was broken. It had been a year of many family crises. My ninety-six-year-old father and his ninety-year-old wife were showing signs of dementia and no longer able to safely manage their lives in Florida, far from family in New Jersey. Our son was in the midst of a divorce; family relationships were very strained; and I was diagnosed with skin cancer on my face. Everywhere I turned there was so much pain and suffering, in my family and in the world. I felt distraught and helpless. Why was I here? Why go on? Everything my life was built around, everything I valued, had collapsed.

Helplessness, anguish, and frustration were my regular companions. It was hard for my husband and I to watch our nine and six-year-old granddaughters live in a war zone, with their divorcing parents still living under one roof. Family life in their household turned into an unrelenting storm of power plays, vindictiveness, unresolved grief, and loss. Their divorce was finalized after two long years in a broken court system that resembled a swamp. Mothers and grandmothers throughout the world had experienced similar pain and suffering before me. I prayed to them daily, seeking courage, strength, and guidance.

I found no beauty, joy, or laughter within this darkness, nor did I feel gratitude, as my normally upbeat, positive, and deeply held spiritual beliefs were challenged and crushed. Thinking about my skin cancer diagnosis, I realized built-up anger inside me was literally getting under my skin. Depression and despair overtook me, and I saw no reason to remain alive. Although I mentally understood the power behind my thoughts, I had little to no *life-force energy* to challenge them.

My unspoken desire to leave this world became a constant in my daily thoughts. The suffering of others became more apparent to me. I understood depression firsthand. I realized why some individuals pursued addictions in order to numb themselves, and why some no longer wanted to be alive. Suffering can become that unbearable.

I was at an emotional and spiritual crossroads, asking, "Why remain here?" Enlightenment came during a session with Bill, my chiropractor. He told me that AIDS patients who asked, "Why remain here?" lived longer. The question opened the door to clarity, options, and conscious choices. For the remainder of our session I fell into a deep state of relaxation. My secret was shared, and I no longer carried this heavy burden alone.

When we remain open, support comes to us in several ways during healing challenges. My dear friend Lawrence, the Guild Certified Feldenkrais Practitioner[CM] I discussed in Chapter Eight, mentioned a book that served him during his dark nights, *The Light Inside the Dark*, by John Tarrant.[3] From the first page, the authenticity of Tarrant's words struck a chord. Tarrant knew the darkness. He, too, had struggled with despair. Somehow Tarrant was with me. His presence brought light and understanding to my path one morning during prayer and meditation. Although it still seemed I was at the bottom of a deep well, I saw a small speck of light as some part of me looked up. That first glimpse revealed the choice I was to make: the journey back into life. My soul work on earth was not yet complete.

Gradually, thin beams of light pierced through the mountains of rubble in the life that had collapsed around me. The light expanded slowly. It became tangible through the hugs and giggles I shared with my granddaughters, Jolie and Mayzie, and through the scent of roses my husband brought me one day. I felt as if a lightning bolt struck me and opened my heart one afternoon while at a craft store. I was looking for something to spark my creativity when a cashier's kindness and smile unexpectedly moved me to tears. In that instant time stood still, and the welcome presence of Spirit filled me through her graciousness. Time together as a family continues to strengthen the love we share. This love is a cherished source of nourishment for each of us. Individually and collectively, our family is learning to embrace the paradox of broken-heartedness and a larger world filled with gratitude, joy, beauty, and love. It is truly a grace-filled miracle that we remained strong and intact during the settlement of our son's divorce and all that remains unsettled in our lives.

I gradually returned to writing and welcomed it like an old friend. Light and darkness have each brought greater authenticity and honesty to my life and creative expression. I am able to take in the beauty around me, reflected in the newly fallen snow that gracefully drapes bare tree branches. Just the day before I wrote this, a deep sigh came forth as I observed the landscape around me after the fourth snowstorm of the winter. In the silence and stillness I was safe. It was then I heard birds chirping, harbingers of spring and nature's reminder that all things pass . . . and new beginnings always emerge.

Questions I asked during these times brought me to vulnerable and fiercely defended places within. I felt unable to do anything to change situations, and was overwhelmed by my own rage and grief when I saw no light at the end of the tunnel. I had been in this place before. I was all too familiar with incomprehensible loss before these family tragedies unfolded, as you know from reading about my earlier journeys. There was nothing for me "to do." Answers no longer came through my mind. I needed to bring Self-compassion to my fiery heart, ablaze with rage, to cool and calm my whole being. I needed space to discharge, and I needed to replenish through deep rest. I could no longer go this route alone. I could no longer remain fiercely independent and invincible. I turned once again to Self-care practices, and made a commitment to remain open to receiving support from external resources.

Psychiatrist and author Viktor Frankl also struggled to find reasons to live, in his case during three years of imprisonment in Auschwitz and other concentration camps. He lost his mother, father, and wife in the camps. After being liberated he wrote about his experiences and developed logotherapy. This form of existential analysis is based on the belief that striving to find meaning in life is the primary and most powerful driving force in a human being. In his book, *Man's Search for Meaning*, Frankl concluded that even in the most painful, dehumanizing conditions and suffering, life has potential and meaning.[4] He believed that our bodies and spirits are liberated when we find meaning and purpose within, beyond pain and suffering, through life-affirming qualities of the joyful heart.

Embracing Grace and the Mystery: Beauty, Gratitude, and the Joyful Heart

Let the beauty of what you love be what you do.
–Rumi

We engage beauty, which brings meaning, pleasure, and satisfaction to us and others, through a spectrum of life experiences. These range from the joyful heart to dark nights of the soul. The latter brings great contrast and challenges relative to acceptance. Dark nights are part of the authentic reality of life. During these times we often find that nothing is beautiful. We experience beauty during life through our senses, relationships, art, music, nature, pets, laughter, and creativity. Beauty is also present during extraordinary moments of Divine grace like sunrises, sunsets, and the giving and receiving of love. Engineer and architect R. Buckminster Fuller stated, "When I am working on a problem I never think about beauty. I only think about how to solve the problem. But when I have finished, if the solution is not beautiful, I know it is wrong."[5]

Author John O'Donohue reminds us that beauty awakens us and opens our heart to the world around us. In his book, *Beauty*, he encourages us to become more intimate with beauty in our life as a way of coming home.[6] During healing beauty can capture our attention, ignite our hearts, and stimulate our life force energy. Ralph Waldo Emerson reminds us to: "Never lose an opportunity of seeing anything that is beautiful; for beauty is God's handwriting – a wayside sacrament. Welcome it in every fair face, in every fair sky, in every fair flower, and thank God for it as a cup of blessing."[7]

Each time I enter the silence and profound stillness within the Great Mystery, and the presence of this in myself, I touch upon beauty within my authentic Self. During such healing moments, the deep gratitude I feel is beyond words. I now realize beauty was present as I silently prayed with my father in the hospital, at his request, before his passing. I am reminded of beauty whenever I silently watch my granddaughters' whole-hearted presence as we draw, paint, and play. I am struck by their total engagement, the beauty that surrounds them, how at home they are, and how I, too, am embraced by the beauty shared in these priceless moments. The thing that is most difficult for me is to hold the paradox of light and darkness when darkness surrounds me. At these times, I need to remember that darkness, too, can enhance awareness and growth.

Author Angeles Arrien describes **gratitude** as "a habit of the heart, an attitude to have toward all of life," in her CD *Gratitude: The Essential Practice for Happiness and Fulfillment*. In this CD Angeles reminds us that gratitude is a choice. Gratitude keeps our hearts open and eliminates envy and comparison, which diminish gratitude. She notes that "practicing gratitude:

- reduces stress and anxiety
- strengthens our immune system
- improves sleep
- enhances creativity, cooperation, collaboration, and productivity at home and at work
- builds trust in relationships
- increases generosity and forgiveness"[8]

Author and Nobel Prize for Peace recipient Elie Wiesel stated, "No one is as capable of gratitude as one who has emerged from the kingdom of night."[9] Wiesel suffered humiliation and loss of faith, family, and any semblance of humanity while in concentration camps in World War II. After the war he expressed gratitude to all those individuals who lived through this with him and made it possible for him to get beyond his own suffering and survival. Wiesel suggested that without gratitude, something is missing from our humanity.

Call to Action: Life-Affirming Gratitude, Grace, and Finding Peace with My Father

Angeles Arrien describes **grace** as the "blessings, kindness, benevolence, mercy, and goodness that life and the Divine freely give us."[10] Gratitude helps us to recognize, honor, and respect grace-filled moments. It has been difficult for me to be open to receiving grace in my life without feeling a need to give back. Growing up, I was conditioned to believe the old adage "It is better to give than receive." In my head, I kept a tally, always wanting to give more so that I owed nothing. When a practitioner and I talked about this, I realized the pride and arrogance in me denied other human beings the opportunity to give. Now, whenever I am open to receiving, I notice that my heart and whole being softens. I am deeply touched when authentic love and compassion are shared with others. I am struck by what occurs at these times beyond the material – a genuine sharing of our humanity and the Great Mystery. I feel blessed to have participated in this with my father before his passing.

My earliest memories of my father are of being afraid of him. I experienced him as a powerful, domineering, and invincible man. He grew up during two world wars and the Depression. He learned early about hard work and survival. From the time I was small, through to the time I married, my father worked two jobs. When he was home, my siblings and I were called for duty. We often joked about being "slave labor" for his garden or building projects around the house. There was little time for fun, and sadly, because of his work schedule, I have no memory of him attending our school events. We had only rare opportunities growing up to experience Dad's sense of humor.

There was no middle path in my relationship with my father; it was either his way or the highway. I frequently stuffed down anger toward him when I helplessly watched my mother withdraw into silence during his spontaneous emotional outbursts. As an adult, my challenging relationship with him came up many times during my therapy and bodywork sessions. Although I worked tirelessly to try to reconcile our relationship within myself before he passed, I never believed it would be possible.

In 2008, my father put out a call for help to our family. After a private nursing agency assessment, my sister, brother-in-law, and I helped Dad and his wife move into independent living in Florida. Unable to adjust after six weeks, my strong-willed ninety-four-year-old father moved them back to their condo and notified us afterward. One year later another cry for help came forth, and we moved them into assisted living. My father's ability to manage their lives was slowly diminishing. He was sadly losing his independence and control of his life.

From the onset, the assisted living facility grossly mismanaged their care. Our family knew it was time to move them to assisted living in New Jersey. We would be closer to them there, and proximity would make it easier for us to oversee their care. The facility we moved them to in New Jersey was excellent, but I watched my father quickly decline and become frail. The invincible man I once knew lost his vision. His hearing diminished, and he shrunk before my eyes.

As fall approached I asked Dad if he wanted to see Bill, my chiropractor. He was eager to go, as he had used chiropractic care his entire life. During sessions with Bill, I watched Dad's body soften and relax. His breath deepened and his chest noticeably expanded more easily and fully with each inhalation. He periodically opened his eyes as if from some deep place inside, and a smile appeared on his face. I sensed my mother's presence in the room during several sessions. I watched in awe as Bill helped midwife Dad's soul during sacred, grace-filled sessions at the end of his life.

Bill's sessions with Dad reminded me of how our children are midwifed into this world when they are born. Our souls, too, need midwifery when we depart this world during our passing. At birth and death we encounter the Great Mystery that accompanies these times. Midwives can bring comfort and peace to both transitions when confusion, worry, or conflict occurs. As described in *Midwife for Souls*, by Kathy Kalina, the pregnant mother and baby need support for a safe birth and a healthy baby. The person facing death also needs support for their process, through the compassionate, loving presence of those around them.[11] Those blessed to assist can bring greater ease and peace to the labor process and transitions that escort us through our passing.

After Bill's sessions it was easier for Dad to get on and off the treatment table. His sleep improved, he felt less pain in his shoulders, he was able to easily walk farther, and he was cold less often. His overall demeanor was more relaxed and peaceful, and I could see this on his face. When I removed Dad's Oriental black cloth shoes during one session, I asked him if they indicated he was a martial artist. "Yes, I am a sensai . . . sense a humor," he replied. Bill and I laughed. It was a treat to experience the joyful heart Dad retained to the end of his life.

I arrived at the assisted living facility one day in the winter to take Dad to a session with Bill. I found him in bed, a staff nurse by his side. She advised me he had severe pain in his thigh, which was very painful to touch. Dad was unable to walk. Shortly thereafter he was admitted to the hospital. Little did I know the next few days would be Spirit-filled moments of reconciliation and the last I would share with my father.

Many signs that week in the hospital revealed that Dad's soul was being prepared for his final passage. As I straightened his bed sheets in the emergency room the first night, I was startled when I noticed the manufacturer's name printed on them, Angelica. Dad was being surrounded and held by "angels." Two days later, I sensed my mother's presence in his hospital room, and the room suddenly became filled with bright daylight. I saw Dad reaching for something and asked, "What do you need?" "Hold my hand," he replied. "We need to say prayers."

Prayer was not something Dad commonly spoke about. And so I held my father's hand, as I had held my mother's hand during her passing, and said prayers with him. As we sat and held hands, I found myself in total awe of the love and light we were amidst in the room. The silence was profound, sacred, and a gift I will always treasure. During this final act of Dad's life we were finally at peace with each other, something I never imagined possible.

As I prepared to speak at Dad's funeral, the part of me that often wondered what I would say at this time came to mind.

Instead of recalling anger and our lifetime of difficulties, I found myself remembering, through my heart, how much Dad loved poetry, learning, music, ceramics, ballroom dancing, doing home repairs, cooking, learning languages, and gardening. I realized he had tilled the soil in his life's garden the best way he knew. I clearly saw what he had taught us, by example, about tenacity, persistence, and commitment to family and life goals. And as I spoke Dad's eulogy, I prayed that he finally realized and took with him the love shared in our family during his lifetime.

Laughter, Play, and Lightness of Being

Years ago I hit burnout. I was angry at myself for letting this happen. When I discovered a clowning class at the local high school, I signed up for it immediately. Once I put on white face and a clown costume I was lost in play. This carried over to my work. I taught wheelchair-bound patients at the hospital how to juggle with scarves and encouraged them to have fun by playing tricks on friends and family members. I saw how they lit up doing this and how renewed they were through playful interaction with others. Laughter and play put problems into perspective. They do not involve competition, and they build strong, trusting, positive connections with others. They help us cope with challenges, energize us, help us think more clearly and creatively, and make us more resilient.

Laughter is a universal language that brings people together. It acts like a tranquilizer and has no side effects, according to musician Victor Borge. Laughter has been described as internal jogging. It boosts our mood, lowers blood pressure and stress hormones, strengthens our immune system, improves oxygen flow to our body and brain, protects our heart, reduces pain, and relaxes our body, mind, and emotions. Being able to laugh and play is a sign of emotional intelligence. Our emotions do not exist in a vacuum. Each emotion influences and is influenced by other emotions. When we block uncomfortable emotions such as fear, anger, or grief, by numbing or distracting ourselves, we also dampen joy. All of our emotions serve us. They warn us, enliven us, alert us, and inform us about what is happening within. Our challenge is to live *with* our emotions, not *from* our emotions by engaging in drama and acting out.

I have felt the impact of laughter and play working with babies and children: tickling them; mimicking their facial expressions; giggling, dancing and moving freely with them; and role playing to help them express their feelings. I have also felt the absence of laughter and play in adults I worked with. When they lost their heart connection the sparkle was missing in their eyes. They described their life as dull, boring, and without joy or excitement. The magic was sadly gone.

As a result of life-changing challenges we face during healing, we can lose our ability to laugh easily and often. Many clients I worked with experienced abuse as children or adults. They rarely lost their ability to laugh. Laughter was a survival skill. Emotional intelligence can be taught and developed, it is *never too late*. I learn much about play and laughter when I watch others, especially children and my grandchildren. Costume parties have been a big hit at our house. Guests are encouraged to bring a three-to-five-minute skit to perform, and everyone shares in the joy, play, and laughter. Game and movie nights are a developing project at our home as our grandchildren get older. I also learn much playing with pets, who are always eager and ready.

Process Acupressure friends and I also shared play and laughter while attending classes taught by Aminah Raheem in Borrego Springs, California. We welcomed opportunities to balance deep process work with levity, and howled with laughter when we sang karaoke at Carlees, a local restaurant. Have you tried Laughter Yoga? Why not get into the habit of arranging a weekly play date? Where would you go? Whom would you invite, or not? What enhances your playfulness? Setting aside regular time to explore play and laughter enables each of us to grow and develop.

Self-healing has shown me that when I wear the mask of a clown, as I have done, it covers my authenticity. However, clowning around as a way of playfully joining with others provides a welcome break from the stress and heaviness in our world. One of my cohorts in crime on my adult jaunts with play and laughter has been my soul friend Katie. Like my grandchildren, she coaxed me out of my shell, and I have never been the same.

Call to Action: Life-Affirming
Katie's Story – The Gift
of Friendship and Laughter

Katie and I met fifteen years ago at the physical therapy practice where we both worked. We became friends instantly, and easily shared our philosophies of life, love of our work with clients, and mutual respect for Dr. Bernie Siegel and his work with people facing terminal illness. We each grew up in large families, and our shared love of home and family sealed the deal on what has become a lifelong, sacred relationship.

My friend Katie is an Irish elf. During manual therapy seminars we attended, we shared mischievous, playful moments, which brought belly laughs and balance to intense study situations. We were in our glory when we found Jack's Joke Shop, in Boston, during one of our classes. We discovered how to make smoke appear magically from our hands; bait classmates with a device that retracted a dollar bill from the floor when they went to pick it up; and create other moments our classmates grew to anticipate – as did we. Katie nudged a repressed part of me from childhood out of its tight shell, a part that loved to play, laugh, and have fun with others.

Our friendship hasn't always included laughter. We have cried, prayed, exchanged bodywork sessions, and walked side by side during difficult times, such as the loss of Katie's father and my parents, my marital separations, our family and work challenges, and Katie's life-long struggle with asthma. When our physical, mental, emotional, and spiritual health have needed compassion and support, we have been there with and for each other. We have shared strength and vulnerability and used laughter and play as a healing salve. We met in our hearts, which cultivated a rare and treasured soul friendship.

Since early on in our relationship, Katie has demonstrated her fighting spirit in the face of death. She began treatment for asthma in junior high school and pushed herself through each episode. Katie was always active in athletics, which brought great joy to her and added fullness to her life. Participation in sports enriched her strong life force. It also taught her to gather and depend on a strong medical team during healing challenges. Asthma continues to plague Katie. There have been multiple trips to the emergency room when she gasped for air. Repetitive use of steroids, orally and in her inhalers, has stabilized Katie. However, their use has thinned and weakened membrane walls throughout her body, especially in her esophagus, lungs, stomach, and colon. As a result, chronic systemic problems have occurred physically and physiologically. Katie's small frame becomes bloated at times. She is often unable to eat and digest a full meal, and she has had problems with elimination. Katie also experiences muscle and organ spasms throughout her body before, during, and after asthmatic episodes.

When Katie was hospitalized with an acute asthma attack during the early years of our friendship, one phone call in particular strengthened our heart-and-soul connection. I reached her by phone through a nurse at her bedside, who told me she was in isolation in ICU and unable to talk or have visitors. Whenever I called, the nurse would hold the phone to Katie's ear and this became our lifeline to each other. Katie clung to our soul connection through my voice. She later told me she had nearly died during that asthma attack. It was her feisty spirit and courage that brought her through that episode and the many that followed. Katie has gone through extensive testing at large teaching hospitals and has been told on too many occasions that there is nothing else that can be done. Katie, who possesses a warrior spirit, has been unwilling to believe this or give up.

One of the highlights in our friendship was attending Katie's marriage to Bruce. Watching their love grow has been a powerful reflection of the strength brought forth in each of them during difficult times. Bruce has been by her side through emergency room visits and has lived with anxiety when he was out of town on business during an attack. He has courageously honored her choice to include alternative healing practices with her medical care – acupuncture, Chinese herbs, Process Acupressure, osteopathy, and integrative manual therapies.

Katie has faced death more than most. During a recent episode she was brought in nearly unconscious and was about to be put on a ventilator by the medical team. She begged to be given one more day to recover with medication and prayed through the night for this to happen. When she awoke the next morning she felt remarkably better. As she looked around her hospital room in ICU, Katie discovered that her room was opposite the one in which her father had passed away just one year earlier.

Katie's family did not initially comprehend the life-threatening nature of her diagnosis or how traumatic each episode was for her body and being. Over the years, Katie had adapted to her mother's less-than-compassionate presence and to being lost in a large family with parents who drank heavily. Her mother's abandonment took a toll on her, and Katie's unresolved grief and anger remained stuffed down, hidden in the very tissues of her being. Like me and like so many of us, Katie wore the mask of the clown to survive, but this no longer fit when death knocked at her door.

On her journey, Katie unexpectedly experienced flashbacks of adolescent trauma, long forgotten and in need of gentleness and compassionate understanding from therapists and herself in order to be healed. We cannot go it alone during healing. We need to create a safety net of core listeners, therapists, bodyworkers, soul friends, and Self-care practices. These establish trust, courage, and strength as we recover from cold, frozen times and thaw out in the warm arms of healing. Katie needed to find her own way. However, she also needed others and to learn new patterns as part of healing. Through sessions with practitioners, Self-compassion, Self-healing practices, and spirituality, Katie reconnected with her heart and a sense of wholeness. This renewed her relationship with her authentic Self and her ability to again participate in what brought heart and meaning to her life.

As we each traveled through darkness and deaths during Self-healing, Katie and I shared tears and priceless moments of laughter and play. This always shifted us back to our hearts and provided a different vantage point, compassion versus toughing things out and resisting. We have sparked and lit our individual and collective soul fires when they went dim. We consider it rare and part of Divine grace to have shared something so precious as our friendship. Together, we have lived an Irish blessing from Katie's ancestry: "May God grant you always . . . a sunbeam to warm you, a moonbeam to charm you, a sheltering Angel so nothing can harm you. Laughter to cheer you. Faithful friends near you. And whenever you pray, Heaven to hear you."[12] May the blessings within this prayer be passed along to you and raise you up during your moments of challenge and healing.

Creativity and Healing

The gift of fantasy has meant more to me than my talent for absorbing positive knowledge.
–Albert Einstein

Pablo Picasso stated that "all children are artists. The problem is how to remain an artist once we grow up."[13] Creativity entails letting our magical, imaginative spirit and our inner child generate something new at any stage of life. This takes us out of everyday living into a place of total focus and absorption. Author Mihaly Csikszentmihalyi calls this state *flow*.[14] He believes we come alive and are rejuvenated in this state of total exhilaration and enjoyment.

I believe the flow state also provides deep healing. Life-affirming qualities of the joyful heart enhance flow and boost physical immunity. They are antidotes to fear, cynicism, and apathy. They empower the human spirit and our ability to interact with uncertainties and challenges that feel foreign to us during healing. These qualities also boost our mental, emotional, and spiritual immunity – how we think, feel, act, and connect with higher forces during healing. Creativity helps us meet and move through struggle and despair, and impacts us by:

- reducing stress
- stimulating the relaxation response
- changing brain wave patterns
- improving heart rate and breathing
- releasing endorphins, which decrease pain and im-prove mood
- enhancing optimism and resilience

Take a few minutes now to remember two or three times in the past several months when your attention was totally focused on an activity. Recall how you were so immersed in this activity that you lost awareness of yourself and time. What were you doing? How did you feel? What do you recall? Make a note of this in your Awareness Journal. Perhaps next time you can learn even more about yourself during these times, such as how it feels when your body, posture, and perhaps your whole being come alive in the flow state of being.

Creativity and Liberation

The painters Renoir, Dufy, Rubens, Klee, Grandma Moses, and Toulouse-Lautrec lived with rheumatoid arthritis, a chronic autoimmune inflammatory disorder that can result in pain, deformity, and disability. In their totally absorbed creative state, their *autonomic nervous system* rebalanced stress and sympathetic nervous system overload by activating their parasympathetic nervous system and promoting relaxation. They found the joyful heart by participating in what they valued, and it produced a cascade of healing chemicals from within their body's pharmacy. These chemicals enhanced blood flow, supported immune function, and greatly improved their quality of life.

Creativity, joy, play, laughter, and gratitude redirect our lives. They help us develop physical courage when we face pain and suffering. It takes courage to listen to and trust messages from our body, especially when we feel it has turned against us. As we stay conscious to body signals and messages when we feel vulnerable, we gain deeper understanding, which helps us remain brave and wholehearted. Your Awareness Journal will support this process.

Each time we follow guidance from our HeartMind, and each time we commit to Self-care intentions and goals, our mental and emotional courage is strengthened. When we add Self-compassion, we stop waging war against ourselves; we stop launching missiles loaded with self-judgment, shame, guilt, and blame. We develop the courage to live from our joyful heart and our authentic, true nature.

When compassion, trust, and intimacy develop in our relationships, so does our courage to be ourselves and speak our truth. In relationships we meet a paradox – our human desire for intimacy and our fear of abandonment, betrayal, and/or being consumed. I was given an opportunity to learn about this during recent facial surgery for skin cancer. After a day of surgery I needed to be seen that evening by a plastic surgeon, as the site was too large for the original surgeon to close. As the plastic surgeon's nurse reached out to hold my hand, while I again received multiple injections to numb my face, my entire body tensed. I felt extremely vulnerable. I was on the receiving end now, outside my normal pattern in relationships. The nurse's touch and empathy sent a wave of reassurance throughout my being, and my entire body let go. I will always remember that brief moment when the nurse's presence established safety and trust. I sensed within myself what I had provided for clients over the years. I was able to sense in the core of my being how kindness and compassion enhance our ability to be courageous during healing challenges.

Erich Fromm noted that "creativity requires the courage to let go of certainties."[15] Julia Cameron states that "creativity – like human life itself – begins in darkness."[16] When we consciously tend to our heart in the face of darkness and uncertainty, a process of internal alchemy begins. Our heart's fire is stirred as we add life-affirming qualities of the joyful heart to our healing journeys. We reinvent ourselves in the process, and a new way of being is molded and strengthened.

Call to Action: Life-Affirming
Julie's Story – Creativity and Self-Healing

I met Julie at an International Women's Writing Guild meeting in New York City. She had an extensive background in the creative arts as a dancer, choreographer, photographer, writer, and poet. Two years before we met, while facing a recurrence of breast cancer, Julie had formed *Women Reading Aloud*, an organization dedicated to the power of the writer's voice.[17] We spoke briefly about her organization and her journey. I was moved by her strength and passion, and we set up a time when I could interview her for *The Heart of Healing*.

When I entered Julie's home, I found myself surrounded by beauty: restful hues, soft carpeting, wooden cabinets that surrounded me with the warmth of nature, sculpted forms that seemed alive within their stillness, paintings with brilliant colors, and large windows that filled each room with light. As Julie shared her arduous journey through breast cancer, it was her inner beauty, strength, authenticity, and courage that touched my heart and soul.

Six years before, Julie had received her first diagnosis of breast cancer. She called this her "rehearsal." Three years later, there was a recurrence. She described healing as "the process of traveling back into the daylight, away from the clutches of darkness. Healing takes time, perhaps forever. Just as a wound closes, a comment or observation breaks it wide open, and the process begins again."

During her first diagnosis, Julie became proactive and read extensively about cancer, radiation, and the impact of treatments. After the second diagnosis, she no longer wanted to read. She was told that she needed to have a mastectomy, and was horrified at the thought of it. Julie knew that if she was to continue living, she would need to find and use her voice in dealing with breast cancer, especially within the medical community. The voice she had found as a parent and writer would now have to carry over into her healing process.

Having her own voice allowed Julie to be in control as much as possible. It enabled her to feel like a human being, not a statistic. She insisted on being called Julie, not by her last name, as she believed the latter would create a distance between her and her physicians and nurses. She also insisted upon walking into surgery on her own two feet versus being wheeled in. After surgery, Julie began chemotherapy and breast reconstruction.

Chemo was "horrific, shocking, and totally without privacy." She found it impossible to remain strong while witnessing the collective grief around her. Julie was hospitalized after a reaction to her first chemo session. At her second session she had her own bed with a curtain in a corner of the room, which created more privacy. Julie was struck by the way her physician made eye contact with her, held her hand, and guided her to filter out her surroundings and come back into herself. Julie hit points of fragility and powerlessness when her blood count dropped and fatigue overwhelmed her. Her devoted husband dressed her when she could barely open her eyelids.

Julie was rushed to the emergency room twice due to weakness. Yoga and artwork steadied her focus when she received painful injections to increase her white blood count. Taking Ativan calmed her body, but knocked her out. Julie began to see the seating arrangements in chemo as a metaphor for the seats and places we take in life. She used this revelation to write *Come Sit by Me*. Julie described this book of personal photographs and stories as a way for her readers to remember what they have seen, where they have been, and whom they have loved.[18] Julie struggled until she met Jean Marie Rosone, an oncology social worker who reached out with compassion, humor, and authenticity*. Julie began to discover what holds us back from being all we can be during healing. Jean Marie provided her with tools and disciplines that stimulated her creativity, validated her, and awakened her joyful heart. These included:

- balancing rest and activity
- writing
- using mind power (focusing, imagery)
- using and enjoying humor
- gaining strength by not traveling the road alone
- finding blessings and gratitude along the way
- pushing through discomfort and the unfamiliar as needed
- spending time alone
- seeing beauty during healthy pauses
- remembering it's okay to take baby steps
- recognizing the power in receiving help

Jean Marie also helped Julie's husband understand the role he could play through listening, validating Julie, and being her "voice trainer." Jean Marie helped Julie organize an "army" to manage her life during this time. Julie joined a weekly support

---

*   See Appendix B

group of nine men and women, who shared aspects of their journey they would not tell their best friends. They caressed each other with laughter and tears, and they learned a significant lesson: the value of getting out of their own space by helping someone else.

Moving away from the fear of cancer was an ongoing process for Julie. Heart connection with her daughters, son, and husband brought greater ease to this. She learned a difficult lesson: Her first responsibility was now to herself, not others. She allowed her children to give to her, and through this she taught them about receiving. Julie was able to rely on her husband's gentle and kind presence, his strength, his ability to continuously listen, and his willingness to defer to her wishes and desire to be proactive.

Julie discovered the benefits of massage therapy, acupressure, and restorative yoga. A strong-hearted hairdresser with great listening skills helped her adjust to losing her hair during chemo and regaining it afterward. She also received help from a woman who lived in her neighborhood, whom she had met only once before. This woman came over when Julie was having an anxiety attack and gave her a foot massage. Someone had done this for her, too, when she needed support while dealing with cancer.

Writing helped bring Julie back from the grip cancer had on her. "Without self-expression I would have shriveled up and died," she said. Poetry empowered Julie. Tools helped her "sew her emotional life together, one stitch at a time, toward healing" and helped her create a magnificent, vivid life tapestry. Creativity strengthened her ability to live life as fully as possible. It helped her remain awake during trying experiences with cancer.

As our time came to a close, Julie emphasized that creativity supports our hopes and dreams, and brings power and joy to healing. She remarked that exercise, dance, and movement keep our body alive and vital, and that everything serves our healing process. Julie continues to live her beliefs through *Mango*, a small stationery and photography business she started as she faced the recurrence of breast cancer, and *Women Reading Aloud*. She also teaches a *Writing to Heal Workshop* series at the Carol G. Simon Cancer Center at Morristown Memorial Hospital in New Jersey. Julie concluded our time together with a powerful statement . . . "Our past is part of who we are, but does not totally define us." She reminded me about her vital discovery that at the heart of healing is joy and love, the joy and love of Self, and the joy and love that we bestow on one another.

The Triumphant Optimist:
Coming Full Circle

Healing is as much a process of coming home to all of life and the joyful heart, as it is one of balancing our body, mind, emotions, and soul. The journey is long and arduous; it may seem impossible; and it is rewarding like no other journey we take. Though we will all experience moments of aloneness, remember that we are never alone. Light exists within darkness. Both serve our ability to remain open to every season of our heart and life – day and night, joy and sadness, life and death. It is through the joyful heart and soul companions along the way that our journey home is graced with unanticipated and unimagined love, joy, beauty, and peace. As Kahlil Gibran wrote, "joy and sorrow are inseparable . . . together they come and when one sits alone with you . . . remember that the other is asleep upon your bed."[19]

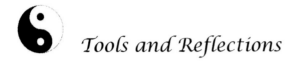

Tools and Reflections

Joy is a net of love by which you can catch souls.
–Mother Teresa

Joy is cultivated when we exchange laughter, play, beauty, creativity, and gratitude in our valued activities and relationships. It affects how we see and interact with ourselves, others, and the world. As we come home and remember our authentic Self, we will need to clarify our values and priorities and bring joy to the process. Self-care practices add Self-compassion, joy, and trust to our healing journeys.

If you could design your life in any way, what would it be like? What are the most important aspects of your life? Which relationships do you value most? If you passed away tomorrow, what would you like others to remember and say about you?

Values reflect what is important to you. They influence your decisions and behavior. Like the rudder on a ship, values give your life direction. Values come from cultures, families, schools, friends, and environmental influences such as advertising and television. They tend to be stable throughout life but may vary during life stages or when change occurs, as during healing. Mahatma Gandhi stated, "Happiness is when what you think, what you say, and what you do are in harmony."[20] Clarifying and prioritizing your values creates greater happiness and makes your life more effective, peaceful, and Self-directed.

Tool 19: Values Clarification

In this Self-care practice you will clarify and prioritize your current values. This will help you determine what you want more of, less of, and who and what are important to you and your life now. Life choices are often compromised when you are out of alignment with your heart and unaware of your true values.

Step 1.   Write a one-page short story about a family member, friend, or someone who has been a role model for you. Let your heart enlighten you about what drew you to them, what values they demonstrated, and why you wanted to model yourself after them.

Step 2.   Select your top five values from Table 4 that follows. List these in order of importance from one to five, one being what you value the most. What activities, habits, or individuals will you bring into your life that will reflect and support your top five values?

Table 4: Values

achievement, adventure, altruism, ambition, approval, authenticity, autonomy, awareness
balance, beauty, belief, belonging
challenge, commitment, compassion, connection, contribution, control, creativity, courage, curiosity
discernment, discipline, discovery, drama, drive
education, empathy, empowerment, enlightenment, excellence, excitement, exercise, expansion
faith, family, feeling, fitness, flexibility, forgiveness, freedom, friendship, fun
generosity, glamour, grace, gratitude, growth, guidance
harmony, health, honesty, honor, hope, humor
imagination, ingenuity, inspiration, integrity, intellect, intimacy, intuition
joy, justice
kindness, knowledge
laughter, leadership, learning, leisure, love, loyalty
magic, mastery, meticulous, money, morality, motivation, movement, music, mysticism
nature, nutrition, nourishment
oneness, openness, order, organization, originality
partnership, patience, peace, perseverance, play, pleasure, power, privacy, prosperity, purpose
recognition, reflection, relaxation, religion, resiliency, responsibility, reverence, risk taking, romance
security, self-actualization, self-esteem, self-expression, sensuality, service, sexuality, sincerity, sleep, solitude, spirituality, spontaneity, stability, strength, structure, support, surrender
thoughtfulness, time, tolerance, touch, transformation, trust, truth
understanding, uniqueness, unity, vision, vitality, vulnerability, well-being, wealth, wholeness, wisdom

Tool 20: Ten Loves

Refer to Appendix A for the worksheet needed to complete this tool. Fill in the worksheet as follows:

- Down the far left column (Activity) list ten activities you enjoy in order of preference. Consider hobbies, sports, stress relievers, clubs, personal and professional activities, and relationships.

- After you complete this list scan across the columns from left to right for each activity. Add additional information about each activity through your responses to the following.

- Place a check in the second column (Past 5 Years) if you have enjoyed the activity for the past five years.

- Place a check in the third column (Next 5 Years) if you anticipate enjoying it for the next five years.

- Place a check in the fourth column (Past 2 Weeks) if you have participated in this activity in the past two weeks.

- Place a check in the fifth column (Want to Improve) if you want to get better at this activity.

- In the sixth column (Cost) indicate the approximate cost to participate in this activity each time.

- In the seventh column (Alone/ With People) put an A if it is an activity you do alone and a P if it is an activity you do with other people, or A/P if both apply.

- Place a check in the last column (Risk) if you believe risk is involved with this activity.

Reflect on your responses. What have you learned about your ten loves? What have you learned about yourself, your values, and how to put them into action? What will you now add to your life that brings pleasure and life-affirming qualities of the joyful heart to you and others?

Tool 21: Gratitude Journals

I have learned silence from the talkative, toleration from the intolerant, and kindness from the unkind; yet, strange, I am ungrateful to those teachers.
–Kahlil Gibran

There are many ways to bring gratitude into daily life as a Self-care practice. Angeles Arrien's book, *Living in Gratitude: A Journey That Will Change Your Life*, offers an inspirational twelve-month program with reflections and practices that will help transform your life and relationships.[21] She brings together wisdom and values from world cultures and reminds us that we are part of something greater than ourselves alone.

Discover unique ideas for gratitude journals on the Internet, or purchase a journal through a local bookstore. I highly recommend *The Simple Abundance Journal of Gratitude* by Sarah Ban Breathnach, noted in the Bibliography. This journal brings daily mindfulness, grounding, and renewal to our frequently hectic lives.

Author Robert Emmons also suggests additional practices to cultivate gratitude: learning prayers of gratitude or writing your own; using our senses, movement, and breathing to experience gratitude; using situations and people to practice gratitude; and noticing how gratitude is expressed by yourself as well as others.[22]

Tool 22: Beauty

Beauty is everywhere. Whether we create beauty, or open to the beauty around us, endless opportunities for Self-healing will emerge. Habitual behaviors and rigid thinking often limit our ability to take in and be nourished by beauty.

Begin this Self-care practice by taking a walk in nature. Notice your surroundings and the beauty around you, which you are part of. Engage this beauty through all your senses, and take pleasure from it with each long, full breath. Use your Awareness Journal and write, draw, or create a collage that grounds this heart-and-soul centered experience for you. What have you discovered that is beautiful within your own nature, which is also reflected in Mother Nature?

Take a few moments to be with all that is beautiful in yourself and the world. Describe what you discover in your Awareness Journal, and bring these insights with you as you return to the outside world.

CHAPTER TEN

Coming Full Circle

Theme Seven: The Common Denominator in All Healing Is Love

The soul would have no rainbow if the eyes had no tears.
–Native American Proverb

*N*ow there was no turning back. As a new soul, about to burst into the world from the Great Mystery, she would remember little of home, the boundless, starry magnificence from whence she came and to which she would return someday as a wise-hearted spiritual warrior. For close to half her life she would seek this infinite origin that permeated all life, the transcendent place of love beyond ego, time, and task. As she lived her life, the realm of the stars would be forgotten or seem separate and far away when she glanced up at the night sky. As she grew and blossomed, she would recall this celestial realm whenever she entered her heart's sacred space. In this space she could see beyond the veil of everyday illusions. She would uncover her original essence and her authentic Self, the Self she carried within her soul when she began her Earth journey. Similar to the journeys of other wise-hearted spiritual warriors, her soul journey would enlighten and guide her return voyage to the Great Mystery. Lessons learned about giving and receiving love would provide stepping-stones.

Much like the archetypal figure in this parable, my Earth journey at times seemed long and distant from my origin in the Great Mystery. At other times it was like a flash in time, a fire burst of indescribable experiences. I was touched by and reminded of the Great Mystery at synchronistic moments. These repeatedly occurred when the wise, creative, playful child within me was activated and when I opened to my heart, love, and the presence of Spirit during healing. At these times I reconnected with my true nature, my soul journey, and the truth that I was loved, safe, and part of everything within the Great Mystery.

In *The Heart of Healing* you have read about what individuals discovered at the heart, or core, of their healing experiences. As beliefs and perspectives changed and/or broadened, many individuals opened to and realized the power and healing potential within the energy we often refer to as "love." This energy flows through all the great mysteries in life and occurs at the heart of all healing. As love weaves through our healing stories a beautiful and vibrantly alive life tapestry emerges. Use the story tapestries throughout this book as a resource to guide you back to center and the sacred wisdom in *your* healing stories and *your* heart. With each heart opening and opportunity for healing you, too, will tap into the infinite power of love that animates all life and your interconnections within the Great Mystery.

This chapter draws on the work of Angeles Arrien and provides opportunities for you to track and enhance heart-centered awareness. Angeles reminds us that indigenous people believe our heart is a bridge between Mother Earth and Father Sky. This bridge connects our personal and spiritual lives. In *The Second Half of Life: Opening the Eight Gates of Wisdom*, Angeles describes four healing rivers that sustain, support, and connect us to our gifts: the river of challenge, the river of surprise, the river of inspiration, and the river of love.[1] Through personal reflection and journaling you will track and explore these rivers as they flow through your life. This will enhance well-being, deepen awareness, and clarify life meaning and purpose. These times of intimate heart-and-soul communion will enhance healing and help you create your own unique life tapestry.

By now you may realize that healing is not a straight, direct path. You may find yourself off your path at times when mindless living occurs, when you overlook your body-mind signals, or when you lose connection with your heart and soul. You are not alone. These experiences happen as part of living and loving consciously in our world. They bring lessons that develop higher consciousness, Self-compassion, Self-trust, and Self-love. Every time you forget your true nature, or betray and abandon yourself through neglecting to listen to yourself, you will also be given opportunities to become aware of and say goodbye to conditioning, beliefs, and habits that no longer serve. Your internal GPS system will be activated during each journey home to your heart. This will provide you with clear directions and wise guidance for life decisions and choices along the way.

Life and relationship challenges are like sand in an oyster. Ultimately, a pearl is created. Many clients took varied routes until they, too, discovered the wisdom in Helen Keller's words: "The marvelous richness of human experience would lose something of rewarding joy if there were no limitations to overcome. The hilltop hour would not be half so wonderful if there were no dark valleys to traverse."[2]

Defining Love

Love is a mysterious, dynamic, universal energy that is often difficult to capture and describe. Love is a choice, made possible by moment-to-moment decisions to open our hearts. The power of love binds our wounds, softens and opens our hearts, dissolves our fears, eases our journeys, inspires and clarifies our dreams, and animates our life meaning and purpose. Love is the common denominator in all healing. As an abundant and continual source, a wellspring, love facilitates the flow of life's internal and external healing waters.

Ralph Waldo Emerson stated: "The reason why all men honor love is because it looks up, and not down; aspires and not despairs."[3] Emanuel Swedenborg noted that "love in its essence is spiritual fire."[4] Dr. Bernie Siegel reminds us that "Life is an opportunity to contribute love in your own way."[5] And during his Nobel Peace Prize speech in 1964, recipient Dr. Martin Luther King, Jr. commented: "Occasionally in life there are those moments of unutterable fulfillment which cannot be completely explained by those symbols called words. Their meanings can only be articulated by the inaudible language of the heart."[6]

Merriam-Webster's dictionary defines love as "positive emotion, affection, devotion, or pleasure; a term of endearment; sexual desire and attraction; wanting good things for another person no matter what." The Greeks described *agape* as unconditional love, and the Persian poet Rumi wrote in Arabic of the ultimate goal, *ishq*, or divine love. In Corinthians, in the New Testament, love is defined as patient and kind, and not envious, boasting, prideful, rude, self-seeking, or easily angered; it is said to keep no record of wrongs and to never fail. We experience love in many forms: romantic love; love of family, pets, and nature; and love of our fellow human beings. Love also comes alive in and through us when we participate in the causes, principles, goals, and activities we enjoy and feel passionate about.

Benjamin Shield, in *Handbook for the Heart*, describes love as our birthright. He states we reclaim our birthright by keeping our hearts open, letting go of past experiences that block forgiveness, and giving and receiving love.[7] This was the process I experienced with my father during his passing, which culminated in the moment when I held his hand on the last day we shared together in the hospital. Love had oiled my stuck places and opened my heart to a new intimacy between my father and me. Love fertilized the soil in which forgiveness could grow in my heart and then extend to my father. Love was the bridge that joined us and brought peace to our relationship at the end of his life, something I never anticipated.

Love is our essential nature, which flows in the world through giving and receiving. Loving others begins with loving ourselves. I am reminded of this each time I fly, when the flight attendant tells passengers to place the oxygen mask on themselves first, before doing so for young children, in an emergency. When love is experienced and realized within us our heart is full, and we are more able to give love to others, our communities, and the world. Love also flows into the world through what we each create, great or small. As our gifts and talents come forth, healing is nourished and enhanced for others as well as ourselves, and we experience a genuine sense of fulfillment.

Like air, love is a continuous life-giving element that nourishes and sustains us. However, when love entails sacrifice beyond healthy limits and boundaries it may be necessary to explore who and what is served by this behavior. When giving is out of balance we betray our authentic Self and resentment, manipulation, or martyrdom may accompany giving. Like many colleagues in the healing arts, I was very good at giving but much less open to receiving. Self-healing experiences taught me the importance of listening to my own heart-and-soul guidance; asking for support; and practicing Self-compassion when I feel stressed, exhausted, or burned out. These actions helped me restore a greater balance between giving and receiving.

Love is a verb as well as a noun. Just as the building of strong muscles requires regular exercise, your heart needs regular practices to strengthen and remind you of your ability to put love into action during healing and everyday life. Your challenge will be to return to your heart and use the energy of love when difficulties arise and your ego builds walls of protection. There may be a tendency to push love away at these times, when it is needed most. Notice how Self-compassion, Self-care, and Self-love break down the walls and build-up your heart's resilience.

Exploring and Touching upon Love

We are all wounded and scarred during life. We fear being unable to bear emotions such as grief, rage, betrayal, abandonment, or even the depth of beauty and love we encounter. We experience heartbreak through pain and suffering, but empathy for others and ourselves also develops. Love challenges us to go deeper, become clearer, and open more fully. Love's challenges admit us to the "scar clan," according to Angeles Arrien. This group of fellow life travelers evolves into wise-hearted spiritual warriors as their hearts soften and break open during healing. They use ancient ways of tracking to remain connected with their four-chambered hearts. These brave ones understand the interconnectedness of all life and how each of us affects, and is affected by, the greater whole. Clan members show us it is possible to grow strong in the broken places with time, patience, compassion, forgiveness, and love.

A common experience on healing journeys is the search for love and belonging. For almost half my life I sought these outside myself through people, work, roles, seminars, teachers, and spiritual quests and connections. When I began to study Process Acupressure, external searching became a deeper, more internal process. I came to respect and trust this process when specific experiences recurred during Process Acupressure sessions: profound internal and external stillness; an all-encompassing sense of peace; and poignant moments of Self-compassion and deep insight. My focus went from head knowledge to heart-and-soul guidance, and my life changed in unimagined ways. I returned to my marriage after an eighteen-month separation and went back to practicing physical therapy as a sole practitioner with a small private practice. In addition, insights from acupressure sessions formulated many of the themes for this book.

Through every transformational process of Self-healing I was opened to connection with Spirit and Divine love, which was vastly different from experiences with romantic and melodramatic love. At times I sensed Spirit's presence travelling vertically through my spine and core Self, which held and supported me between heaven and Earth. I also sensed Spirit's presence as a horizontal place of union when my heart-and-soul were touched in relationships and by Mother Nature. I began to experience a limitless, infinite relationship with Spirit in my Self, others, and all of life. Only then did I appreciate the depth and breadth of love that I had plugged into within the Great Mystery during prayer, meditation, and moments of heart-centered presence.

I find myself in the presence of this love as I watch my granddaughters. Their tiny hands and eager imaginations magically transform a simple egg carton into a caterpillar. When the playful, joyous child in me joins them, I am again filled with curiosity, innocence, and wonder. Their treasured works of art grace our home and remind us that love-filled moments strengthen our hearts and well-being, individually and as a family collective.

I am reminded of who I am and why I am here through this sacred relationship with Spirit. My life takes on greater meaning and purpose with every awakening and heart opening in this co-creative relationship, which asks me to contribute to the world. Without sacred connections our untended hearts can become closed and brittle. As a result we may numb ourselves through addictions, or get lost in drama, or choose power, recognition, and achievement as substitutes for love. I witnessed the choice of power over love when mothers and therapists interacted with children during therapy sessions. Task and goal-oriented therapy often became power plays between parent and child or therapist and child. When unconditional love and compassion accompanied goals the love of power shifted to the power of love, and healing materialized through trust versus fear and control.

Call to Action: Loving Challenges of the Heart – Healing and Evolving Through Love

In *Transitions, Making Sense of Life's Changes*, William Bridges describes endings as "the first phase of the transition process and a precondition of self-renewal."[8] Challenges of the heart bring darkness and endings, but they also bring light and new beginnings. Unresolved personal and/or family challenges often arise with endings. Heart-centered process and bodywork bring clarity and insight to these times, as baggage that has been carried is unpacked, healed, and laid to rest. As in our gardens, it is necessary to clear what no longer serves or has died off before planting new growth.

Challenges of the heart also bring opportunities for liberation and transformation. They provide lessons through which we grow and evolve, where love becomes a teacher. My father was a great teacher about love and forgiveness. I struggled with his patriarchal and domineering ways for almost half of my life. However, beneath my father's stern exterior there was a very sensitive heart. This became evident to me when I recalled the beauty he created in his gardens and how he raised canaries when I was young. He gently and patiently fed each newborn canary with a small eyedropper until they could eat on their own weeks later. I also watched my father become a playful child around his grandchildren and missed not experiencing this part of him when I was growing up. When I became a grandparent I gained a broader perspective about this, and my beliefs shifted. Through healing I surrendered long-held judgment toward my father, which did not serve him, our relationship, or me. Because of our difficult relationship, and heart-challenging experiences with him, I explored healing and forgiveness for years before my father passed away. He may not have changed over the years, but I changed in response to him and that made all the difference.

My mother, too, helped me to heal and evolve through love. When I visited her in the nursing home one day during her final months of life, I asked her to dance with me. My hope was that this would stir her memories of dancing at family functions and permeate her now silent and vacant veneer. I held Mom close, felt our bodies sway as our hearts touched, quietly sang to her, and ached to awaken and connect with some remnant of her former self. My efforts were in vain. I can still recall the tightness throughout my body and being as I struggled to hold back and control what felt like an overwhelming tsunami of tears.

During subsequent therapy sessions a lifelong history of controlling my emotions became evident to me, and I also gained deeper insight about my relationship with my mother. With time and support I allowed myself to let go of controlling my emotions and opened to places where I felt vulnerable. This birthed me into new ways of being with my emotions. As I worked through grief regarding my mother's passing, I became aware of other emotions beneath the surface. I sensed the emotional distance and loneliness I felt in my relationship with my mother as a young child and the unconscious anger that accompanied these experiences. Alongside all this was the deep love I felt for my mother. I was challenged to open my heart once again and restore inner peace through healing and resolution of deep emotional issues with my mother. I became aware of situations and relationships that I had attracted in my life to recreate and heal this relationship. Most of all, healing guided me to a limitless reservoir of love and acceptance within my authentic Self and with Spirit. Each time I call upon and connect with this infinite supply I am in awe of how much love is always available.

My family stories are not unique. They are interconnected in the web of life with other family stories of pain, loss, vulnerability, and suffering. I now call upon my wise-hearted spiritual warrior for guidance when strong emotions surface: grief for the loss of hopes and dreams; grief for family losses; and anger and fear when I feel betrayed, abandoned, disillusioned, or vulnerable.

When there is nothing to hold on to or lean on, I move inward to my authentic Self, my heart, and my soul. As I surround myself with Self-compassion, acceptance, and Divine love, light and higher awareness enters the darkness. It is then that I am more willing to trust and open my heart and love becomes oxygen for my soul.

Being gentle with yourself as you learn and integrate acceptance, surrender, and forgiveness is always a work in progress. You may become more conscious of unprocessed emotions and resistance, but actualizing virtues such as forgiveness will take time, patience, and practice. Heart-centered guidance and Self-compassion will assist your process and allow you to see life from different vantage points. As you walk "a path with heart," described by Buddhist teacher Jack Kornfield, you will be shown that there is an easier, gentler path to freedom at the heart of healing.

What have you learned about acceptance, surrender, forgiveness, and your wise-hearted spiritual warrior? Who have been your greatest teachers? How have obstacles and discoveries served you and your highest healing? Write your reflections in your Awareness Journal

Enhancing Heart-Centered Awareness: The Four Rivers

Wisdom from indigenous cultures can help us to build trust and forgiveness, integrate learning, enhance well-being, and stay connected with our life force. The ancient tool of tracking helped individuals determine if they were alive and strong or settling and "walking the procession of the living dead," according to Angeles Arrien. Through tracking the four rivers you, too, will strengthen your four-chambered heart. This will awaken you to your greatest capacities to give and receive love and to create.[9] Keep your Awareness Journal nearby.

The River of Challenge

Your pain is the breaking of the shell that encloses
your understanding.
–Kahlil Gibran

On the river of challenge we are invited to stretch, grow, and move beyond the familiar and knowable. We become new learners and explorers here. We are initiated into new ways of being when we leave or are taken out of our comfort zones and revert back to old patterns or beliefs.

Few of us expect to change our identity in our sixties, but that is indeed what occurred as I concluded writing this book. A depression descended on me like a shroud, causing me to question my life purpose. I sunk into aimlessness for the first time in my life, initially with little self-compassion. I missed all that had been beautiful, joyful, and loving in my life, and I couldn't fathom that I was turning into a cynical old woman. A morning ritual of prayer, meditation, journaling, gratitude, and a commitment to cultivate a joyful heart helped rebuild Self-trust and brought Self-compassion into my process. I soon was in a very different life stream. I felt a deeper empathy for all humanity and a renewed respect for the Divine strength and support that guided me through the river of challenge.

Reflect now on your unique healing challenges. Recall Charles, from Chapter Two, who became quadriplegic after a car accident and perceived life as a new adventure versus a life sentence. Remember Mark, from Chapter Eight, who redefined himself after he lost parts of his hand in a life-changing work injury.

Who or what is asking you to stretch and challenging you to grow in your life now? Write your reflections in your Awareness Journal.

The River of Surprise

The river of surprise reveals where we remain open and delighted by surprise in our lives. It is also where the Divine child within us stays connected to wonder, awe, and curiosity. As adults we often lose touch with and avoid surprises. We become cynical, jaded, and controlling, which disconnects us from life-affirming qualities of the joyful heart. Along with curiosity and flexibility, these qualities are essential when facing life's adventures and challenges.

My granddaughters Jolie and Mayzie teach me how joyful it is to share secrets and surprises through play. Each spring we go to playgrounds at nearby parks. I feel whole and alive again with each raindrop we catch and taste in our mouths, each flower and rock we collect for memory jars, and each new hiding place we discover. We also wrap silk scarves around our heads and faces for our famous "babushka dancing." While playing this one day, their costumes suddenly reminded me of women in burkas throughout the world, unable to participate in the same lighthearted singing, dancing, and freedom. I felt as if my heart would burst and tears began to flow. I felt gratitude for my granddaughters' freedom as well as heavyheartedness for all the girls and women who are unable to experience these joys and liberties. As my granddaughters reached out to wipe my tears, I was astonished by the pure compassion these young innocents brought forth. In that moment I was reminded how we are frequently touched by angels in disguise – when we take time to notice and receive their blessings.

How do you relate to surprise now in your life? How do you handle surprise? Who and/or what has been your greatest surprise or teacher about surprise this year? Write your reflections in your Awareness Journal.

The River of Inspiration

The river of inspiration shows who and what excites, uplifts, and inspires us and helps bring forth our life purpose. Without inspiration we go into malaise, atrophy, and cynicism. Cultivating optimism in our hearts is the antidote for each of these.

Many heroes live in our communities and give service from their hearts without much ado. Like these heroes, each of us can be a significant source of inspiration. Linda and Marion, from Chapter Six, inspired many individuals as they walked their paths with heart and courage during life-threatening illness, breast cancer and colon cancer respectively.

My friend Katie, from Chapter Nine, meets challenges with humor. She lives life through the wisdom in Henry Ward Beecher's comment "A person without a sense of humor is like a wagon without springs. It's jolted by every pebble on the road."[10] Katie continues to be an inspiration to her friends and family. Just before Christmas one year she was brought into the hospital emergency room nonresponsive and was placed on a ventilator. Miraculously, she returned home after four days. When we spoke afterward she told me her lungs were clear, and she did not experience fear at any moment during this crisis. Katie continues to work with her pulmonology specialists, who are astounded by the status of her lungs. She is creating major inroads in allopathic medicine's understanding and treatment options relative to asthma. She is an example of how valuable complementary medicine options can be when used along with traditional care. Time I share with Katie is a priceless reminder of the power and gifts love brings to Self-healing.

Who and/or what inspires you now in your life? Where are you deeply touched, moved, and inspired? Write your reflections in your Awareness Journal.

The River of Love

But let there be spaces in your togetherness and let the winds of the heavens dance between you. Love one another but make not a bond of love: let it rather be a moving sea between the shores of your souls.
–Kahlil Gibran

The river of love involves matters of the heart. Life's experiences are teachers of the heart, and they help us learn to use the arms of love described by Angeles Arrien: acknowledgment, acceptance, recognition, validation and gratitude.[11] These powerful resources will provide support during life and healing.

My husband is one of my greatest teachers about love. Through the highs and lows of our relationship I have learned that love is "as perennial as the grass," and arises anew with each ending and new beginning.[12] I am humbled and graced by the love we share. Beneath our differences our hearts have many similarities. We each develop courage, compassion, strength, and hope through our struggles. This helps us as we walk through minefields of uncertainty and doubt in our lives and relationships. Each time we return home to our hearts and authentic selves, and consciously open to one another through heart-centered time together, we appreciate the blessings of love we have cultivated through second chances.

My children and family continue to teach me about love and the need for roots and wings in loving relationships. Kahlil Gibran beautifully describes this in a favorite passage of mine from *The Prophet*: "Your children are not your children. They are the sons and daughters of Life's longing for itself. They came through you but not from you and though they are with you yet they belong not to you."[13] I have learned valuable lessons about love and letting go through my children since the moment of their birth when they left the womb. This is also true for relationships with clients as they heal and move on with their lives.

When I notice that giving and receiving is out of balance in my relationships, I am reminded to stop, look, and listen. At these times healthy detachment allows time and space for objectivity, clear heartedness, and higher insight to develop. Through this process I reconnect with my authentic Self as I journey on the river of love.

Time and poetry shared during therapy sessions with Cessy, whom you met in Chapter Seven, reveal how much he extended the arms of love through his presence. Cessy gave me the following poem in 1983 at our last session. His words still remind me of the real, indestructible love we all have a right to, which we can find and touch upon at the heart of healing.[14]

Dimples – Smiles – Laughter
You always seem so full of "spunk"

Like the Sun on a Mid Summer Day –
Shining through the Forest of Green

Leafed Sycamore Trees or like Sparkling Waters
of a Water Fall bounding off

The clay granite rocks of various colors . . .
Each dazzle of water that falls, lands like Cotton . . .

Within your "Heart" – "Mind" and your "Soul" –
that makes you easy to Love also . . .

We all know that there is life within you –
A life that Bears Strength – Draws Strength –
Strength – that grows stronger through

Nourishment and nourishing Love –
A Love that you have Full right to.

What are you learning about love this year? Who are the teachers of your heart? What do you want your children and/ or significant others to know about love? Where are you being touched and moved by love in your life? Write your reflections in your Awareness Journal.

Trust, Intimacy, and the Arms of Love

I've learned that you shouldn't go through life with
a catcher's mitt on both hands; you need to be able
to throw something back.
–Maya Angelou

Our heart is an instrument of vision that will heighten awareness during life and healing. It is a container for intimacy, a place where trust can be reestablished when it has been challenged, weakened, or undone in relationships. Without awareness love can become a means of control, manipulation, or a power play. This can also occur when love is withheld as punishment, repeatedly tested, or not tended to consistently. Self-awareness and Self-care practices enhance our ability to use love as an antidote to fear, anger, denial, and whatever separates us from our authentic Self.

The arms of love (acknowledgment, acceptance, recognition, validation, gratitude) carry us through times of despair and times when we encounter what is unresolved in our lives. They help us to remain present with pain and suffering. My dear friend Lu, a wise and creative teacher, Reiki practitioner/drummer, and poet, writes, "In the loss of love, despair becomes an unwelcome guest. Despair, like love, is universal, and if one denies the antithesis of love one in a way also denies love."[15] Bring the arms of love and the wisdom within your heart and authentic Self to pain and suffering, which inevitably show up. Witness the healing and transformation that occurs as pain and suffering are embraced by love.

The arms of love are like fertilizer. They feed our hearts and souls and nourish our life force. They help us grow strong roots that ground us in Mother Earth as well as wings that enable us to fly. Every act of love anchors, broadens, and reflects the interconnectedness and oneness of all life on planet Earth and within the Great Mystery.

The arms of love need to be practically and consistently applied in daily life. Acknowledgment validates and strengthens love in relationships. Recognition brings love alive and can be expressed many ways: verbally and through touch; placing love notes in lunch bags; putting notes to ourselves or someone else on a desk or near a bedside; and planning creative surprises that bring joy and love for no special reason. Gratitude also brings a sense of renewal, optimism, and trust to difficult times. Gratitude reminds us of what remains joyful and beautiful in our lives.

Who are the healing agents and catalysts in your life? How can you use the arms of love to serve others and yourself?

What are your unique gifts and talents waiting to be expressed, which will strengthen, open, clarify, and fill your heart and the heart of our world? Write your reflections to the above in your Awareness Journal.

Everything and everyone serves our healing journeys. Healing manifests through the integration of light and darkness, love and loss, and life and death. Usually, it is in retrospect that we are able to look upon times of loss and discover greater insight. As we witness and participate in suffering, our own and others, it can be like spinning straw into gold. Compassion, forgiveness, respect, and empathy will emerge and blossom through this process.

Beneath our everyday thinking mind, which fences with chaos and ego-defensive behaviors, heart intelligence and spiritual guidance are always available. Remember to call upon them. Your heart-and-soul connection will be rejuvenated as you awaken; renew connection with your authentic Self; appreciate how precious life is; and realize how blessed you are each time you discover and live what Kahlil Gibran spoke of, "your own power to rise and become whole."[16]

Tools and Reflections

I offer you peace. I offer you love. I offer you friendship. I see your beauty. I hear your need. I feel your feelings. My wisdom flows from the Highest Source. I salute that Source in you. Let us work together for unity and love.
–Mahatma Gandhi

Welcome to this final section. Your courageous commitment to conscious healing and living an awakened life is a gift to you and our world. It is through the arms of love that your discoveries and creative evolution will flow and reverence for all life will deepen.

Begin this time for Self-care with any mindfulness practice that creates sacred space for you such as prayer, breathing, meditation and/or movement. Bring your hands to your heart and gently focus on the life force present there. Breathe into your heart and feel the rich human emotions and experiences that reside there. Take a few moments to breathe what you discover into every cell of your being, and let this spill over and connect with other hearts.

Self-care practices will empower you and bring forth the legacy within your heart. Please reread your Awareness Journal responses from chapter three now, where you explored and tracked your four-chambered heart. Do this before proceeding with the next tool.

Tool 23: Revisiting Your Four-Chambered Heart

Your current and future paths will unfold and manifest through guidance from your four-chambered heart. After you read your responses from Chapter Three, notice if anything has changed or if any new awareness surfaces. Now reflect and write about the following in your Awareness Journal. Consider what resources and support will best serve you in each area. You may want to do this over four sessions.

- We learn about love, compassion, and tolerance through an open heart. Where are you open-hearted in your life and healing journey? Where and with whom have you closed your heart? How can you reopen your heart to yourself and others through forgiveness?

- We learn about authenticity, commitment, and Self-expression through a full heart. Where are you full-hearted in your life and healing journey? Where are you half-hearted? How can you bring these aspects of your life into greater harmony?

- We learn about integrity and discernment through a clear heart. Where are you clear-hearted in your life and healing journey – for example, in your beliefs, roles, actions, and relationships? Where are you confused and uncertain? How can you resolve your concerns and move ahead?

- We learn about courage through a strong heart. Where are you strong-hearted in your life and healing journey – for example, in your beliefs, roles, actions, and relationships? Where are you weak-hearted, and where do you have difficulty speaking your truth and standing by your convictions? What will strengthen your heart?

Tool 24: Visualization and Creativity

Someday, after mastering the winds, the waves, the tides and gravity, we shall harness for God the energies of love, and then, for a second time in the history of the world, man will have discovered fire.
–Teilhard de Chardin

When you engage vision and creativity through Self-care practices, your triumphant optimist and wise-hearted spiritual warrior are nourished, inspired, and empowered. One way you can do this is by creating a vision board, also called a treasure map or collage. A vision board is a visual representation of what and whom you want to manifest in your life. It will help you draw attention daily to your vision and your intention. This tool will also stimulate action when opportunities present themselves.

Consider what has been awakened in your consciousness as you journeyed through *The Heart of Healing*. What lights up your life? What brings joy and excitement to your life path? What do you want to manifest in your life and healing over the next six to twelve months? You may also want to revisit the dimensions of wellness chart, the Ten Loves, your Awareness Journal, or anything that has touched and opened your heart and soul vision.

Before you begin, put on some easy-listening music. Gather a large assortment of magazines; a pair of scissors; glue, rubber cement, or a glue stick; and poster board. Sit quietly and focus on your breathing and your heart. Ask your authentic Self to clarify your life vision and your intention for the next six to twelve months. Notice any words, images, emotions, sounds, or movement that arises. Be with this for several minutes as your ego steps aside and your soul vision emerges through your Divine authentic Self. In the sacred silence that surrounds you take time to embrace your vision with your senses, your heart, and your soul. Look, listen, and feel into your vision. Breathe life, excitement, joy, and passion into it. When your vision and intention are clear, continue with the steps that follow.

Step 1.   Have fun as you go through magazines and cut or tear out pictures or words that speak to you about your vision and intention. Cut away anything extraneous on the pictures. When you are finished go through your pile and select pictures and words that speak to your heart, ones that impact you emotionally. Eliminate any that do not feel appropriate now. Let your intuition, heart, and authentic Self guide your choices.

Step 2.   Lay your pictures on the poster board. Play with the arrangement until you feel heart-and-soul connection with the way they are grouped. There is no right or wrong way to do this. When you feel ready, glue your pictures onto the board. Add whatever personal writing or drawing you desire. Give your vision board a title, and sign and date it.

Step 3.   Place your vision board in a strategic location that allows you to see it as much as possible during the day. Keep it in a safe place if you desire, to avoid comments that may not serve. Update your vision board to keep it dynamic and to infuse it with new insights, inspiration, and passion. Take moments in silence daily to be with your next creative adventure, your soul vision, as it unfolds.

♥   Love and enjoy the magnificence of your dreams!

♥   May your magical, sacred journeys continue to be blessed, and a blessing you share with the world.

Epilogue

Once you have flown, you will walk the earth with
your eyes turned skyward for there you have been,
there you long to return.
–Leonardo DaVinci

We are all in this together. Lessons learned on your healing journeys are like talismans. They will remind you of who you really are as you journey home. Place your lessons and insights from your journey through *The Heart of Healing* on the altar of your inner and outer sanctuaries. Retreat to these sacred spaces of stillness for guidance and insight. Let each lesson fuel the eternal flame that burns on your altar. Let the ashes there be a reminder of the phoenix rising within you. Let there be hope with each rebirth, and triumph with each remembrance of your authentic Self and Divine soul nature.

The Self-healing journey is rigorous. It will ultimately reconnect you with your heart, soul, authentic Self, and your Divine essence. Each of these will sustain you when wintry storms blanket the landscape of your life. You will be well equipped for storms as you embody life-affirming qualities of the joyful heart: creativity, laughter, play, beauty, and gratitude. These qualities will furnish you with roots and wings, roots that ground you and wings that lift you to new vantage points. This will impact your perceptions, attitudes, and beliefs. During bleak times, when you feel lost, alone, and overwhelmed, or your Spirit feels broken, these sacred moments will nourish your heart and soul and light the way home.

As you embark on your journey beyond this book, know that you will not journey alone. Our healing journeys are always intertwined. When you awake in a strange land, like Dorothy in the *Wizard of Oz*, know that individuals and/or situations will help you find the heart, brains, and courage for healing. You may encounter menacing witches as the shadow side of your psyche arises for healing. However, you will also meet virtuous witches and wise-hearted spiritual warriors who will provide guidance. Remember Dorothy's discovery that her power to return home is a power she already possesses. Like Dorothy, your journey to the heart of healing will ultimately lead you within.

As you journey ahead in healing, let your heart guide you like the North Star. Your heart will align your deepest intentions and highest aspirations with your authentic Self, your true nature, and your Divine essence. We often know our aspirations through our dreams, which bring us visions of what our lives can be. Your dreams will reveal your deepest intentions and create a fulcrum in your life, around which your visions can manifest. Your heart will align your intentions with love and create an internal navigation system you can always consult.

Your heart is at the center of it all, the ultimate elixir of healing. Your journey beyond this book will take you through terrains of darkness and light. There will be times when you will be called to be a wise-hearted spiritual warrior, but the secret is to always navigate back to your heart and Divine essence. We heal and find peace through strong, indestructible places within. The wise-hearted spiritual warrior in all of us resides in these places. At times, your wise-hearted spiritual warrior may appear to be asleep. At other times, this warrior will awaken and amplify the magical life-force elixir produced within your heart, which courses through your whole being. Connection and communication with your heart will keep internal passageways open and allow this elixir to flow. As it flows through you, it will cultivate health and well-being for yourself, your family, your friends, your communities, and the world.

How do we heal? The process is as miraculous and mysterious as when a child is born into this world and changes and grows into adulthood. The Self-healing journey continuously changes and evolves. As it takes us through the Great Mystery, it changes us and the way we respond. Every time we "do small things with great love," as Mother Teresa suggested, healing pathways are fortified as this elixir flows through them. When we remain open, curious, patient, and enhance our response ability, this elixir activates the Great Mystery, which infuses all life and healing.

Spiritual teacher Gangaji reminds us that when we discover our true nature and stop warring against ourselves, we will finally begin to see the end of war and a return to peace. The journey through our suffering, which leads to inner peace, is the journey of Self-healing. This journey takes us from our heads to our hearts. Remember the seven themes encountered in any Self-healing process:

- Healing involves showing up and being present.
- Healing is a journey, a process, versus a single event.
- Healing involves Self-healing and coming home to your heart and your authentic Self.
- Healing is a lifelong process of growth and development.
- Healing involves change and movement.
- Healing is stimulated by life-affirming qualities of the joyful heart: creativity, play, laughter, beauty, and gratitude.
- The common denominator in all healing is love.

The Self-healing journey is one of moving from awakening to awakening to awakening. Each awakening provides a stepping-stone to the next. It is my hope and prayer that you will integrate and embody the Self-care practices from each chapter into your life and healing journey. Look and listen through the eyes and ears of your heart. Become present with your wise-hearted spiritual warrior. Take to heart the Awareness Journal and your commitment to Self-care practices. These are portals that will guide your journey through your body and mind, and ultimately to your heart. These practices are lamplights that will lead you to power places where you can pause for rest, regeneration, renewal, and insight. When your wise-hearted spiritual warrior is activated, your response ability and connection with Divine guidance and the Great Mystery will be enhanced.

May your healings reconnect you with the unique and beautiful soul you are, why you are here, and the love you uniquely bring from the Great Mystery. May you be awakened to the beauty, grace, and Divinity within, and may your reflection help others realize this in themselves, others, and our magnificent universe.

Namaste,

Gina

Glossary

Acupressure: The application of fingertip or hand pressure to specific energetic or conductive points on the body, to relieve tension or pain, alleviate fatigue, and promote healing. Acupressure is based upon the ancient principles of acupuncture.

Acupuncture: A Chinese medical practice that treats illness, relieves pain, or provides local anesthesia by the insertion of needles at specific sites on the body.

Allopathic medicine: A system that aims to combat a dis-ease by use of drugs, surgery, or therapies that produce effects different from or incompatible with those produced by the dis-ease.

Archetypes: Repetitive, universally observed patterns of thought and behavior, often recognized through images and emotions.

Asanas: Yoga postures.

Attunement: An interactive human process, vital to health, in which the individuals in the exchange are sensitive to one another's verbal and nonverbal cues. As a result of attunement, emotions are met and reciprocated with compassion and acceptance.

Authentic Self: Who and what we are in our core being, true nature, or essential Self; the aspect of our Self that transcends conditioning, roles, personality, attitudes, and beliefs; the Divine within our human nature that exists alongside our Divine soul nature.

Autonomic nervous system (ANS): Division of the central nervous system composed of two branches that control involuntary, unconscious actions of smooth and cardiac muscle and glands; the branches have opposite actions, often complementary to each other. The ANS provides almost every organ with branches from the sympathetic and parasympathetic nervous systems. See: parasympathetic nervous system and sympathetic nervous system.

Body-oriented psychotherapies: See somatic therapies.

Bodywork: Touch or manipulation of the body that uses specialized therapeutic techniques or methods.

Burnout: Exhaustion of physical, emotional, or mental strength or motivation, usually as a result of prolonged stress or frustration.

Cell memory: Unconscious aspects of prior trauma stored within cells of the body.

Chakras: The seven major energy vortexes located midline in the subtle energy body, which receive, organize, assimilate, and express life-force energy. Chakras correspond to nerve ganglia that extend out from major branches of the nervous system along the spinal column, from the base of the spine to the top of the skull. Chakras influence the subtle or energy body as well as the physical body. The word *chakra* is from the Sanskrit, meaning "wheel" or "disk."

Chakra Tai Chi (CTC): Movement meditation designed by Aminah Raheem, Ph.D., to activate and enlighten all parts of the being – body, mind, emotions, and soul. This practice stimulates and aligns the chakras and energy from the base of the body to the crown of the head, to bring more consciousness through, for integration of the whole person. Insight into the whole being, and body wisdom, become more accessible through CTC.

Codependency: The learned behaviors and tendency to behave in overly passive or excessively caretaking ways, where one's own needs are given a lower priority than those of others. This behavior can negatively impact relationships and quality of life and can affect the ability to have healthy, mutually satisfying relationships. Individuals with codependency often form or maintain one-sided relationships that are emotionally destructive and/or abusive.

Conditioning: A process in which a person learns to behave in certain ways in response to events that occur in their environment.

Consciousness: The state of being aware of something within oneself or externally.

Core being: See authentic Self.

Craniosacral therapy: A system of gentle touch designed to enhance the functioning of the membranes, tissues, fluids, and bones surrounding or associated with the brain and spinal cord.

Dis-ease: A lack of ease in our being or any departure from health.

Edge: Any experience where the unknown is faced, often accompanied by feelings of fear, stress, and tension. No patterns of thinking or behaving exist in our awareness relative to the experience. An edge provides an opportunity to bring what is unconscious to conscious awareness, for healing and wholeness.

Energetic healing: Holistic therapeutic techniques that stimulate the body's natural healing ability and facilitate growth and Self-awareness through clearing, repairing, and balancing the body's energy systems. Practices look to the physical and energetic systems in the body (meridians and chakras), where the blocks, beliefs, trauma, and stress that cause dis-ease may be stored, limiting full potential. Types of energetic healing include: acupuncture, chakra balancing, crystal healing, flower essences, kinesiology, Process Acupressure, reflexology, Reiki, the Feldenkrais Method®, the Trager® Approach, Zero Balancing, and other forms of bodywork.

Energy centers: See chakras and meridians

Energy cysts: Encapsulated and adapted places in the body where physical, mental, and/or emotional trauma has occurred.

Essential touch: A term that describes a *quality* of touch, rather than a particular, specific method. This right-brain oriented form of touch helps practitioners contact the energy field, and movement of energy, of the individual receiving a bodywork session.

Feldenkrais Method®: An approach to human movement, learning, and change that is based on physics, neurology, physiology, and neuromuscular reeducation. The Feldenkrais Method® explores the biological and cultural aspects of movement, posture, and learning. A process of organic learning, movement, and sensing is used to free individuals from habitual patterns and allow new patterns of thinking, moving, and feeling to emerge.

Flow: A state of total focus, absorption, exhilaration, and enjoyment in which we come alive and are rejuvenated.

Gestalt psychotherapy: An existential form of psychotherapy that emphasizes personal responsibility and focuses on the individual's present-moment experience; self-awareness of emotions, perceptions, and behaviors; the therapist-client relationship; the environmental and social contexts of a person's life; the self-regulating adjustments people make as a result of their overall situation; and better recognition of these aspects to satisfy current needs.

Goal: Step(s) or plan(s) one has in mind to use, in order to manifest an intention(s).

Grace: The kindness, blessings, benevolence, mercies, and goodness life freely gives us.

Gratitude: An attitude of appreciation and thankfulness toward all of life, referred to as "a habit of the heart" by Angeles Arrien.

Great Mystery: The intrinsic aliveness and wisdom in all creation; the interconnectedness of everything in the universe with Spirit.

Healing: A lifelong process of growth and development; a journey of Self-discovery and empowerment.

Health: Optimal daily functioning; the presence of physical, mental, emotional, and social balance and well-being, not only the absence of dis-ease.

HeartMind: The integration of higher mind, intuition, and the feeling Self, or heart. Referred to in Chinese medicine as xin.

Higher Mind: An aspect of mind we are born with that connects us to Spirit or Source. It houses divine awareness and higher consciousness. We often become disconnected from Higher Mind because of distractions and/or impulses in our conscious mind. We can learn to access Higher Mind and the bigger picture through healing.

Inner child healing: According to Aminah Raheem, "the process of identifying, discharging, and healing past childhood traumas through validation, tissue release, and repatterning of old, obstructive thinking and behaviors with loving touch."

Intention: The ultimate end or purpose desired.

Interface: The place where a practitioner's hands and whole being meet the structure and energy of a client during bodywork; also exists "off the table" during communication interactions between individuals. Interface requires clear boundaries, specific intention, now presence, and grounding; it is challenged by beliefs, intentions, lack of clarity, trust, and/or awareness.

Intimacy: A close, familiar, and usually affectionate or loving personal relationship with another individual or group.

Intuition: The perception of fact, truth, knowledge, cognition, or insight, independent of rational thought and reasoning; the power or faculty of gaining direct knowledge without evident rational thought and inference.

Jungian psychotherapy: A form of psychotherapy aimed at growth and realigning the conscious and unconscious aspects of the personality, toward enhanced psychological balance, life meaning and purpose, sense of wholeness, and relief of suffering.

Lab work: Practical integration of awareness and insights gained from the healing process, through use of Self-care practices such as yoga breathing, mindfulness, journaling, therapeutic exercise, movement, and bodywork.

Life-force energy: Vital, life-sustaining forces – known in Indian traditions as *prana* and in Chinese practices as *chi* – that flow through a network of subtle channels in all living forms. When low, there is greater susceptibility to stress and illness. When high, there is greater tendency toward health and happiness.

Lymphatic mobilization: A gentle, conservative therapy that treats localized swelling by using gentle superficial stretching to improve the activity of the lymphatic system. This therapy opens pathways and helps congested fluid move into central lymph vessels and the venous system.

Masks: The persona or outer appearance we present to the world; the parts we play in families, society, relationships, and life; and the personal qualities that fit our work or roles, which provide a sense of distinction or dignity. Masks often separate us from our authentic Self. They may also appear in dreams.

Meditation: Internal practices to quiet and train the mind, or to induce a mode of consciousness. Meditation can center on cultivating a feeling or internal state, such as compassion; or it can center on attending to a specific focal point, such as a word, candle, or mantra. There are many styles of meditation practice.

Meridians: Twenty major energy pathways (twelve organ and eight extraordinary meridians) described in acupuncture and Chinese medicine models of the body.

Mind-body medicine: A form of medicine that uses the power of thoughts and emotions to influence physical health, through practices such as biofeedback, cognitive behavioral therapy, relaxation techniques, meditation, hypnosis, and spirituality. The key to any mind-body medicine practice is training the mind to focus on the body without distraction, in order to improve health. Mind-body medicine arose in the 1960s and 1970s, through Dr. Herbert Benson's work with meditation and the relaxation response, followed by psychologist Robert Ader's work in 1975 showing that mental and emotional cues can affect the immune system.

Mindfulness: One of the three pillars of Buddhist practice (mindfulness, virtue, and wisdom) also known as concentration, which is practiced to develop well-being and for growth and self-realization. Mindfulness involves the development of skillful attention to our outer and inner worlds.

Movement therapies: A broad range of Eastern and Western approaches used to promote physical, mental, emotional, and spiritual well-being. Movement therapy can bring about changes in attitude and emotions, increase self-esteem and self-image, increase tolerance, and enhance openness and creativity. Western movement therapies developed from dance, physical therapy, psychology, and bodywork. Eastern movement therapies – such as yoga, qigong, and tai chi – began as spiritual or self-defense practices and evolved into healing therapies.

Myofascial release: Soft-tissue therapy used to treat physical dysfunction, pain, and restricted movement by reducing muscle contractions, increasing circulation and venous and lymphatic drainage, and stimulating the stretch reflex in muscles and fascia.

Neural mobilization: A therapeutic technique used to restore and enhance pain-free mobility of the nerves in the central and peripheral nervous systems.

Parasympathetic nervous system (PNS): One of two main divisions of the autonomic nervous system; the PNS, which operates during normal situations, acts to lower activity, permit digestion, and conserve energy; the PNS brings about relaxation and renewal within the body, and is responsible for recuperation and return to a balanced state when pain or stress are experienced. See: autonomic nervous system and sympathetic nervous system.

Pranayama: Breathing exercises practiced in hatha yoga to control the flow of life force energy. The term is made up of the words *prana* (life force) and *ayama* (control).

Process: Movement of information to and from a person, through what is experienced, perceived, and expressed in the now.

Process Acupressure (PA): A hands-on acupressure approach to the body with psychological and psychospiritual processing of the psyche, with a focus on soul or Higher Self. This holistic method helps individuals understand and process who they are, and assists with growth and development of body, mind, emotions, and soul consciousness. PA provides a way to derive meaning and purpose from personal history and supports connection with soul guidance.

Psyche: The forces in an individual (self, personality, and ego) that influence thought, emotions, and behavior, and consciously or unconsciously adjust or mediate how the body responds.

Psychoneuroimmunology: A branch of medicine that deals with the influence of emotional states and nervous system activities on immune function, especially in relation to the onset and progression of dis-ease.

Qigong: An ancient Chinese healing art involving meditation, controlled breathing, and movement exercises.

Response ability: Our ability to respond to, versus react to, life situations and challenges.

Restorative Yoga: Restful yoga postures that stimulate the parasympathetic nervous system and help balance and return the body to equilibrium and health. These practices lower heart rate and blood pressure, stimulate the immune system, and keep the endocrine system operating in a balanced manner. When the parasympathetic nervous system is exhausted, or underactive, illness can more readily occur.

Reverence for life: A philosophy developed from observation of the world around us, in which we find ourselves in awe of the mystery of life that surrounds us. All living things have the capacity for reverence for life, which connects us all as brothers and sisters. When practiced, reverence for life brings awareness and responsibility to our actions.

Self-healing: A process and journey of coming home to our authentic Self.

Shadow: Described by Carl Jung as part of our unconscious, unknown mind. The shadow contains repressed ideas and latent desires, instincts, and shortcomings. It is present in everyone, though often denied and projected onto others. The shadow can appear in dreams and visions as demons, dragons, or wild, exotic figures.

Somatic therapies: Therapies that integrate physical, mental, emotional, and spiritual aspects of our whole being by increasing body, breath, and sensory awareness of what we are experiencing in the now. These therapies often provide cues that tap into current or prior experiences and assist us with making aware choices and decisions. Somatic therapies include: craniosacral therapy, The Feldenkrais Method®, Process Acupressure, The Trager Approach®, and Zero Balancing.

Soul: The nonmaterial essence or energy that animates life; the Divine aspect within our core being that carries wisdom and our life purpose.

Soul actualization: Realization of the soul's potential; the fullest expression and activation of the soul's capacities.

Soul guidance/wisdom: Knowledge and insight from the human and Divine aspects of our soul.

Source energy: See Spirit.

Spirit: The formless energy that encompasses and embraces all creation. Also referred to as the Divine, G-d, or Source.

Strain-counterstrain: A therapeutic technique where the body is placed in positions that decrease pain and muscle spasms and normalize muscle tone. It is effective in the treatment of cranial, spinal, sacral, pelvic, rib cage, and extremity joint pain and dysfunction.

Stress-hardy personality: Learned personality characteristics or traits described by Suzanne Kobasa, which protect people from stress and enhance their quality of life. These traits include: commitment, a sense of control, and the viewing of change as a challenge and opportunity for growth and learning.

Sympathetic nervous system (SNS): One of two main divisions of the autonomic nervous system located in the thoracic and lumbar segments of the spinal cord; the SNS activates and prepares the body for activity, stress, and emergencies, which can be experienced as a "fight or flight" response. See: autonomic nervous system and parasympathetic nervous system.

Tachyon crystals: Crystals used to heal injuries, restore organ function, bolster a weak immune system, enhance meditation capabilities, improve athletic performance, and treat chronic health conditions. These crystals are used as tools to stimulate the appropriate subtle organizing energy fields (SOEF) and alter energetic frequencies, rebalance energetic flow, and convert higher energies into appropriate healing frequencies. This approach to healing is based on quantum physics.

Tracking: A tool that develops the aware ego through the nonjudgmental witnessing of life experiences and relationships; a skill that develops objectivity, discernment, a sense of safety, and deep intimacy with our authentic Self and our relationships.

Trager Approach®: An approach to movement education created and developed by Milton Trager, M.D., which uses bodywork and Mentastics® (movement) to: release deep-seated physical and mental patterns; facilitate deep relaxation; increase physical mobility; and enhance mental clarity.

True nature: See authentic Self.

Values: Ideals, beliefs, and customs that reflect what is important to an individual, group, or society. Values influence decisions and behavior. Values are derived from cultures, families, schooling, friends, and environmental influences; values may be positive (for example: cleanliness, freedom, education) or negative (for example: cruelty, crime, blasphemy).

Visceral mobilization: A gentle hands-on therapy developed by French osteopath Jean-Pierre Barral, M.D., which locates restrictions or imbalances involving the organs (viscera), their supportive connective tissue (fascia), and the musculoskeletal system of the body. This approach helps to restore normal organ function and tone and often relieves chronic pain.

Well-being: A natural state of feeling good throughout one's being.

Wise-hearted spiritual warrior: An individual who embodies heart and Spirit through their vision, commitment, discipline, courage, integrity, service, and wholeheartedness.

Yoga: An ancient philosophy and practice developed in India more than 5,000 years ago. Yoga uses meditation, breath, and postures to achieve well-being and balance of body, mind, emotions, and soul.

Zen: A school of Buddhism that emphasizes experiential wisdom in the attainment of enlightenment. Zen emphasizes direct realization through meditation and dharma practice (religious observances, conformity to the law, and duty) over theoretical knowledge.

Zero Balancing (ZB)®: A mind-body holistic therapy developed by Fritz Frederick Smith, M.D. in the early 1970s. ZB applies finger pressure and gentle fulcrums to tension in bones, joints, and soft tissue. These fulcrums create points of balance around which the body can relax and reorganize. ZB is designed to balance the structure and the energy of the body; clear blocks in the body's energy flow; enhance postural alignment; and increase vitality.

Endnotes

Introduction: How to Use This Book

¹ Angeles Arrien, *The Four-Fold Way: Walking the Paths of the Warrior, Teacher, Healer and Visionary* (San Francisco: HarperCollins, 1993), 50–51.

² A. Zubko, Editor, *The Wisdom of James Allen* (California: Laurel Creek Press, 2004), 22.

Chapter 1: The Whole Heart

¹ ThinkExist.com Quotations. "Helen Keller quotes". <u>ThinkExist.com Quotations Online</u> 1 Nov. 2011. 29 Dec. 2011, http://en.thinkexist.com/quotes/helen_keller/.

² Paul Pearsall, *The Heart's Code* (New York: Broadway Books, 1998), 55.

³ Roger Jahnke, *The Healing Promise of Qi: Creating Extraordinary Wellness Through Qigong and Tai Chi* (New York: Contemporary Books, 2002), 65, 69, 122, 134, 135.

⁴ ThinkExist.com Quotations. "Rene Descartes quotes". <u>ThinkExist.com Quotations Online</u> 1 Nov. 2011. 29 Dec 2011, http://en.thinkexist.com/quotes/rene_descartes/.

⁵ A. Jaffe, Editor, *Memories, Dreams, and Reflections* (New York: Vintage Books, 1961), 247.

⁶ Institute of HeartMath®, Boulder, Colorado, http://www.heartmath.org, 6 Jan 2012.

⁷ Candace B. Pert, *Molecules of Emotion* (New York: Scribner, 1997).

[8] ThinkExist.com Quotations. "Rainer Maria Rilke quotes". ThinkExist.com Quotations Online 1 Nov. 2011. 29 Dec. 2011, http://en.thinkexist.com/quotes/rainer_maria_rilke/.

[9] Max DePree, *Leadership Is An Art* (New York: Random House, 2004), 16-17.

[10] Elizabeth Baker and Susan Popiel. "Dearest Diary... The Awareness Journal." AHNA Journal Beginnings 29 (Spring 2009), 10-11.

[11] Joseph Emet, 2010 Booklet published for Thich Nhat Hanh's 84th birthday. Mindfulness Meditation Centre, 29 Dec 2011, http://www.mindfulnessmeditationcentre.org/ Thich.htm.

[12] Rick Hanson and Richard Mendius, *Buddha's Brain: The Practical Neuroscience of Happiness, Love, & Wisdom* (Oakland: New Harbinger Publications, Inc.), 13.

[13] Steven Goodheart, "Mindfulness of Breathing — a short teaching by Thich Nhat Hanh" Metta Refuge, 29 Dec 2011, http://mettarefuge.wordpress.com/2010/02/08/, mindfulness-of-breathing-a-short-teaching-by-thich-nhat-hanh.

Chapter 2: The Journey

[1] Vidyavachaspati V. Panoli, Translator,"108 Upanishads: Katha Upanishad, 1-lll-14". Vedanta Spiritual Library, http://www.celextel.org/108upanishads/ 29 Dec 2011.

[2] "Jung's Archetypes." ChangingMinds.org, 29 Dec 2011, http://changingminds.org/org/explanations/identify/jung_archetypes.html.

[3] ThinkExist.com Quotations. "Norman Cousins quotes". ThinkExist.com Quotations Online 1 Nov. 2011. 31 Dec. 2011, http://en.thinkexist.com/quotes/Norman_Cousins/.

Chapter 3: Recovering Reverence for Life

[1] ThinkExist.com Quotations. "Ralph Waldo Emerson quotes". ThinkExist.com Quotations Online 1 Nov. 2011. 31 Dec. 2011, http://en.thinkexist.com/quotes/ralph_waldo_ emerson/3.html

[2] Ibid., "Albert Einstein quotes". ThinkExist.com Quotations Online 1 Nov. 2011. 31 Dec. 2011, http://en.thinkexist.com/ quotes/albert_en.thinkexist.com/9. html.

[3] Ibid., "T.S. Eliot quotes". ThinkExist.com Quotations Online 1 Nov. 2011. 31 Dec. 2011, http://en.thinkexist.com/ quotes/t.s._eliot/2.html.

[4] QuotationsBook.com. "Problems quotes." QuotationsBook.com Online, 31 Dec. 2011, http:// quotationsbook.com/quote/32470/.

[5] ThinkExist.com Quotations., "Michael Nolan quotes". ThinkExist.com Quotations Online 1 Nov. 2011. 31 Dec. 2011, http://en.thinkexist.com/quotes/michael_nolan/.

Chapter 4: Theme One

[1] Dianne M. Connelly, *All Sickness is Home Sickness* (Maryland: Traditional Acupuncture Institute, 1983), 9.

[2] Wikiquote.org., "Inferno (Dante)." Wikiquote.org Online, 31 Dec 2011, http://en.wikiquote.org/wiki/Inferno_(Dante).

Chapter 5: Theme Two

[1] ThinkExist.com Quotations., "Carl Rogers quotes". ThinkExist.com Quotations Online 1 Nov. 2011. 31 Dec. 2011, http://en.thinkexist.com/quotes/carl_rogers/.

[2] Ibid., "Helen Keller quotes". ThinkExist.com Quotations Online 1 Nov. 2011. 31 Dec. 2011, http://en.thinkexist.com/quotes/helen_keller/3.html.

[3] Ibid., "Charles Darwin quotes". ThinkExist.com Quotations Online 1 Nov. 2011. 31 Dec. 2011, http://en.thinkexist.com/quotes/charles_darwin/.

[4] David Richo, *The Five Things We Cannot Change...and the Happiness We Find by Embracing Them*. (Massachusetts: Shambhala, 2005), 11.

[5] Marilyn Schlitz & Tina Amorok, *Consciousness & Healing: Integral Approaches to Mind-Body Medicine*. (Missouri: Churchill Livingstone, 2005), Dedication.

[6] Gloria Steinem, *Revolution From Within: A Book of Self-Esteem*. (Massachusetts: Little Brown & Company, 1993), 389.

Chapter 6: Theme Three

[1] Lewis Carroll, *Through the Looking Glass*. (London: Macmillan & Company, 1872), Chapter 5.

Chapter 7: Theme Four

[1] ThinkExist.com Quotations., "Thomas Alva Edison quotes". ThinkExist.com Quotations Online 1 Dec. 2011. 23 Jan. 2012, http://en.thinkexist.com/quotes/thomas_alva_edison/6.html.

[2] George E. Vaillant, *Aging Well: The Landmark Harvard Study of Adult Development*. (Boston: Little, Brown, and Company, 2002).

[3] John W. Travis and Regina Sara Ryan, *The Wellness Workbook*. (California: Ten Speed Press, 1991), xiv.

[4] ThinkExist.com Quotations., "Saint Bartholomew quotes". <u>ThinkExist.com Quotations Online</u> 1 Dec. 2011. 23 Jan. 2012, http://en.thinkexist.com/quotes/saint_bartholomew/.

[5] Mimi Guarneri, *The Heart Speaks: A Cardiologist Reveals the Secret Language of Healing.* (New York: Simon & Schuster, 2006), 106.

[6] ThinkExist.com Quotations., "Albert Schweitzer quotes". <u>ThinkExist.com Quotations Online</u> 1 Dec. 2011. 30 Jan. 2012, http://en.thinkexist.com/quotes/albert_schweitzer/2.html.

[7] Suzanne C. Kobasa, "Stressful Life Events, Personality, and Health: An Inquiry Into Hardiness," *Journal of Personality and Social Psychology,* 37 (1979): 1-11.

[8] Cessy Morris, personal note to author, 1983.

[9] ThinkExist.com Quotations., "Kahlil Gibran quotes". <u>ThinkExist.com Quotations Online</u> 1 Dec. 2011. 30 Jan. 2012, http://en.thinkexist.com/quotes/kahlil_gibran/5.html.

[10] Daniel Stern, "The Process of Therapeutic Change Involving Implicit Knowledge: Some Implications of Developmental Observations for Adult Psychotherapy," *Infant Mental Health Journal,* 19 (1998): 300-308.

[11] Paul Sibcy, *Healing Your Rift With God: A Guide to Spiritual Renewal and Ultimate Healing.* (Oregon: Beyond Words Publishing, Inc., 1999).

[12] Gangaji, *The Diamond in your Pocket: Discovering Your True Radiance.* (Colorado: Sounds True, Inc., 2005).

[13] David V. Erdman, Editor, *The Complete Poetry & Prose of William Blake.* (New York: Anchor books, 1988), 490.

Chapter 8: Theme Five

[1] National Archives, "Charters of Freedom: Declaration of Independence," 30 Jan 2012, http://www.archives.gov/ exhibits/ charters/declaration_transcript.html.

[2] Russell Delman, "The Embodied Life: Twelve Somatic Journeys based on the Feldenkrais® Method," read by Russell Delman, © 1993 Feldenkrais® Recordings.

[3] Fritz Frederick Smith, *Inner Bridges: A Guide to Energy Movement and Body Structure*. (Georgia: Humanics New Age, 1986), 78-79, 109.

[4] Soul Lightening International, "Accupressure for Anyone Workshop Descriptions". http://www.soulightening.com. (accessed 10 March, 2012).

[5] ThinkExist.com Quotations., "Mahatma Gandhi quotes". ThinkExist.com Quotations Online 1 Dec. 2011. 30 Jan. 2012, http://en.thinkexist.com/quotes/mahatma_gandhi/.

[6] Ibid., "Anais Nin quotes". ThinkExist.com Quotations Online 1 Dec. 2011. 30 Jan. 2012, http://en.thinkexist.com/ quotes/anais_nin/.

[7] Ibid., "Anne Frank quotes". ThinkExist.com Quotations Online 1 Dec. 2011. 30 Jan. 2012, http://en.thinkexist.com/ quotes/anne_frank/.

[8] Elisabeth Sifton, *The Serenity Prayer: Faith and Politics in Times of Peace and War*. (New York: W.W. Norton & Company, 2005), 277.

[9] Parker J. Palmer, *Let Your Life Speak: Listening for the Voice of Vocation*. (California: Jossey-Bass, 2000), 22-36.

Chapter 9: Theme Six

[1] Vaillant, *Aging Well*, 15.

[2] Gene D. Cohen, *The Creative Age: Awakening Human Potential in the Second Half of Life*. (New York: Harper Collins, 2000).

[3] John Tarrant, *The Light Inside the Dark: Zen, Soul, and the Spiritual Life*. (New York: Harper Collins, 1998).

[4] Viktor E. Frankl, *Man's Search For Meaning: An Introduction to Logotherapy*. (New York: Simon & Schuster, 1984).

[5] ThinkExist.com Quotations., "Richard Buckminster Fuller quotes". <u>ThinkExist.com Quotations Online</u> 1 Dec. 2011. 31 Jan. 2012, http://en.thinkexist.com/quotes/richard_buckminster_fuller/.

[6] John O'Donohue, *Beauty: The Invisible Embrace*. (New York: Harper Collins, 2004).

[7] ThinkExist.com Quotations., "Ralph Waldo Emerson quotes". <u>ThinkExist.com Quotations Online</u> 1 Dec. 2011. 31 Jan. 2012, http://en.thinkexist.com/quotes/ralph_waldo_emerson/24.html.

[8] Angeles Arrien, "Gratitude: The Essential Practice for Happiness and Fulfillment," read by Angeles Arrien, 2009 Sounds True.

[9] ThinkExist.com Quotations., "Elie Wiesel quotes". <u>ThinkExist.com Quotations Online</u> 1 Dec. 2011. 31 Jan. 2012, http://en.thinkexist.com/quotes/elie_wiesel/2.html.

[10] Angeles Arrien, "Gratitude: The Essential Practice for Happiness and Fulfillment."

[11] Kathy Kalina, *Midwife For Souls: Spiritual Care For The Dying*. (Massachusetts: Pauline Books & Media, 1993), 22-23.

[12] ThinkExist.com Quotations., "Irish Blessings quotes". ThinkExist.com Quotations Online 1 Dec. 2011. 31 Jan. 2012, http://en.thinkexist.com/quotes/irish_ blessings/.

[13] Ibid., "Pablo Picasso quotes". ThinkExist.com Quotations Online 1 Dec. 2011. 31 Jan. 2012, http://en.thinkexist.com/ quotes/pablo_picasso/3.html.

[14] Mihaly Csikszentmihalyi, *Finding Flow: The Psychology of Engagement With Everyday Life*. (New York: Perseus Books, 1997).

[15] ThinkExist.com Quotations., "Erich Fromm quotes". ThinkExist.com Quotations Online 1 Dec. 2011. 31 Jan. 2012, http://en.thinkexist.com/quotes/erich_fromm/2.html.

[16] Ibid., "Julia Cameron quotes". ThinkExist.com Quotations Online 1 Dec. 2011. 31 Jan. 2012, http:// en.thinkexist.com/quotes/julia_cameron/.

[17] Women Reading Aloud, http://www.womenreadingaloud. com/, 6 Jan 2012.

[18] Julie Maloney, *Come Sit By Me*. (New Jersey: Mango Press LLC, 2004).

[19] ThinkExist.com Quotations., "Kahlil Gibran quotes". ThinkExist.com Quotations Online 1 Dec. 2011. 31 Jan. 2012, http://en.thinkexist.com/quotes/kahlil_gibran/2.html.

[20] Ibid., "Mahatma Gandhi quotes". ThinkExist. com Quotations Online 1 Dec. 2011. 31 Jan. 2012, http:// en.thinkexist.com/quotes/mahatma_gandhi/5.html.

[21] Angeles Arrien, *Living in Gratitude: A Journey That Will Change Your Life*. (Boulder: Sounds True, 2011).

[22] Robert A. Emmons, *Thanks! How Practicing Gratitude Can Make You Happier*. (Massachusetts: Houghton Mifflin, 2008), 185-207.

Chapter 10: Theme Seven

[1] Angeles Arrien, *The Second Half of Life: Opening the Eight Gates of Wisdom*. (Boulder: Sounds True, 2007), 118-122.

[2] ThinkExist.com Quotations., "Helen Keller quotes". <u>ThinkExist.com Quotations Online</u> 1 Jan. 2012. 2 Feb. 2012, http://en.thinkexist.com/quotes/helen_keller/6.html.

[3] Ibid., "Ralph Waldo Emerson quotes". <u>ThinkExist.com Quotations Online</u> 1 Jan. 2012. 2 Feb. 2012, http://en.thinkexist.com/quotes/ralph_waldo_emerson/ 10.html.

[4] Spiritual Quotes to Live By, "Enchanting and Expressive Love Sayings and Verse," 2 Feb 2012, http://www.spiritual-quotes-to-live-by.com/love-sayings.html.

[5] Helping Quotes, Service Quotes, Help and Service Sayings at <u>JoyofQuotes.com</u>, 2 Feb 2012, http://www.joyofquotes.com/helping_quotes.html.

[6] "Martin Luther King – Acceptance Speech". Nobelprize. org. 17 Jan 2012. http://www.nobelprize.org/ nobel_prizes/peace/laureates/1964/king-acceptance.html.

[7] Richard Carlson & Benjamin Shield, *Handbook for the Heart: Original Writings on Love*. (Massachusetts: Little Brown & Company, 1996), 67-72.

[8] William Bridges, *Transitions, Making Sense of Life's Changes*. (Massachusetts: Addison-Wesley Publishing Company, 1980), 90.

[9] Angeles Arrien, Four-Fold Way® Program, January, 1997-September, 1997, Creative Energy Options, Spring House, Pennsylvania.

[10] ThinkExist.com Quotations., "Henry Ward Beecher quotes". ThinkExist.com Quotations Online 1 Jan. 2012. 3 Feb. 2012, http://en.thinkexist.com/quotes/henry_ward_beecher/.

[11] Arrien, *The Four-Fold Way*, 49

[12] Wikipedia.org., "Desiderata. Wikipedia.org Online, 26 Jan 2012, http://en.wikipedia.org/wiki/Desiderata.

[13] Wikiquote.org., "The Prophet." Wikiquote.org Online, 10 Nov 2011, http://en.wikiquote.org/wiki/The_Prophet.

[14] Cessy Morris, personal note to author, 1983.

[15] Lu Pierro, personal interview with author, 2011.

[16] 4umi.com., "Khalil Gibran, Jesus the Son of Man: Philemon, A Greek Apothecary," 3 Feb 2012, http://4umi.com/gibran/jesus/philemon.

Bibliography

Allen, James. *As a Man Thinketh*. New York: Tribeca Books, 2011.

Arrien, Angeles. *Signs of Life: The Five Universal Shapes and How to Use Them*. New York: Jeremy P. Tarcher/Putnam, 1981.

Bach, Richard. *Jonathan Livingston Seagull*. New York: MacMillan, 1970.

Barasch, Marc Ian. *The Healing Path: A Soul Approach to Illness*. New York: Jeremy P Tarcher/Putnam,1993.

Barks, Coleman. *The Illuminated Rumi*. New York: Broadway Books, 1997.

Bays, Jan Chozen. *Mindful Eating: A Guide to Rediscovering a Healthy and Joyful Relationship with Food*. Boston: Shambhala Publications, 2009.

Beattie, Melody. *The New Codependency: Help & Guidance for Today's Generation*. New York: Simon & Schuster, 2009.

Benson, Herbert. *Timeless Healing: The Power and Biology of Belief*. New York: Scribner, 1996.

Blum, Jeanne Elizabeth. *Woman Heal Thyself: An Ancient Healing System for Contemporary Women*. Boston: Charles E. Tuttle Co., Inc., 1995.

Bolen, Jean Shinoda. *Close to the Bone: Life-Threatening Illness and the Search for Meaning*. New York: Scribner, 1996.

Borysenko, Joan. *Guilt is the Teacher, Love is the Lesson*. New York: Time Warner, 1990.

———. *Minding the Body, Mending the Mind*. Philadelphia: Da Capo Books, 2007.

Braden, Gregg. *Awakening to Zero Point: The Collective Initiation*. Bellevue, WA: Radio Bookstore Press, 1997.

———. *The Divine Matrix: Bridging Time, Space, Miracles, and Belief*. Carlsbad: Hay House, 2007.

Breathnach, Sarah Ban. *The Simple Abundance Journal of Gratitude*. New York: Time Warner, 1996.

Buscaglia, Leo. *Love*. Greenwich, Connecticut: Fawcett Crest Books, 1972.

Cameron, Julia. *The Artist's Way*. New York: GP Putnam's Sons, 1992.

Campbell, Don. *The Harmony of Health: Sound Relaxation for Mind, Body, and Spirit*. Audio CD. Carlsbad: Hay House, Inc., 2006.

Carlson, Richard, and Benjamin Shield, Editors. *Healers on Healing*. New York: Jeremy P. Tarcher/Putnam, 1989.

———. *Handbook for the Soul*. Boston: Back Bay Books, 1996.

———. *Handbook for the Spirit*. Novato, CA: New World Library, 1997.

Carroll, Lewis. *Alice's Adventures in Wonderland and Through the Looking-Glass*. New York: Penguin Putnam, 1997.

Chödrön, Pema. *When Things Fall Apart*. Boston: Shambhala Publications, 1997.

———. *The Places That Scare You: A Guide to Fearlessness in Difficult Times*. Boston: Shambhala Publications, 2001.

———. *Practicing Peace in Times of War*. Boston: Shambhala, 2006.

Chopra, Deepak. *Quantum Healing: Exploring the Frontiers of Mind/Body Medicine*. New York: Bantam Books, 1989.

———. *Perfect Health: The Complete Mind/Body Guide Revised and Updated*. New York: Three Rivers Press, 2001.

Claire, Thomas. *Body Work: What Type of Massage to Get and How to Make the Most of It.* Laguna Beach, CA: Basic Health Publications, Inc., 2006.

Cohen, Andrea Joy. *A Blessing in Disguise: 39 Life Lessons from Today's Greatest Teachers.* New York: Berkley Trade, 2008.

Connelly, Dianne M. *Traditional Acupuncture: The Law of the Five Elements.* Laurel, MD: Tai Sophia Institute, 1979.

Cousins, Norman. *Anatomy of an Illness as Perceived by the Patient.* New York: W. W. Norton & Company, Inc., 1979.

————. *The Healing Heart: Antidotes to Panic and Helplessness.* New York: W. W. Norton & Company, 1983.

Dalai Lama, His Holiness the. *Essential Teachings.* Berkeley: North Atlantic Books, 1995.

————, and Howard C. Cutler. *The Art of Happiness: A Handbook for Living.* New York: Penguin Group, 1998.

————, and Jeffrey Hopkins, Editor. *How to Practice: The Way to a Meaningful Life.* New York: Simon & Schuster, Inc., 2002.

Dechar, Lorie Eve. *Five Spirits: Alchemical Acupuncture for Psychological and Spiritual Healing.* New York: Lantern Books, 2006.

Devi, Nischala Joy. *The Healing Path of Yoga: Alleviate Stress, Open Your Heart, and Enrich Your Life.* New York: Three Rivers Press, 2000.

Dispenza, Joseph. *The Way of the Traveler: Making Every Trip a Journey of Self-Discovery.* Emeryville, California: Avalon Travel Publishing, 2002.

Dolowich, Gary. *Archetypal Acupuncture: Healing With the Five Elements.* Aptos, CA: Jade Mountain Publishing, 2003.

Dossey, Larry. *Recovering the Soul: A Scientific and Spiritual Search*. New York: Bantam Books, 1989.

Duerk, Judith. *Circle of Stones: Woman's Journey to Herself*. San Diego: Lura Media, 1989.

Dyer, Wayne. *The Shift: Taking Your Life From Ambition to Meaning*. Carlsbad, CA: Hay House, Inc. 2010.

Eden, Donna. *Energy Medicine*. New York: Jeremy P. Tarcher/Putnam, 1998.

_____. *Energy Medicine for Women: Aligning Your Body's Energies to Boost Your Health and Vitality*. New York: Jeremy P. Tarcher/Penguin, 2008.

Emoto, Masuro. *The Hidden Messages in Water*. Hillsboro, OR: Beyond Words Publishing, Inc., 2004.

Estes, Clarissa Pinkola. *Women Who Run With the Wolves: Myths and Stories of the Wild Woman Archetype*. New York: Ballantine Books, 1992.

Fields, Rick, editor. *The Awakened Warrior: Living with Courage, Compassion & Discipline*. New York: Tarcher/Putnam Books, 1994.

Feldenkrais, Moshe. *Awareness through Movement*. New York: Harper & Row, 1972.

Foundation for Inner Peace. *A Course in Miracles*. Tiburon, CA: Foundation for Inner Peace, 1975.

Gardner, Howard. *Multiple Intelligences, The Theory in Practice*. New York: Basic Books, 1993.

Gerber, Richard. *A Practical Guide to Vibrational Medicine: Energy Healing and Spiritual Transformation*. New York: HarperCollins, 2000.

Gershon, David, and Gail Straub. *Empowerment: The Art of Creating Your Life as You Want It*. West Hurley, NY: High Point, 1989.

Gibran, Kahlil. *The Prophet*. New York: Knopf, 1923.

Goldsmith, Joel. *Practicing the Presence: The Inspirational Guide to Regaining Meaning and a Sense of Purpose in Your Life*. New York: HarperCollins, 1991.

Goleman, Daniel. *Emotional Intelligence*. New York: Bantam Books, 1995.

Gottlieb, Daniel. *Learning from the Heart: Lessons on Living, Loving, and Listening*. New York: Sterling Publishing, 2008.

Green, Joey. *The Zen of Oz: Ten Spiritual Lessons from Over the Rainbow*. New York: Renaissance Books, 1998.

Haas, Elson M. *Staying Healthy with the Seasons*. Berkeley: Celestial Arts, 2003.

Hay, Louise L. *You Can Heal Your Life*. Santa Monica: Hay House, 1984.

Hillman, James. *The Soul's Code: In Search of Character and Calling*. New York: Time Warner Company, 1996.

Hunt, Valerie V. *Infinite Mind: Science of the Human Vibrations of Consciousness*. Malibu, CA: Malibu Publishing Co., 1989.

Ihnen, Anne, and Carolyn Flynn. *The Complete Idiot's Guide to Mindfulness*. New York: Alpha Books, 2008.

Jahnke, Roger. *The Healer Within: Using Traditional Chinese Techniques to Release Your Body's Own Medicine*. San Francisco: HarperCollins, 1997.

Jampolsky, Gerald. *Love is Letting Go of Fear*. Millbrae, CA: Celestial Arts, 1979.

———. *Teach Only Love: The Seven Principles of Attitudinal Healing*. New York: Bantam, 1983.

Johanson, Greg, and Ron Kurtz. *Grace Unfolding: Psychotherapy in the Spirit of the Tao-te ching*. New York: Bell Tower, 1991.

Judith, Anodea. *Eastern Body Western Mind: Psychology and the Chakra System as a Path to the Self*. Berkeley, CA: Celestial Arts Publishing, 1996.

———. *Chakra Balancing: A Guide to Healing and Awakening Your Energy Body*. Boulder, CO: Sounds True, 2003.

Juhan, Deane. *Job's Body: A Handbook for Bodywork*. Barrytown, NY: Station Hill, 1987.

_____. *Touched by the Goddess: The Physical, Psychological, and Spiritual Powers of Bodywork*. Barrytown, NY: Station Hill, 2002.

Jung, Carl G. *Memories, Dreams, Reflections*. New York: Pantheon, 1963.

Kabat-Zinn, Jon. *Full Catastrophe Living: Using the Wisdom of Your Body and Mind to Face Pain, Stress, and Illness*. New York: Delta, 1990.

———. *Coming to Our Senses: Healing Ourselves and the World Through Mindfulness*. New York: Hyperion, 2005.

———. *Wherever You Go, There You Are*: Mindfulness Meditation in Everyday Life. New York: Hyperion, 2005.

Katie, Byron. *Loving What Is: Four Questions That Can Change Your Life*. New York: Three Rivers Press, 2002.

Kaufman, Barry Neal. *Son-Rise: The Miracle Continues*. Novato, CA: H. J. Kramer, 1994.

Keenan, Father Paul. *Stages of the Soul: The Path of the Soulful Life*. Chicago: Contemporary Books, 2000.

Kelder, Peter. *Ancient Secret of the Fountain of Youth Book 1*. New York: Doubleday, 1985.

———. *Ancient Secret of the Fountain of Youth Book 2*. New York: Doubleday, 1985.

Klein, Allen. *The Healing Power of Humor: Techniques for Getting through Loss, Setbacks, Upsets, Disappointments, Difficulties, Trials, Tribulations, and All That Non-So-Funny Stuff*. Los Angeles: Jeremy P. Tarcher, Inc., 1989.

———. *The Courage to Laugh: Humor, Hope, and Healing in the Face of Death and Dying*. New York: Jeremy P. Tarcher/Putnam, 1998.

Koller, Alice. *The Stations of Solitude*. New York: William Morrow & Company, Inc., 1990.

Kornfield, Jack. *A Path with Heart: A Guide through the Perils and Promises of Spiritual Life*. New York: Bantam, 1993.

———. *After the Ecstasy, the Laundry: How the Heart Grows Wise on the Spiritual Path*. New York: Bantam, 2000.

Kübler-Ross, Elisabeth. *On Death and Dying*. New York: Macmillan, 1969.

———. *To Live Until We Say Goodbye*. Englewood Cliffs, NJ: Prentice-Hall, 1978.

Kurtz, Ron. *Body-Centered Psychotherapy: The Hakomi Method*. Mendocino, CA: Liferhythm, 1990.

LaVoie, Karla Lee. *For Time and All Eternity: Love Never Dies*. West Conshohocken, PA: Infinity Publishing, 2006.

Lasater, Judith. *Relax & Renew: Restful Yoga for Stressful Times*. Berkeley, CA: Rodmell Press, 2011.

Leonard, George. *Mastery: The Keys to Success and Long-Term Fulfillment*. New York: Penguin, 1991.

Lesser, Elizabeth. *Broken Open: How Difficult Times Can Help Us Grow*. New York: Villard, 2004.

Levine, Barbara Hoberman. *Your Body Believes Every Word You Say: The Language of the Body-Mind Connection*. Lower Lake, CA: Aslan Publishing, 1991.

Levine, Stephen. *A Gradual Awakening*. New York: Anchor Books, 1979.

———. *Turning Toward the Mystery: A Seeker's Journey*. San Francisco: HarperCollins, 2002.

——— and Ondrea Levine. *Who Dies?* New York: Anchor Books, 1982.

Lindbergh, Anne Morrow. *Gift from the Sea*. New York: Pantheon Books, 1955.

Lipton, Bruce. *The Biology of Belief: Unleashing the Power of Consciousness, Matter & Miracles*. Carlsbad, CA: Hay House, Inc., 2005.

Lowen, Frank. *The Roots & Philosophy of Dynamic Manual Interface: Manual Therapy to Awaken the Inner Healer*. Berkeley, CA: North Atlantic Books, 2011.

Mairi, Audrey. *Trager for Self Healing: A Practical Guide for Living in the Present Moment*. Novato, CA: New World Library, 2006.

Maloney, Julie. *Private Landscape*. New Jersey: Arseya Publishing, 2007.

Mandino, Og. *The Greatest Salesman in the World*. New York: Bantam Books, 1974.

———. *The Greatest Miracle in the World*. New York: Bantam, 1983.

Mannheimer, Jeffrey S., and Regina M. Rosenthal. "Acute and Chronic Postural Abnormalities as Related to Craniofacial Pain and Temporomandibular Disorders." *The Dental Clinics of North America*, 35, no. 1 (January 1991): 185-208.

McTaggart, Lynne. *The Field: The Quest for the Secret Force of the Universe*. New York: HarperCollins, 2002.

Millman, Dan. *No Ordinary Moments: A Peaceful Warrior's Guide to Daily Life*. Tiburon, CA: H J Kramer, Inc., 1992.

Mindell, Arnold. *Working on Yourself Alone: Inner Dreambody Work*. London, UK: Arkana, 1990.

———. *Dreambody: The Body's Role in Revealing the Self*, 2nd edition. Portland, OR: Lao Tse Press, 1998.

Moustakas, Clark E. *Loneliness*. New York: Prentice Hall Press, 1961.

Muller, Wayne. *Sabbath: Finding Rest, Renewal, and Delight in Our Busy Lives*. New York: Bantam Books, 1999.

Myss, Caroline. *Anatomy of the Spirit: The Seven Stages of Power and Healing*. New York: Harmony/Crown, 1996.

———. *Sacred Contracts: Awakening Your Divine Potential*. New York: Harmony Books, 2001.

———. *Entering the Castle: Finding the Inner Path to God and Your Soul's Purpose*. New York: Free Press, 2007.

Nyima Rinpoche, Chokyi, and Shlim, David R. *Medicine & Compassion: A Tibetan Lama's Guidance for Caregivers*. Boston: Wisdom Publications, 2006.

Ornish, Dean. *Dr. Dean Ornish's Program for Reversing Heart Disease*. New York: Ballantine Books, 1990.

———. *Love and Survival: 8 Pathways to Intimacy and Health*. New York: HarperCollins, 1998.

Oz, Mehmet C. *Healing from the Heart: A Leading Surgeon Combines Eastern and Western Traditions to Create the Medicine of the Future*. New York: Penguin Books, 1998.

Pearson, Carol S. *Awakening the Heroes Within: Twelve Archetypes to Help Us Find Ourselves and Transform Our World*. San Francisco: Harper Collins, 1991.

Pipher, Mary. *Seeking Peace: Chronicles of the Worst Buddhist in the World*. New York: Riverhead Books, 2009.

Progoff, Ira. *At a Journal Workshop: The Basic Text and Guide for Using the Intensive Journal*. New York: Dialogue House Library, 1981.

Ram Dass. *Still Here: Embracing Aging, Changing, and Dying*. New York: Riverhead Books, 2000.

Rico, Gabriele. *Pain and Possibility: Writing Your Way Through Personal Crisis*. New York: Putnam, 1991.

Riso, Don Richard. *Discovering Your Personality Type: The New Enneagram Questionnaire*. New York: Houghton Mifflin Company, 1995.

Rogers, Carl R. *On Becoming a Person*. Boston: Houghton Mifflin Co., 1961.

Rother, Steve, and The Group. *Re-member: A Handbook for Human Evolution*. Poway, CA: Lightworker Publications, 2000.

Rowe, John W., and Robert L. Kahn. *Successful Aging*. New York: Dell Publishing, 1998.

Ruby, Margaret. *The DNA of Healing: A Five-Step Process for Total Wellness and Abundance*. Charlottesville, VA: Hampton Roads Publishing, 2006.

Ruiz, Don Miguel. *The Four Agreements: A Practical Guide to Personal Freedom, A Toltec Wisdom Book*. San Rafael: Amber-Allen Publishing, 1999.

Sams, Jamie. *Dancing the Dream: The Seven Sacred Paths of Human Transformation*. San Francisco: Harper, 1998.

Santorelli, Saki. *Heal Thy Self: Lessons on Mindfulness in Medicine*. New York: Bell Tower, 1999.

Schaef, Anne Wilson. *Living in Process: Basic Truths for Living the Path of the Soul*. New York: Ballantine, 1998.

Schneider, Meir, and Maureen Larkin. *The Handbook of Self-Healing: Your Personal Program for Better Health and Increased Vitality*. New York: Penguin Books, 1994.

Schwartz, Morrie. *Letting Go: Morrie's Reflections on Living While Dying*. New York: Dell Publishing, 1996.

Schwartz-Salant, Nathan. *The Mystery of Human Relationship: Alchemy and the Transformation of the Self*. New York: Routledge, 1998.

Seale, Alan. *Soul Mission Life Vision: Recognize Your True Gifts and Make Your Mark in the World*. Boston: Red Wheel, 2003.

Siegel, Bernie. *Love, Medicine & Miracles*. New York: Harper Perennial, 1986.

———. *Peace, Love, and Healing*. New York: Harper Collins, 1989.

Simpkinson, Anne, Charles Simpkinson, and Rose Solari, Editors. *Nourishing the Soul: Discovering the Sacred in Everyday Life*. San Francisco: HarperCollins, 1995.

Simonton, O. Carl, Stephanie Matthews-Simonton, and James Creighton. *Getting Well Again*. New York: Bantam, 1980.

Sinetar, Marsha. *A Way without Words: A Guide for Spiritually Emerging Adults*. New York: Paulist Press, 1992.

Singh, Tara. *A Gift for All Mankind: Learning the First Ten Lessons of a Course in Miracles*. New York: Ballantine Books, 1986.

———. *Nothing Real Can Be Threatened: Exploring A Course in Miracles*. Los Angeles: Life Action Press, 1989.

Smith, Fritz Frederick. *The Alchemy of Touch: Moving Towards Mastery Through the Lens of Zero Balancing*. Taos: Complementary Medicine Press, 2005.

Snowdon, David. *Aging with Grace: What the Nun Study Teaches Us about Leading Longer, Healthier, and More Meaningful Lives*. New York: Bantam Books, 2001.

Stevens, Barry. *Don't Push the River — Gestalt Therapy and the Ways of Zen*. Moab, UT: Real People Press, 1970.

Stone, Hal, and Sidra Stone. *Embracing Our Selves: The Voice Dialogue Manual*. Mill Valley, CA: Nataraj Publishing, 1989.

———, and Sidra Winkelman. *Embracing Each Other: Relationship as Teacher, Healer & Guide*. Mill Valley, CA: Nataraj Publishing, 1989.

Storr, Anthony, selector. *The Essential Jung*. New York: MJF Books, 1983.

Straub, Gail. *The Rhythm of Compassion: Caring for Self, Connecting with Society*. Boston: Tuttle Publishing, 2000.

Taylor, Jill Bolte. *My Stroke of Insight: A Brain Scientist's Personal Journey*. New York: Viking, 2006.

Thich Nhat Hahn. *The Miracle of Mindfulness*. New York: Beacon Press, 1975.

———. *Peace is Every Step: The Path of Mindfulness in Everyday Life*. New York: Bantam Books, 1991.

Tolle, Eckhart. *The Power of Now: A Guide to Spiritual Enlightenment*. Novato, CA: New World Library, 1999.

———. *Practicing the Power of Now*. Novato, CA: New World Library, 2001.

———. *A New Earth: Awakening to Your Life's Purpose*. New York: Plume, 2005.

Trager, Milton and Cathy Hammond. *Movement as a Way to Agelessness: A Guide to Trager Mentastics*. Barrytown, NY: Station Hill, 1987.

Truman, Karol K. *Feelings Buried Alive Never Die...* Las Vegas: Olympus Distributing, 1991.

Wauters, Ambika. *Chakras and Their Archetypes: Uniting Energy Awareness and Spiritual Growth*. Freedom, CA: The Crossing Press, 1997.

Walsch, Neale Donald. *The Little Soul and the Sun: A Children's Parable Adapted from Conversations with God*. Charlottesville, VA: Hampton Roads Publishing Co., Inc., 1998.

Weil, Andrew. *Healthy Aging*. New York: Alfred A. Knopf, 2005.

Wiesel, Elie. *The Night Trilogy: Night, Dawn, Day*. New York: Hill and Wang, 1972.

Williamson, Marianne. *A Return to Love: Reflections on the Principles of A Course in Miracles*. New York: HarperCollins, 1992.

Young, William Paul. *The Shack*. Newbury Park, CA: Windblown Media, 2007.

Zi, Nancy. *The Art of Breathing: Six Simple Lessons to Improve Performance, Health and Well-Being*. Berkeley: Frog Ltd., 1986.

Zweig, Connie and Jeremiah Abrams, Editors. *Meeting the Shadow: The Hidden Power of the Dark Side of Human Nature*. New York: Jeremy P. Tarcher/Putnam, 1991.

Appendix A: Ten Loves

Activity	Past 5 Years	Next 5 Years	Past 2 Weeks	Want to Improve	Cost	Alone/With People	Risk
1.							
2.							
3.							
4.							
5.							
6.							
7.							
8.							
9.							
10.							

APPENDIX B
Internet Resources

Body-Mind Training Centers

Center for Mindfulness in Medicine, Health Care, and Society
University of Massachusetts Medical School
http://www.umassmed.edu/cfm/home/index.aspx

Emotional Freedom Technique® (EFT)
http://www.emofree.com

The Tapping Solution
http://www.thetappingsolution.com/index.php

Eden Energy Medicine
http://www.innersource.net

Esalen Institute
http://www.esalen.org

Feldenkrais® Educational Foundation of North America and the Feldenkrais Guild® of North America
http://www.feldenkrais.com

Himalayan International Institute of Yoga, Science and Philosophy
Honesdale, PA
http://www.himalayaninstitute.org

Institute of HeartMath®
http://www.heartmath.org

Institute of Integral Qigong and Tai Chi
http://www.instituteofintegralqigongandtaichi.org

Institute of Integrative Manual Therapy
http://www.instituteofimt.com

Institute of Noetic Sciences (IONS)
http://www.noetic.org

Kripalu Center
Massachusetts
http://www.kripalu.com

Lowen Systems. Dynamic Manual Interface: Embracing the Wisdom of the Body and its Rhythms
http://lowensystems.com

Omega Institute
Rhinebeck, New York
http://www.eomega.org

Soul Lightening International.®
Process and Clinical Acupressure, Spirit of Seva Project, Acupressure for Anyone™, Chakra Tai Chi
http://www.soullightening.com

Trager® International
http://www.trager.com.

Upledger Institute
Palm Beach Gardens, Florida
http://www.upledger.com

Zero Balancing.® Zero Balancing Health Association
http://www.zerobalancing.com

Organizations

Association for Applied and Therapeutic Humor
http://www.aath.org

American Comedy Institute
http://www.comedyinstitute.com

American School of Laughter Yoga
http://www.laughteryogaamerica.com

National Comedy Hall of Fame
http://www.comedyhall.com

Older Jokes for Older Folks
http://www.seniors-site.com/funstuff/jokes97.html

American Holistic Health Association
http://www.ahha.org

American Holistic Nurses Association
http://www.ahna.org

Association for Research & Enlightenment
http://www.are-cayce.cp

Center on Aging, Health & Humanities
http://www.gwumc.edu/cahh

Circle of Life Health Coaching™
http://www.healthandwellnesscoaching.org

Elderhostel
http://www.elderhostel.org

Integrative Practitioner
Online community for integrative healthcare professionals
http://www.integrativepractitioner.com

International Women's Writing Guild
http://www.iwwg.org

Jazzercise®
http://www.jazzercise.com

William T. Kelly, Sr., D.C.
Red Bank, NJ

National Certification Board for Therapeutic Massage & Bodywork
http://www.ncbtmb.org

National Center for Complementary and Alternative Medicine
http://nccam.nih.gov

National Institute of Health
http://www.nih.gov

National Qigong Association
http://nqa.org/

National Wellness Institute
http://www.nationalwellness.org

New York Open Center
http://www.opencenter.org

Nia®: Sensory-based Movement Practice
http://www.nianow.com

The Options Institute
Sheffield, Massachusetts
http://www.option.org

Senior Corps
Washington, DC
http://www.cns.gov/senior/index.html

The Institute of Transpersonal Psychology
Stanford, CA
http://www.itp.edu

Wholistic Healing Research
http://www.wholistichealingresearch.com

Individual Resources

Angeles Arrien, Ph.D
http://www.angelesarrien.com

Brene Brown, Ph.D.
http://www.ordinarycourage.com

Pema Chodren
http://www.shambhala.org/teachers/pema/

Charles Fleisher
Beyond Wheels: http://www.beyondwheels.org
Inspirational Speaking: http://www.theopportunitiesguy.com

Maren Good, LMT
Scent and Sound Works, NJ
http://www.scentandsoundworks.com

The Work of Byron Katie
http://www.thework.com/index.php

Bruce Lipton, PhD.
http://www.brucelipton.com

Dean Ornish, M.D.
Preventive Medicine Research Institute
http://www.pmri.org/index.html

Lawrence Phillips and Myron McClellan
http://www.onebodyspirit.net

Patrick O'Neill. "Extraordinary Conversations"
http://www.extraordinaryconversations.com

Perelandra Center for Nature Research
http://www.perelandra-ltd.com

Lu Pierro
http://www.lifecoachingpierro.com
http://www.lupierro.wordpress.com
http://sat-acttesttaking.com/wordpress

Rachel Naomi Remen, M.D.
http://www.rachelremen.com

Jean Marie Rosone, LCSW
Coordinator of Integrative Oncology, Carol G. Simon Cancer
Center, Morristown Memorial Hospital, NJ

Dr. Martin Seligman, Director
Positive Psychology Center
University of Pennsylvania
http://www.authentichappiness.sas.upenn.edu

APPENDIX C:

Healing Questionnaire

1. How do you define healing – physically, mentally, emotionally, and/or spiritually?

2. What internal or external healing challenges have you encountered?
   - physical struggles
   - emotional upheavals
   - mental beliefs, attitudes, and perceptions
   - spiritual or life-force factors

3. What and/or who assisted your healing process?
   - self-awareness, personal strengths, practices used (i.e. exercise, prayer, meditation, journaling, hobbies, music, arts, pets, nature, sports)
   - mentors, role models, internal and external resources and support
   - relationships, friendships
   - physical, mental, emotional, and/or spiritual factors

4. What have you learned about yourself and your life path and purpose through healing experiences?

5. Describe your greatest lessons and insights about healing.

6. What new intentions, goals, and dreams have emerged as a result of your healing process?

7. What do you want medical and health-care professionals to know about the healing process, personally and professionally, to enhance their awareness and presence with those they serve?

Acknowledgments

I am appreciative of the rich legacies left by wise ancestors, and guides who set a strong foundation for my growth and development. I am grateful to my parents, who gave me the gift of life and taught me many lessons about family, work, and values. I cherish the heart-filled memories of Aunt Lilly, who demonstrated how to live joyfully with a full, open, clear, and strong heart.

Many courageous individuals shared their hearts and healing challenges with me. Each of them showed me how education and Self-care can maximize healing, and how necessary healing partnerships are in the health-care process. I express deep appreciation to: Alec, Brody, Cessy, Charles, Cheryl, Frank, Howard, John, Julie, Katie, Kathy, Linda, Lois, Marion, Mark, Maxine, Melissa, Pat, Susan, Terri, Tom, and countless others whom I have been blessed to walk beside.

My life has been transformed and deeply enriched by Angeles Arrien. Her authenticity, generosity, wisdom, and grace-filled presence have been a beacon of light for me and numerous others in a rapidly changing world. This book is a way of paying it forward, with gratitude to Angeles, for all she has brought to my life and our world.

Many teachers, mentors, therapists, and soul friends had faith in me, at times greater than I had in myself. I am grateful to various individuals who supported me and reminded me to steward my own healing as part of being of service in the world. Thank you: Katie Alexander, Betsy Baker, Maria De St Croix, Donna Eden, Sharon Weiselfish Giammatteo, Maxine Guenther, Roger Jahnke, Bill Kelly, Sr., Frank Lowen, Jeff Mannheimer,

Rebecca McLean, Cathy Miller, Lawrence Phillips, Lu Pierro, Aminah Raheem, Lydia Salant, Kathleen Rose Schival, Fritz Smith, Carol Wetherill, Cassie White, the Soul Lightening International community, and Geoffrey White.

I am also grateful for the presence of midwives, who took me through labor and delivery relative to this book. Thank you Peggy Jaegly, Carolyn Flynn, Vanessa Mickan, and Amy Collins. I could not have done this without you! Donna Miller and Gwyn Snider brought their extensive knowledge, artistic talents, creativity, patience, and dedication to the cover and interior design of this book. I am grateful to them for the beauty and clarity they helped bring to these pages. I also wish to thank the readers who reviewed what I thought was a final version – Betsy, Deanna, Katie, Kathleen Rose, Marcia, Michael, Mimi, Peggy, and Stanley. Your insights mined the "gold" for what was published.

My life partner, Stanley, has been one of my greatest teachers about giving and receiving love. His patience, love, and support were invaluable to me in completing this book. His willingness to remain open and present with me facilitated my learning the heart of healing themes firsthand.

Michael and Laurie, my adult children, bring lessons and blessings into my life. Each of them is living proof of our ability to remain afloat amidst life's challenges, and to heal in the face of adversity. The times we share as a family are priceless.

My beautiful grandchildren – Jolie, Mayzie, and Noah – your sparkle, magic, sweetness, joy, and honesty are a breath of fresh air. I see wonder and beauty again through your eyes, and the laughter we share tickles my whole being. Your presence transports me home to my heart, and reminds me of the authentic Divine Self that is present within each of us.

And to all of you who now hold *The Heart of Healing* in your hands and hearts . . . may your awakenings and healing bring you compassion, joy, peace, and love, and may this ripple out into our world and infinite universe.

ABOUT THE AUTHOR

Regina Rosenthal, PT, MA, has been a physical therapist, teacher, and writer for three decades. Her fascination with the universe as a youngster grew into a spiritual journey, bringing experiences with yoga, meditation, and many healing modalities. Each encouraged her to be more consciously present in daily life, and use this to educate others about Self-healing and transformational practices. She founded Dimensions of Wellness in 1992, offering clients, professionals, and the community opportunities to maximize well-being through body-mind manual therapies and Self-care practices. Regina has worked in hospital, university, home care, and private practice settings, and has taught seminars nationally and internationally. She developed and taught a Chronic Pain Self-Help class as part of her Master's Thesis in Counselor Education at Kean University, New Jersey. In addition, she instituted a Stress Management program at the Facial Pain Clinic, New Jersey University of Medicine and Dentistry. Regina lives with her husband near the Jersey Shore. Her journey continues to unfold as she teaches, writes, and becomes present with the heart of healing as it emerges in individuals she sees through her private practice.

Discover more through her blog and workshops on her website: www.reginarosenthal.com